Time on the Cross

Books by Robert William Fogel and Stanley L. Engerman

THE UNION PACIFIC RAILROAD:
A CASE IN PREMATURE ENTERPRISE

(by Robert William Fogel)

RAILROADS AND AMERICAN ECONOMIC GROWTH:
ESSAYS IN ECONOMETRIC HISTORY

(by Robert William Fogel)

THE REINTERPRETATION OF AMERICAN ECONOMIC HISTORY

(by Robert William Fogel, Stanley L. Engerman, and others)

RACE AND SLAVERY IN THE WESTERN HEMISPHERE:
QUANTITATIVE STUDIES

(edited by Stanley L. Engerman and Eugene D. Genovese)

THE DIMENSIONS OF QUANTITATIVE RESEARCH IN HISTORY

*(by Robert William Fogel, W. O. Aydelotte,
A. G. Bogue, and others)*

TIME ON THE CROSS:
THE ECONOMICS OF AMERICAN NEGRO SLAVERY
and EVIDENCE AND METHODS — A SUPPLEMENT

(by Robert William Fogel and Stanley L. Engerman)

WITHOUT CONSENT OR CONTRACT:
THE RISE AND FALL OF AMERICAN SLAVERY

(by Robert William Fogel)

WITHOUT CONSENT OR CONTRACT:
THE RISE AND FALL OF AMERICAN SLAVERY—
EVIDENCE AND METHODS

*(by Robert William Fogel, Ralph A. Galantine,
Richard L. Manning, and others)*

WITHOUT CONSENT OR CONTRACT:
THE RISE AND FALL OF AMERICAN SLAVERY—TECHNICAL PAPERS:
MARKETS AND PRODUCTION (VOLUME I)

(by Robert William Fogel, Stanley L. Engerman, and others)

WITHOUT CONSENT OR CONTRACT:
THE RISE AND FALL OF AMERICAN SLAVERY—TECHNICAL PAPERS:
CONDITIONS OF SLAVE LIFE AND
THE TRANSITION TO FREEDOM (VOLUME II)

(by Robert William Fogel, Stanley L. Engerman, and others)

Time on the Cross

The Economics
of American Negro Slavery

by Robert William Fogel
and Stanley L. Engerman

W. W. Norton & Company
New York • London

First published as a Norton paperback 1989; reissued 1995

Library of Congress Cataloging-in-Publication Data

Fogel, Robert William.
    Time on the cross : the economics of American Negro slavery / by
Robert William Fogel and Stanley L. Engerman.—New ed.
        p.   cm.
    Includes bibliographical references.

        1. Slavery—Economic aspects—United States.   I. Engerman,
Stanley L.   II. Title.
E449.F65   1989
331.11´734´0973—dc20   89-35275
                                                            CIP

ISBN 0-393-31218-6

W. W. Norton & Company, Inc., 500 Fifth Avenue, New York, N.Y. 10110
W. W. Norton & Company Ltd., 10 Coptic Street, London WC1A 1PU

1 2 3 4 5 6 7 8 9 0

To Mary Elizabeth Morgan's first daughter:
She has always known that black is beautiful

Publisher's Note

This is the primary volume of *Time on the Cross*.

For the convenience of the general reader and student, *Time on the Cross* has been divided into two volumes. This primary volume, subtitled *The Economics of American Negro Slavery*, contains the full and complete text of *Time on the Cross*, as well as pertinent charts, maps, and tables, an index, and all acknowledgments.

A supplementary volume for *Time on the Cross*, subtitled *Evidence and Methods*, is also available. The supplementary volume contains all source references for the work, together with comprehensive appendixes that discuss in detail the technical, methodological, and theoretical bases for the writing of *Time on the Cross*.

Contents

Tables

Figures

Time on the Cross

Prologue.

Slavery and the Cliometric Revolution

The years of black enslavement and the Civil War in which they terminated were our nation's time on the cross. Certainly if any aspect of the American past evokes a sense of shame, it is the system of slavery. And no war in our history, including World Wars I and II, took more American lives, was more devastating to our economy, or more threatening to our national survival, than the Civil War. The desire of scholars to lay bare the economic, political, and social forces which produced the tensions of the antebellum era and exploded into the worst holocaust of our history is not difficult to appreciate.

A vast literature has accumulated on the operation of the slave economy. Hundreds of historians have examined virtually every aspect of the institution. While scholars have disagreed on many points, a broad consensus has gradually emerged. By the midpoint of the twentieth century the consensus had been repeated so often that it had earned the status of a traditional interpretation. This interpretation is taught in most high school and college classes across the nation. It is the view that has been accepted by most of the readers of this book.

What is not generally known is that the traditional interpretation of slavery has been under intensive critical review for almost a decade and a half by historians and economists who are trained in the application of quantitative methods to historical problems. This review involves the processing of large quantities of numerical data. Although these data have been available for some time, the techniques required to analyze and interpret them systematically were not perfected until after the close of World War II. Then a series of rapid advances in economics, statistics, and applied mathematics, together with the availability of high-speed computers, put information long locked in obscure archives at the disposal of a new generation of scholars.

The review based on these new techniques and hitherto neglected sources has contradicted many of the most important propositions in the traditional portrayal of the slave system. As significant as the correction of past errors is the new information brought to light on the conditions of black bondage. Though the investigations are still in progress, enough have been completed so that the main features of the actual operation of the slave economy are now clear. The reconstruction which has emerged is so much at variance with common beliefs, and its implications are so central to the understanding of contemporary issues, that we believe the new findings should no longer be restricted to the pages of esoteric scholarly journals.

The following are some of the principal corrections of the traditional characterization of the slave economy:

1. Slavery was not a system irrationally kept in existence by plantation owners who failed to perceive or were indifferent to their best economic interests. The purchase of a slave was generally a highly profitable investment which yielded rates of return that compared favorably with the most outstanding investment opportunities in manufacturing.

2. The slave system was not economically moribund on the

eve of the Civil War. There is no evidence that economic forces alone would have soon brought slavery to an end without the necessity of a war or some other form of political intervention. Quite the contrary; as the Civil War approached, slavery as an economic system was never stronger and the trend was toward even further entrenchment.

3. Slaveowners were not becoming pessimistic about the future of their system during the decade that preceded the Civil War. The rise of the secessionist movement coincided with a wave of optimism. On the eve of the Civil War, slaveholders anticipated an era of unprecedented prosperity.

4. Slave agriculture was not inefficient compared with free agriculture. Economies of large-scale operation, effective management, and intensive utilization of labor and capital made southern slave agriculture 35 percent more efficient than the northern system of family farming.

5. The typical slave field hand was not lazy, inept, and unproductive. On average he was harder-working and more efficient than his white counterpart.

6. The course of slavery in the cities does not prove that slavery was incompatible with an industrial system or that slaves were unable to cope with an industrial regimen. Slaves employed in industry compared favorably with free workers in diligence and efficiency. Far from declining, the demand for slaves was actually increasing more rapidly in urban areas than in the countryside.

7. The belief that slave-breeding, sexual exploitation, and promiscuity destroyed the black family is a myth. The family was the basic unit of social organization under slavery. It was to the economic interest of planters to encourage the stability of slave families and most of them did so. Most slave sales were either of whole families or of individuals who were at an age when it would have been normal for them to have left the family.

8. The material (not psychological) conditions of the lives of slaves compared favorably with those of free industrial workers. This is not to say that they were good by modern standards. It merely emphasizes the hard lot of all workers, free or slave, during the first half of the nineteenth century.

9. Slaves were exploited in the sense that part of the income which they produced was expropriated by their owners. However, the rate of expropriation was much lower than has generally been presumed. Over the course of his lifetime, the typical slave

field hand received about 90 percent of the income he produced.

10. Far from stagnating, the economy of the antebellum South grew quite rapidly. Between 1840 and 1860, per capita income increased more rapidly in the South than in the rest of the nation. By 1860 the South attained a level of per capita income which was high by the standards of the time. Indeed, a country as advanced as Italy did not achieve the same level of per capita income until the eve of World War II.

Even this partial summary of corrections raises the question of how those who fashioned the traditional interpretation of the slave system could have been so wrong. The historians whose views are now under criticism were conscientious and diligent scholars; they were highly intelligent and perceptive; and they strove to portray the history of the antebellum South as it actually was. The explanation of how such men were misled does not turn on issues of personal bias or other idiosyncratic behavior — even if, in some instances, bias has been a contributing factor. It hinges to a large extent on certain broad methodological questions, and particularly on the role of mathematics and statistics in historical analysis. For some of the most telling revisions of the new work turn on technical mathematical points, points which despite their obscurity are vital to the correct description and interpretation of the slave economy.

Antebellum slavery is not the only aspect of American economic history which has undergone radical revision as a result of the application of mathematical and statistical methods. The reexamination of slavery is part of a more ambitious effort to reconstruct the entire history of American economic development on a sound quantitative basis. Those engaged in this enterprise are called "new economic historians," "econometric historians," and "cliometricians." The first definitely formulated expression of the new approach was set forth in a pair of essays written in 1957 by Alfred H. Conrad and John R. Meyer, who were then young assistant professors at Harvard. Since the appearance of these papers, the number of scholars attempting to apply mathematical and statistical methods to history increased from less than a score to several hundred. As their numbers have proliferated so have their iconoclastic findings.

The cliometricians have downgraded the role of technological change in American economic advance; they have controverted the claim that railroads were necessary to the settlement and exploitation of the West; they have contended that the boom and bust of the 1830s and early 1840s were the consequences of developments in Mexico and Britain rather than the policies of Andrew Jackson; and they have rejected the contention that the Civil War greatly accelerated the industrialization of the nation.

Today the findings and methods of the new economic history are routinely taught at the graduate level at Harvard, Yale, Chicago, the University of California, and other leading universities which together produce most of the Ph.D.s in the field. This does not mean that the controversy over the cliometric approach has come to an end. There are still a significant number of eminent economic historians who are deeply skeptical of the usefulness of mathematical methods.

But even the most skeptical critics of the "mathematical craze" have had to concede that the cliometricians have performed a service in searching out and systematically sifting through huge quantities of data of direct relevance to the understanding of U.S. economic development. And nowhere has this passion for numbers been more vigorously pursued than in the study of the economics of slavery.

For more than a decade several scores of scholars have been exploring every conceivable source of information bearing on the operation of the slave system. The search led them into the deepest recesses of the National Archives and of various state archives where the original, handwritten schedules of information collected by the census takers of 1850 and 1860 were stored. These documents contain quite detailed information about every plantation then extant as well as about the slaves who were born, lived, and died in those years. The cliometricians also scoured the papers of the historical societies of various southern states and some states in the North, where are deposited the family papers and business records of the largest planters. The wills and other legal documents of the estates of planters have been particularly valuable. In addition to yielding prices on tens of thousands of slaves, these records have been one of the principal bases for determination of the structural characteristics of black families. Pursuit of this body of evidence eventually led even to such places as the Wasatch Mountains of Utah, where the Genealogical Society of the Church of Jesus Christ of Latter-Day Saints has stored microfilms of probate records gathered from hundreds of county courthouses.

As a result of the search, the cliometricians have amassed a more complete body of information on the operation of the slave system than has been available to anyone interested in the subject either during the antebellum era or since then. It is this enormous body of evidence which is the source of many of their new discoveries.

Some of the discoveries were at one time as unbelievable to the cliometricians as they will be to the readers of this volume. Indeed, many of the findings presented in the chapters that follow were initially discounted, even rejected out of hand. But when persistent efforts to contradict the unexpected discoveries failed, these scholars were forced into a wide-ranging and radical reinterpretation of American slavery.

This will be a disturbing book to read. It requires forbearance on the part of the reader and a recognition that what is set forth represents the honest efforts of scholars whose central aim has been the discovery of what really happened. We believe that this forbearance will prove worthwhile. For the findings we discuss not only expose many myths that have served to corrode and poison relations between the races, but also help to put into a new perspective some of the most urgent issues of our day.

In considering the evidence presented in this book, readers should keep in mind certain caveats regarding the advantages and limitations of cliometric methods. The advantage of the application of quantitative methods to history is not that it provides unambiguous answers to all questions. Not all questions have unambiguous answers. And many of those questions which in principle have unambiguous answers cannot be resolved because of the absence of crucial bodies of data, because the retrieval of some bodies of data are too expensive to be practical, or because the analysis of a given body of data poses problems that cannot be treated by the mathematical and statistical methods that have thus far been developed.

It is, for example, much easier to obtain data bearing on the frequency with which slave families were broken up by the interregional slave trade than on the inner quality of the family life of slaves. Similarly, the evidence on the number of slaves per slave house is more direct and complete than the evidence available on the cleanliness and healthfulness of that housing. And, while the cliometricians have been able to construct reasonably reliable indexes of the material level at which blacks lived under slavery, it has been impossible, thus far, to devise a meaningful index of the effect of slavery on the personality or psychology of blacks.

In other words, cliometrics provides a set of tools which are of considerable help in analyzing an important but limited set of problems. Many vital issues in the economics of slavery lie beyond the range of these tools. This does not mean that issues such as the quality of slave family life or the psychological effects of slavery on black personalities should be ignored, but that discussion of these issues must of necessity continue to be shrouded in more uncertainty than discussion of such questions as the nutritional adequacy of the slave diet, the profitability of investments in slaves, and the efficiency of slave labor.

This book not only presents the principal findings of the cliometricians but also attempts to interpret them. In the pages that follow, we reconsider many aspects of the prevailing interpretation of the slave experience and of black history in light of the new findings. It is important that readers keep in mind this distinction between the principal findings of the cliometricians and our attempt to interpret them. The findings and the interpretation do not stand on the same level of certainty. Interpretation sometimes involves additional data which are quite fragmentary and assumptions which, though they are plausible, cannot be verified at present. Hence, even when readers accept the validity of one or another of the principal findings, they may disagree with the significance that we attach to it.

There is no such thing as errorless data. The questions with which cliometricians must always grapple are the nature of the errors contained in the various bodies of data that they employ and the biases that such errors will produce in estimates based on data containing them. When evaluated from this standpoint, evidence falls not into just two categories (good and bad), but into a complex hierarchy in which there are many categories of evidence and varying degrees of reliability.

Our aim has been to base our statements on evidence drawn from as high up in this hierarchy of reliability as possible. We have least confidence in fragmentary evidence which is based on unverifiable impressions of individuals whose primary aim was the defense of an ideological position. Fragmentary evidence from objective sources, such as impressionistic reports of "detached" observers, may be more believable, but is still of a low order of reliability since it is usually not possible to submit such evidence to systematic statistical tests.

Data which can be subjected to systematic statistical tests

(which we will refer to as "systematic data"), even when they are biased, are frequently more useful than fragmentary data. For if the nature or direction of the bias is known, it is frequently possible to design statistical procedures which will yield valid tests of important historical issues. For example, in chapter 4 we present an estimate of the nutritional content of the slave diet on large plantations. The first step in the estimation procedure involved the determination of the total supply of food available for human consumption on the designated plantations. The second step required the separation of the consumption of slaves from that of the whites who lived on the plantations. Since no systematic information on the diets of these whites was available, we resolved the issue by assuming that their consumption of particular foods was substantially in excess of national averages. This "overfeeding" resulted in an estimated daily intake for whites of 5,300 calories — a figure which is clearly in excess of any feasible level of consumption for the relatively inactive, upper-class whites living on plantations. While the "overfeeding" of whites leads to an underestimation of slave consumption, the error is relatively small (less than 5 percent of the per capita consumption of slaves), since whites formed a small percentage of the population of large plantations. Moreover, correction of this small error would not change the conclusion that the nutritional content of the slave diet was quite high. Quite the contrary, correction of the error would only serve to buttress that conclusion.

We use fragmentary, impressionistic evidence in two ways: to illustrate and make more vivid results that have been established by more precise methods, and to fill in gaps in evidence where it has not been possible thus far to obtain systematic data. Arguments that rest on impressionistic, fragmentary evidence must be considered to be on a relatively low level of reliability, regardless of the objectivity of the source of this evidence.

In order to encourage the widest possible discussion of the findings of the cliometricians, we have attempted to present them in as nontechnical a manner as possible. Popularization has its costs. Those who are familiar with cliometric writings know that one of its principal hallmarks is "sensitivity analysis." "Sensitivity analysis" refers to the investigation of the quantitative effects on findings of possible biases in the data, in the behavioral equations, and in the assumptions of the estimating techniques. However, if we attempted to introduce such analysis into the main body of the text, the book would quickly become too technical.

Instead we have included a technical appendix (appenddix B) which discusses the data on which the principal findings are based, as well as the techniques employed in the analyses of these data. While not all of the technical issues are included in appendix B, we deal there with the most important issues, or at least with the most controversial ones. Those readers who desire more complete information should consult the various scientific papers on which this book is based. Papers that have already been published or that will soon be published are referred to in appendixes B or C and are cited in the list of references.

Appendixes B and C and the list of references, as well as an appendix on the role of science in the study of history, are to be found in the companion volume to *Time on the Cross*, which is subtitled *Evidence and Methods: A Supplement*.

One.

The International Context of United States Slavery

The Origins of the Atlantic Slave Trade

Slavery is not only one of the most ancient but also one of the most long-lived forms of economic and social organization. It came into being at the dawn of civilization, when mankind passed from hunting and nomadic pastoral life into primitive agriculture. And although legally sanctioned slavery was outlawed in its last bastion — the Arabian peninsula — in 1962, slavery is still practiced covertly in parts of Asia, Africa, and South America.

Over the ages the incidence of slavery has waxed and waned. One high-water mark was reached during the first two centuries of the Roman Empire when, according to some estimates, three out of every four residents of the Italian peninsula — twenty-one million people — lived in bondage. Eventually Roman slavery was transformed into serfdom, a form of servitude that mitigated some of the harsher features of the older system. Serfs were perpetually tied to land and owed a certain amount of labor service to

Figure 1

The Distribution of Slave Imports in the New World, 1500-1870

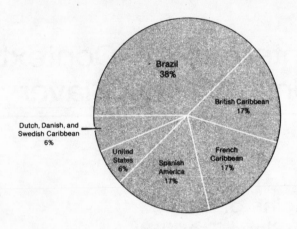

the lords of the estates to which they belonged. But unlike slaves, serfs had such personal freedoms as the right to marry, to establish separate households, and to own personal property. Moreover, the lord of an estate was limited in the punishment he could inflict on his serfs, no longer having the power to take the lives of those in bondage.

While serfdom was the most characteristic condition of labor in Europe during the Middle Ages, slavery was never fully eradicated. The Italians were quite active in importing slaves from the area of the Black Sea during the thirteenth century. And the Moors captured during the interminable religious wars were enslaved on the Iberian peninsula, along with Slavs and captives from the Levant.

Black slaves were imported into Europe during the Middle Ages through the Moslem countries of North Africa. Until the Portuguese exploration of the west coast of Africa, however, such imports were quite small. Beginning about the middle of the fifteenth century, the Portuguese established trading posts along the west coast of Africa below the Sahara with the aim of capturing or making relatively large purchases of black slaves. Soon the average imports of slaves into the Iberian peninsula and the Iberian-controlled islands off the coast of Africa (the Canaries, the Madeiras, the Cape Verde archipelago, and São Thomé) rose to about a thousand per year. By the time Columbus set sail on his first expedition across the Atlantic, accumulated imports of Negro slaves into the Old World were probably in excess of twenty-five thousand. Although Negroes continued to be imported into the Old World until the beginning of the eighteenth century, it was the New World that became the great market for slaves.

It is customary to date the beginning of the New World traffic in Africans in the year 1502 when the first references to blacks appear in the documents of Spanish colonial administrators. The end of this trade did not come until the 1860s. Over the three and one half centuries between these dates, more than 9,500,000 Africans were forcibly transported across the Atlantic. Brazil was by far the largest single participant in the traffic, accounting for 38 percent of the total. British- and French-owned colonies in the Caribbean and the far-flung Spanish-American empire were the destination of 50 percent. Dutch, Danish, and Swedish colonies took another 6 percent. The remaining 6 percent represent the share of the United States (or the colonies which eventually became the United States) in the Atlantic slave trade.

To those who identify slavery with cotton and tobacco, the small U.S. share in the slave trade may seem unbelievable. Consideration of the temporal pattern of slave imports, however, clearly reveals that the course of the Atlantic slave trade cannot be explained by the demand for these crops. The temporal pattern of the slave trade is displayed in figure 2. It shows that 80 percent of all slaves were imported between 1451 and 1810. This fact clearly rules out cotton as

Figure 2

Imports of Negro Slaves by Time and Region

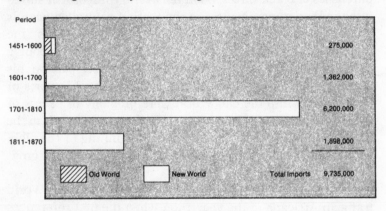

a dominant factor in the traffic since the production of cotton was still in its infancy in 1810. Figure 2 also shows that there was an enormous increase in the extent of the slave trade during the eighteenth century. This fact rules out the possibility of a major role for tobacco. For during the eighteenth century, tobacco imports into Europe increased at an average annual rate of about 350 tons per annum. Since an average slave hand could produce about a ton of tobacco, the total increase in the tobacco trade over the century required an increase of about seventy thousand hands, a minuscule fraction of the six million slave imports during the same period.

It was Europe's sweet tooth, rather than its addiction to tobacco or its infatuation with cotton cloth, that determined the extent of the Atlantic slave trade. Sugar was the greatest of the slave crops. Between 60 and 70 percent of all the Africans who survived the Atlantic voyages ended up in one or the other of Europe's sugar colonies.

The first of these colonies was in the Mediterranean.

Sugar was introduced into the Levant in the seventh century by the Arabs. Europeans became familiar with it during the Crusades. Prior to that time honey was the only sweetening agent available to them. After taking over the Arab sugar industry in Palestine, the Normans and Venetians promoted the production of sugar in the Mediterranean islands of Cyprus, Crete, and Sicily. From the twelfth to the fifteenth centuries these colonies shipped sugar to all parts of Europe. Moreover, the sugar produced there was grown on plantations which utilized slave labor. While the slaves were primarily white, it was in these islands that Europeans developed the institutional apparatus that was eventually to be applied to blacks.

The rapid growth of European demand led the Spanish and Portuguese to extend sugar cultivation to the Iberian peninsula and to the Iberian-owned Atlantic islands off the coast of Africa. Here, as in the Mediterranean, it was slaves employed on plantations who provided the labor for the new industry. While some of these bondsmen were natives of the newly conquered islands, as in the Cape Verde archipelago, most were blacks imported from Africa. For the first century of the Atlantic slave trade, the scope of imports was determined almost exclusively by the needs of the sugar planters in the Cape Verdes, the Madeiras, and São Thomé. Of the 130,000 Negro imports between 1451 and 1550, 90 percent were sent to these islands and only 10 percent to the New World.

During the last half of the sixteenth century, the center of sugar production and of black slavery shifted across the Atlantic to the Western Hemisphere. By 1600 Brazil had emerged as Europe's leading supplier of sugar. Cane was also grown in substantial quantities in Mexico, Peru, Cuba, and Haiti. Although the Old World colonies continued to plant the crop, their absolute and relative shares of the European market declined rapidly. By the close of the seventeenth century sugar production all but disappeared from

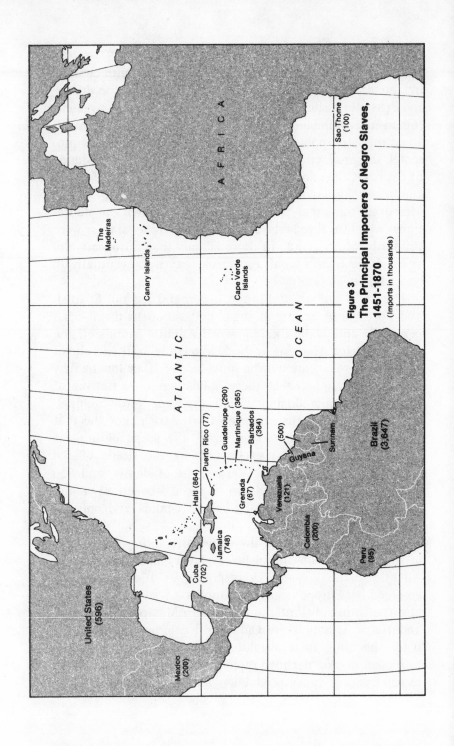

Figure 3
The Principal Importers of Negro Slaves, 1451-1870
(Imports in thousands)

United States (596)

Mexico (200)

Cuba (702)

Jamaica (748)

Haiti (864)

Puerto Rico (77)

Guadeloupe (290)

Martinique (365)

Barbados (364)

Grenada (67)

Venezuela (121)

Colombia (200)

Peru (95)

Guyana (500)

Surinam

Brazil (3,647)

The Madeiras

Canary Islands

Cape Verde Islands

Sao Thome (100)

A F R I C A

A T L A N T I C   O C E A N

the Madeiras, the Cape Verde Islands, the Canaries, and São Thomé. The end of sugar production also marked the end of slave imports into these territories.

The sugar monopoly of the Spanish and Portuguese was broken during the seventeenth century when the British, French, and Dutch became major powers in the Caribbean. The British venture into sugar production began in Barbados during the second quarter of the seventeenth century. In 1655 the British seized Jamaica from the Spanish, and shortly thereafter began the development of sugar plantations on that island. During the eighteenth century the output of sugar grew rapidly, not only in these colonies but throughout the British West Indies. By 1770 the annual yield of the sugar crop in the British Caribbean territories stood at 130,000 tons, more than three times as much as the output of Brazil in the same year.

The development of the sugar culture in French Caribbean possessions was even more spectacular. Haiti (then called Saint Domingue) was the principal sugar colony of the French. The French promoted plantations in that territory from the early seventeenth century until the Haitian revolution in 1794. By 1770 Haiti was producing 107,000 tons, nearly as much as the entire British output. Production elsewhere brought the sugar output of French Caribbean possessions in 1770 to 151,000 tons. The Dutch were a poor fourth (after the French, the British, and the Portuguese) in the international sugar trade in 1770, with an output of 15,000 tons, nearly all of which was produced in Dutch Guiana, located on the north-central coast of South America in terrain which embraces the modern nations of Guyana and Surinam. The Danes produced a total of 11,000 tons of sugar, nearly all of it on the island of Saint Croix. By 1770 Spain had been squeezed out of the international sugar trade. The sugar produced in Spanish colonies was consumed largely by the local population. However, Spain re-emerged as a major sugar supplier in the nineteenth century with the development of extensive plantations in Cuba and Puerto Rico.

Thus, the great majority of the slaves brought into the British, French, and Dutch Caribbean colonies were engaged, directly and indirectly, in the sugar industry. In Brazil, 40 percent of slave imports were involved in sugar culture, and in Spanish America the share was probably between 30 and 50 percent. Mining, which probably stood second to sugar in the demand for labor, claimed about 20 percent of the slaves in Brazil. The balance of the blacks brought to the New World were utilized in the production of such diverse crops as coffee, cocoa, tobacco, indigo, hemp, cotton, and rice. Of the relatively small percentage of Africans engaged in urban pursuits, most were usually servants or manual laborers, although some became artisans. However, it is probable that by the mid-eighteenth century most of the urban slaves were Creoles, slaves born in the New World, rather than recent imports.

The Evolution of Slavery in the United States

The United States stands apart from the other slave-importing territories, not only because of its comparatively small share in the Atlantic slave trade, but also because of the minor role played by its sugar industry in the growth of U.S. slavery. The commercial production of sugar in Louisiana did not begin until 1795, barely a decade before the U.S. withdrew from the international slave trade. At the time of the U.S. annexation of Louisiana, sugar production was a mere five thousand tons. Even at its antebellum peak, sugar was never more than a minor southern crop which utilized less than 10 percent of the slave labor force.

Figure 4

Negroes as a Percentage of the Total Population in Four Regions

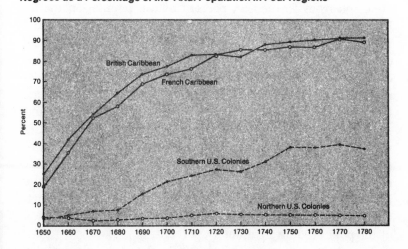

The absence of the sugar culture had a profound effect on the development of slavery in the U.S. colonies. For one thing, it affected the rate at which the slave labor force grew, both in absolute numbers and in relative importance. While African labor was introduced into Virginia earlier than in Barbados, there were six times as many Negroes in the British Caribbean in 1700 as there were in all of the North American colonies. Some eighty years after the first group of slaves landed in Virginia, the Negro population of that colony was just sixteen thousand, while all the other North American colonies contained a mere eleven thousand Negroes. In the British Caribbean the slave population climbed to sixty thousand within thirty years after the beginning of the British presence. It took the U.S. colonies a hundred and ten years to reach the same absolute level, despite the extremely favorable rate of natural *increase* of slaves in British North America and the high rate of natural *decrease* in the Caribbean.

Even more striking are the differences of the ratios of Negro to total population among the colonies. As early as 1650, Negroes formed 25 percent of the population in the British Caribbean. By 1770 the ratio stood at 91 percent. The experience in the French Caribbean was similar. By contrast, Negroes formed only 4 percent of the population of the North American colonies in 1650, and rose to a pre-revolutionary peak of 22 percent in 1770. In the southern U.S. colonies the percentages for 1650 and 1770 were 3 and 40, respectively. Thus, while Negroes were the overwhelming majority of the population and labor force of the Caribbean during most of the colonial era, they were always a minority of the population of the U.S. colonies, and for most of the colonial period a relatively small minority. Midway through the colonial period, even in the South, the Negro proportion of the population was under 15 percent.

The absence of a sugar industry in the U.S. colonies also affected the size of the units on which slaves lived. Sugar production was big business by the standards of the time. Not only were considerable sums of capital necessary, but the optimum size of the labor force of a productive unit was quite large. Some plantations in the Caribbean ran to five hundred slaves and beyond. The *average* size of a sugar plantation in Jamaica toward the end of the eighteenth century was about a hundred and eighty slaves. By contrast, the average size of a holding in Virginia and Maryland at that time was less than thirteen slaves. Blacks in Jamaica and the other Caribbean islands had little contact with the European culture of the white slaveowner both because of the small percentage of whites who lived on these islands and because of the enormous size of the typical sugar planta-tion. But blacks in the U.S. colonies were typically a minority of the population and lived on small units which brought them into continuous contact with their white masters.

Figure 5

Foreign-born Negroes as a Percentage of the U.S. Negro Population, 1620-1860

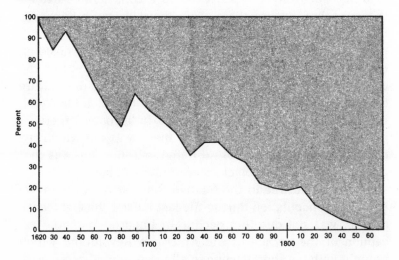

U.S. slaves were not only in closer contact with European culture, they were also more removed from their African origins than were slaves in the Caribbean. Down through the end of the eighteenth century and into the nineteenth century, the great majority of the slave populations of the British and French Caribbean islands were born in Africa. Indeed, as late as 1800, one quarter of the populations of Jamaica, Barbados, and Martinique consisted of Africans who had arrived in the New World *within the previous decade.* On the other hand, native-born blacks made up the majority of the slave population in the U.S. colonies as early as 1680. By the end of the American Revolution, the African-born component of the black population had shrunk to 20 percent. It hovered at this share from 1780 to 1810 and then rapidly headed toward zero. By 1860 all but one percent of U.S. slaves were native-born, and most of them were second, third, fourth, or fifth generation Americans. These Americans not only had no personal experience with Africa but were generally cut off from contact with persons who had such direct experience. To a considerable extent, the word that reached them about their African origins was filtered through minds and emotions of parents, grandparents, and great-grandparents who had always walked on the North American continent. This is not to deny the contribution of an African heritage in shaping the culture of blacks, but rather to stress the extent to which black culture had, by 1860, been exposed to indigenous American influences. There were, of course, many ways in which the culture of whites and blacks differed in 1860. One was that a larger proportion of blacks were American-born.

The rapid decline in the relative share of Africans in the U.S. Negro population during the last half of the eighteenth century was not due to a decline in imports. With the exception of the decade of the American Revolution, which brought with it a short decline in all international commerce, the trend in imports of slaves into the United States was strongly upward from 1620 until the end of legal U.S. involvement in the international slave trade in 1808. It has been frequently asserted that slavery was dying in the United States from the end of the Revolution to 1810, and that if it had not been for the rise of the cotton culture, slavery would have passed from existence long before the Civil War. This proposition rests partly on erroneous but widely cited estimates of slave imports for the period from 1790 to 1810 put forward by Henry Carey. Revised estimates show that far from declining, slave imports were higher in this period than in any previous twenty-year period of U.S. history. There were in fact about as many Africans brought into the United States during the thirty years from 1780 to 1810 as during the previous hundred and sixty years of the U.S. involvement in the slave trade.

Figure 6

U.S. Imports of Slaves per Decade, 1620-1860

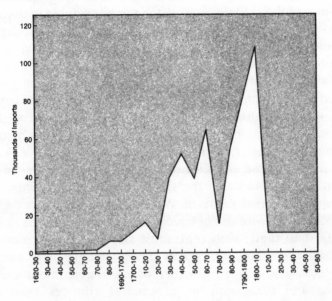

While the imports of Africans certainly contributed to the growth in the slave population of the U.S. colonies, they were of secondary importance in explaining that growth after 1720. Natural increase was by far the more significant factor during the eighteenth and nineteenth centuries. This is another respect in which the U.S. experience differed from that of Latin America. In the British and French West Indies, in Dutch Guiana, and in Brazil, the death rate of slaves was so high, and the birthrate so low, that these territories could not sustain their population levels without large and continuous importations of Africans. The rate of natural decrease in the West Indies varied from 5 to 2 percent per annum during most of the eighteenth century. Over time, the rate of decrease moved toward zero. But it was not until well into the nineteenth century that the black population of the West Indies became demographically self-sustaining.

What were the factors which made the demographic experience of the U.S. slaves so much more favorable than that of their Caribbean counterparts? To Americans who have a penchant for finding the silver linings of clouds, it is tempting to cast the explanation in terms of the relative humaneness of the treatment of slaves in the U.S. colonies. While there is some evidence to support this view, evidence that will be considered in a later chapter, much of the explanation turns on factors that were independent of the kindness or cruelty of the masters. No doubt poorer food and more intense work schedules contributed to the high death rate of blacks in the Caribbean. But these only increased the vulnerability of West Indian slaves to an epidemiological environment which in any case was much more severe than that which confronted slaves in the territories to the north. Malaria, yellow fever, tetanus, dysentery, smallpox, and a score of other diseases were more widespread and more virulent in tropical climates than in temperate ones. Moreover, the high ratio of Africans to native-born slaves in the Caribbean meant that only a relatively small percentage of the black population had acquired the immunities needed to resist diseases that were prevalent in the American environment. White Europeans also suffered high death rates in the Caribbean. Indeed, the death rates among European troops in West Indian colonies exceeded that of slaves.

The large proportion of Africans in the slave population also served to reduce the birthrate in the Caribbean territories. For males and females were not brought to the New World in equal numbers. Less than 40 percent of imports were female. Even if African-born women had been as fertile as Creole women, the imbalance in the sex ratio among Africans would have resulted in a relatively low

Figure 7

Actual U.S. Negro Population Compared with the Population that Would Have Existed If the U.S. Had Duplicated the Demographic Experience of the West Indies

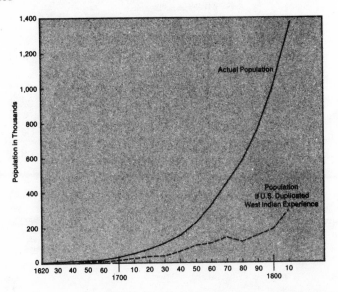

birthrate. But the fertility of African women was substantially below that of Creoles. Thus, while the Creole population was not only able to reproduce itself but to grow at moderate rates, the African population could not. The combination of an unbalanced sex ratio with low fertility made the African birthrate much too low to offset the very high African death rate. The relative importance of various social, cultural, and physiological factors in explaining the low fertility rates of Africans is obscure. Emotional shock, generally poor health, venereal disease, abortion, infanticide, and the distortion of family life created by the unbalanced sex ratio have all been cited as possible causes.

Whatever the factors responsible for the favorable demographic experience of U.S. slaves, its consequences were clear. Despite their low rates of importations, which initially

Figure 8

A Comparison of the Distribution of the Negro Population (Slave & Free) in 1825 with the Distribution of Slave Imports, 1500-1825

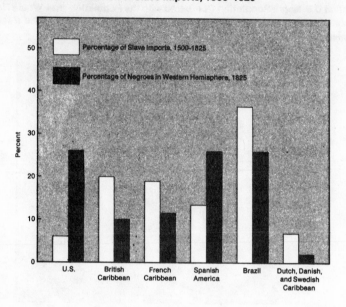

Figure 9

The Distribution of Slaves in the Western Hemisphere, 1825

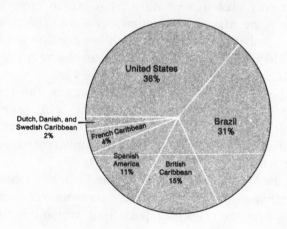

caused the growth of the U.S. slave population to lag behind that of the Caribbean, the U.S. colonies not only overtook but far exceeded the rate of growth of the slave populations elsewhere in the hemisphere. By 1720, the annual rate of natural increase in the U.S. was greater than the annual increase due to importations. And during the last half century of legal U.S. involvement in the slave trade, although the absolute level of importations was high compared with earlier U.S. experience, importations contributed only half as much to the growth of the black population as did natural increase. Even these statements underestimate the impact of the favorable demographic experience. For they fail to take into account the unfavorable demographic experience elsewhere. In 1800 there were 1,002,000 Negroes in the United States. But if the U.S. had duplicated the demographic experience of the West Indies, its Negro population in 1800 would have been only 186,000.

Thus, the United States became the leading slave power of the Western world, not because it participated heavily in the slave trade but because of the unusually high rate of natural increase of its slave population. By 1825 there were about 1,750,000 slaves in the southern United States. This represented over 36 percent of all of the slaves in the Western world in that year. Despite its peripheral role in the Atlantic slave trade the U.S. was, during the three decades preceding the Civil War, the greatest slave power in the Western world and the bulwark of resistance to the abolition of slavery.

The Course of Emancipation

For nearly three thousand years — from the time of King Solomon to the eve of the American Revolution — virtually every major statesman, philosopher, theologian, writer, and critic accepted the existence and legitimacy of slavery. The word "accepted" is chosen deliberately. For these men of affairs and molders of thought did not excuse, condone, pardon, or forgive the institution. They did not have to; they were not burdened by the view that slavery was wrong. Slavery was considered to be part of the natural scheme of things. "From the hour of their birth," said Aristotle, "some are marked out for subjection, others for rule."

It is true that Christian theologians and others were concerned with the possible dichotomy between servitude and the "divine law of human brotherhood." But this apparent contradiction was neatly resolved by treating slavery as a condition of the body rather than of the spirit. In the spiritual realm "all men were brothers in union with God," but in the temporal realm slavery was "a necessary part of the world of sin." Thus, "the bondsman was inwardly free and spiritually equal to his master, but in things external he was a mere chattel."

The Catholic Church not only rationalized the possession of slaves by others, but was itself a major owner of slaves. Even before the Jesuits began to encourage the importation of Africans into the New World, the Church actively promoted slavery. In 1375, Pope Gregory XI, viewing bondage as a just punishment for those who resisted the papacy, ordered the enslavement of excommunicated Florentines whenever they were captured. And in 1488 Pope Innocent VIII accepted a gift of a hundred Moorish slaves from Ferdinand of Spain and then distributed them to various cardinals and nobles. Nor was it merely the conservative members of the hierarchy who countenanced human bondage. No less a humanist than Thomas More held slavery to be an appropriate state for the "vyle drudge," the "poore laborer," and the criminal. He therefore included slavery in his vision of *Utopia*.

Differences on the legitimacy of servitude were not among the issues that motivated the Protestant Reformation. "When

Swabian serfs appealed for emancipation in 1525, holding that Christ had died to set men free, Martin Luther was as horrified as any orthodox Catholic." He considered that demand to be a distortion of Scripture which, if permitted, would confuse Christ's spiritual kingdom with the world of affairs. He reaffirmed Saint Paul's dictum that "masters and slaves must accept their present stations, for the earthly kingdom could not survive unless some men were free and some were slaves."

Acceptance of slavery was not less common in the secular than in the religious world. As prominent a champion of the "inalienable rights of man" as John Locke wrote a provision for slavery into his draft of the "Fundamental Constitutions of Carolina," and also became an investor in the Royal African Company, the organization that enjoyed the British monopoly of the African slave trade. Thus, the man who formulated the theory of natural liberty, and whose thesis regarding the moral obligation of men to take up arms in defense of liberty later inspired many revolutionaries and abolitionists was, nevertheless, a staunch defender of slavery. This paradox is attributed by David Brion Davis to Locke's belief that

the origin of slavery, like the origin of liberty and property, was entirely outside the social contract. When any man, by fault or act, forfeited his life to another, he could not complain of injustice if his punishment was postponed by his being enslaved. If the hardships of bondage should at any time outweigh the value of life, he could commit suicide by resisting his master and receiving the death which he had all along deserved.

The last quarter of the seventeenth and the first three quarters of the eighteenth century were a watershed between the routine acceptance of slavery and the onset of a concerted, successful movement for the abolition of human bondage. The early outspoken critics of slavery were easily ignored. Such men as Judge Samuel Sewall, a Puritan from

Massachusetts who in 1700 published an antislavery tract entitled *The Selling of Joseph,* were viewed by most of their contemporaries not as prophets, but as men of questionable integrity, if not sanity, who for inexplicable reasons had set out to controvert both the Scripture and the natural order. Even in the Society of Friends, where doctrinal considerations made the minds of its members more open to abolitionist arguments than in other circles, the opponents of slavery were rebuffed for three quarters of a century — from 1688, when the Germantown Quakers issued their condemnation of human bondage as a violation of the Golden Rule, until the 1758 Yearly Meeting of Quakers in Philadelphia, which, for the first time, condemned not only the slave trade but slavery itself, and threatened to exclude from positions of responsibility within the society any members who participated in that trade.

It is amazing how rapidly, by historical standards, the institution of slavery gave way before the abolitionist onslaught, once the ideological campaign gained momentum. The moment at which abolitionism passed over from apparently ineffectual harangues by isolated zealots to a significant political movement cannot be dated with precision. Nevertheless, the year in which the English Society of Friends voted to expel any member engaged in the slave trade (1774) seems to be a reasonable, although not a unique, occasion to mark the onset of concerted political action to end slavery. Slavery was abolished in its last American bastion — Brazil — in 1888. And so, within the span of a little more than a century, a system which stood above criticism for three thousand years, was outlawed everywhere in the Western world.

While the struggle to end slavery was often associated with violence, it was only in the United States that slaveowners resorted to full-scale warfare to halt the abolitionist trend. And only in Haiti did a whole colony of slaves obtain liberation through bloody revolution. Much of the violence

Table 1

A Chronology of Emancipation, 1772–1888

1772   Lord Chief Justice Mansfield Rules that Slavery Is Not Supported by English Law, Thus Laying the Legal Basis for the Freeing of England's 15,000 Slaves.

1774   The English Society of Friends Votes the Expulsion of Any Member Engaged in the Slave Trade.

1775   Slavery Abolished in Madeira.

1776   The Societies of Friends in England and Pennsylvania Require Members to Free Their Slaves or Face Expulsion.

1777   The Vermont Constitution Prohibits Slavery.

1780   The Massachusetts Constitution Declares That All Men Are Free and Equal by Birth; a Judicial Decision in 1783 Interprets This Clause as Having the Force of Abolishing Slavery.

    Pennsylvania Adopts a Policy of Gradual Emancipation, Freeing the Children of All Slaves Born after November 1, 1780, at Their Twenty-eighth Birthday.

1784   Rhode Island and Connecticut Pass Gradual Emancipation Laws.

1787   Formation in England of the "Society for the Abolition of the Slave Trade."

1794   The French National Convention Abolishes Slavery in All French Territories. This Law Is Repealed by Napoleon in 1802.

1799   New York Passes a Gradual Emancipation Law.

1800   U.S. Citizens Barred from Exporting Slaves.

1804   Slavery Abolished in Haiti.
    New Jersey Adopts a Policy of Gradual Emancipation.

1807   England and the United States Prohibit Engagement in the International Slave Trade.

1813   Gradual Emancipation Adopted in Argentina.

1814   Gradual Emancipation Begins in Colombia.

1820   England Begins Using Naval Power to Suppress the Slave Trade.

1823   Slavery Abolished in Chile.

1824   Slavery Abolished in Central America.

1829   Slavery Abolished in Mexico.

1831   Slavery Abolished in Bolivia.

1838   Slavery Abolished in All British Colonies.

1841   The Quintuple Treaty Is Signed under Which England, France, Russia, Prussia, and Austria Agree to Mutual Search of Vessels on the High Seas in Order to Suppress the Slave Trade.

1842   Slavery Abolished in Uruguay.

1848   Slavery Abolished in All French and Danish Colonies.

1851   Slavery Abolished in Ecuador.
        Slave Trade Ended in Brazil.

1854   Slavery Abolished in Peru and Venezuela.

1862   Slave Trade Ended in Cuba.

1863   Slavery Abolished in All Dutch Colonies.

1865   Slavery Abolished in the U.S. as a Result of the Passage of the Thirteenth Amendment to the Constitution and the End of the Civil War.

1871   Gradual Emancipation Initiated in Brazil.

1873   Slavery Abolished in Puerto Rico.

1886   Slavery Abolished in Cuba.

1888   Slavery Abolished in Brazil.

---

elsewhere was not the consequence of emancipation *per se* but of nationalist revolutions. In countries such as Colombia and Venezuela the emancipation of slaves became an instrument of the revolutionaries who sought state power. With many of the nationalist leaders of these movements drawn from the wealthy landholding and slaveholding classes, abolition was generally a protracted process. Indeed, the majority of slaves — those in the northern United States, the British colonies, Puerto Rico, Cuba, and Brazil, among others — were emancipated under more or less peaceful conditions and with, at least, the begrudging acquiescence of substantial parts of the slaveowning classes. This is not to say that slavery merely faded away, but to emphasize that its demise was the result of the cumulative impact of the ideological and political, rather than military, pressure of the abolitionists.

Considering the large proportion of the wealth of slaveholders represented by their bondsmen, what needs to be explained is not so much why the slavocracy of the U.S. resorted to open warfare but why other slavocracies did not. A full and rigorous answer to the question is beyond the scope of this volume. However, economic factors are not without consequence in explaining the submission of slaveholders to the eventuality of abolition.

In this connection it should be noted that many, perhaps most, of the slaves outside of the southern United States were freed under programs of gradual emancipation. These schemes usually involved the freeing, not of adults, but of children born on some date after the emancipation law was enacted. Moreover, the freeing of slave children was delayed until their eighteenth, twenty-first, or in some cases, twenty-eighth birthday. Under such arrangements, slaveholders suffered no losses on existing male slaves or on female slaves who were already past their childbearing years. Having control over the services of a newly born child until his or her twenty-first or twenty-eighth birthday meant that most, if not all, of the costs of rearing such slaves would be covered by the income they earned between the onset of their productive years and the date of their emancipation. Thus, the major loss imposed on slaveowners was a consequence of the fall in value of slave women whose childbearing years still lay before them. For reasons explained in chapter 3 and appendix B the loss on these women probably did not exceed 15 percent of their value, and these women made up about one third of the labor force. In other words, gradual abolition imposed an average cost on slaveholders which was probably less than 5 percent of the initial value of their slaves; the average loss may, in fact, have been quite close to zero. Even when emancipation was carried out at a relatively rapid rate, as in the British colonies, a combination of factors served to reduce the losses of slaveowners to low levels. Under the enactment of the British Parliament, total emancipation was scheduled to take place six years after the passage of the law. At rates of return which prevailed in the West Indies, even such a relatively short delay permitted slaveowners to recover 50 percent of the initial value of their chattel. In addition, slaveowners received average payments from the British government as compensation for emancipation which were estimated at 40 percent of the initial value of the slaves. Here again, emancipation was planned in such a way as to limit the losses of slaveowners to approximately 10 percent of the value of their chattel. The actual loss could have been further reduced by increases in the intensity of labor and a deterioration in the level of slave maintenance. Such efforts to increase the income of slaveholders, and the protests they engendered, help to explain why the so-called "period of apprenticeship" was cut from six to four years.

The mounting pressure for emancipation produced substantial success. By 1830, more than a third of the Negroes in the Western Hemisphere were free. The greatest inroads were made in Spanish and French America. Only 25 percent of blacks in the colonies or former colonies of Spain were still slaves. And the revolution in Haiti had freed 80 percent of the slaves under French rule. Before the decade of the thirties was over, all the slaves of the British colonies were freed. The fervor for slavery seemed to be ebbing even in Brazil. At any rate, slave imports into Brazil during the decade of the thirties fell to 65 percent of the level which obtained in the twenties.

But in the southern United States, slavery continued with

undiminished vigor. Indeed, in this region it became more and more deeply entrenched during the last three decades of the antebellum era. With servitude crumbling all around them, and with their peculiar institution under increasing attack from abolitionists in the North, southern politicians moved to strengthen the legal bulwarks of their system. In eleven states the death penalty was imposed on slaves who participated in insurrections. In thirteen states it became a capital crime for free men to incite slaves to insurrection. Stricter laws and more severe penalties were also legislated against anyone who helped a slave to run away or who gave him asylum after he escaped.

At the same time, various barriers to voluntary manumission were erected. Several states passed laws requiring the consent of the legislature to validate a manumission. Seven states required emancipated slaves to leave their territory, and thirteen states barred freedmen from immigrating. Other limitations put on free Negroes by state, county, or city governments included the right to bear arms, to sell liquor, to travel beyond the borders of the county of which they were residents, to own real estate, and to assemble in public meetings.

There was also a marked deceleration in the rate of increase of the free Negro population after 1830. As a consequence, the proportion of the Negro population of the South that was free fell from slightly over 8 percent in 1830 to less than 6 percent in 1860. There was little in these figures or, as we shall soon see, in the economic statistics of the South over the same span, to encourage the view that southern slavery was on the brink of its own dissolution.

Two

Occupations and Markets

The Structure of Occupations

During the last three decades of the antebellum era, slaves were involved in virtually every aspect of southern economic life, both rural and urban. They were not only tillers of the soil but were fairly well-represented in most of the skilled crafts. In the city of Charleston, for example, about 27 percent of the adult male slaves were skilled artisans. In several of the most important crafts of that city — including carpentry and masonry — slaves actually outnumbered the whites. Some bondsmen even ascended into such professions as architecture and engineering. Of course, only a relatively small percentage of slaves (about 6 percent) lived in cities and towns of one thousand or more persons. One should not, however, leap from this fact to the conclusion that the entry of slaves into skilled occupations was special to the urban setting and therefore atypical of those who lived in rural areas.

The fact is that slaves also held a large share of the skilled jobs in the countryside. Indeed, on the large plantations slaves actually predominated in the crafts and in the lower

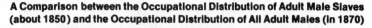

Figure 10

A Comparison between the Occupational Distribution of Adult Male Slaves
(about 1850) and the Occupational Distribution of All Adult Males (in 1870)

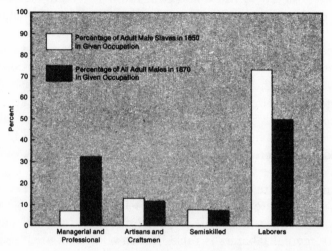

managerial ranks. To a surprising extent, slaves held the
top managerial posts. Within the agricultural sector, about
7.0 percent of the men held managerial posts and 11.9
percent were skilled craftsmen (blacksmiths, carpenters,
coopers, etc.). Another 7.4 percent were engaged in semiskilled and domestic or quasi-domestic jobs: teamsters,
coachmen, gardeners, stewards, and house servants. Occupational opportunity was more limited for women. About
80 percent of slave women labored in the fields. Virtually
all of the 20 percent who were exempt from field tasks
worked as house servants or in such quasi-domestic positions as seamstresses and nurses.

Comparison of the skill distribution of adult male slaves
with that of all adult males shortly after the Civil War reveals the way in which slavery limited opportunity. The

proportion of the labor force in the professional and managerial category was only one fifth as large for slaves as it was for all males in 1870. This was partly due to the fact that slaves were completely excluded from such choice professions as law, politics, and education. The main barrier to the entry of slaves into the top occupational category, however, was the exclusion of slaves from landownership. For three quarters of all men in the managerial and professional class in 1870 were landowning farmers. The exclusion of slaves from the top of the occupational pyramid pushed a larger proportion into the category of laborers. Laborers accounted for 73 percent of the male slaves in the labor force in 1850, but in 1870 only 49 percent of all males in the labor force were laborers.

While slavery clearly limited the opportunities of bonds-men to acquire skills, the fact remains that over 25 percent of males were managers, professionals, craftsmen, and semiskilled workers. Thus, the common belief that all slaves were menial laborers is false. Rather than being one undifferentiated mass, slave society produced a complex social hierarchy which was closely related to the occupational pyramid. It was out of this class of skilled workers that many of the leaders of the slave community arose. In normal times slave managers and craftsmen led in establishing and enforcing codes of behavior in the slave quarters, as well as in shaping patterns of black culture. They also represented the slave community in negotiating various prerogatives with masters and in restraining the excesses of white overseers. This upper occupational stratum may have provided, as a number of historians have argued, a disproportionately large share of the leaders of protests, desertions, insurrections, and rebellions.

Neglect of the fact that more than one out of every five adult slaves held preferred occupational positions, which involved not only more interesting and less arduous labor but also yielded substantially higher real incomes, has encouraged still another oversight: that is, the failure to recognize the existence of a flexible and exceedingly effective incentive system that operated within the framework of slavery. The notion that slaveowners relied on the lash alone to promote discipline and efficiency is a highly misleading myth. In slave, as in free society, positive incentives, in the form of material rewards, were a powerful instrument of economic and social control. Although slavery restricted economic and social mobility for blacks, it did not eliminate it.

While the great majority of slaves were agricultural laborers, it is not true that these agriculturalists were engaged only in a very few, highly repetitive tasks that involved no accumulation of skills. With the exception of entrepreneurial decisions regarding the allocation of resources among alternative uses and the marketing of crops and livestock, slaves engaged in the full range of agricultural activities. These included the planting, raising, and harvesting of virtually every type of crop, as well as animal husbandry, dairying, land improvement, use and maintenance of equipment and machinery, and the construction of buildings. Participation in a variety of activities was the rule rather than the exception.

The belief that slaves on plantations were mainly occupied in picking or raising cotton is also without foundation in fact. This popular misconception is partly attributable to the widely cited, but badly misinterpreted, statement of the superintendent of the U.S. census for 1850 that the 2,800,000 slaves in the agricultural sector were distributed among farms producing the great southern staples in the following proportions:

Cotton	73 percent
Tobacco	14 percent
Sugar	6 percent
Rice	5 percent
Hemp	2 percent

Although this distribution of the farm population of slaves is roughly correct, it does not follow that the 2,000,000 slaves on cotton plantations (0.73 × 2,800,000) spent all of their *labor time* in raising and picking cotton. In the first place, approximately one third of the slaves on cotton plantations were children under ten who were generally exempt from regular labor tasks. Of the remaining 1,400,000 slaves, about 20 percent were (as previously noted) artisans, semiskilled workers, or domestics who were not engaged in field tasks. Moreover, not all of the labor time of the remaining 1,150,000 field hands was spent in producing cotton. Even on farms in which cotton was the primary *market crop*, most of the labor time of slaves was devoted to other activities than the growing of cotton. This paradox is easily resolved. Nearly 100 percent of all cotton was shipped off the farm, but most of the output of grains, vegetables, and meat was consumed on the farm.

Cotton was, of course, the single most important crop on large cotton plantations, requiring about 34 percent of the labor time of slaves. However, the rearing of livestock (including the raising of feed) took nearly as much of the labor time of slaves — about 25 percent. Corn bound for human consumption took another 6 percent. The remaining 34 percent of the working time of slave hands was divided among land improvement, the construction of fences and buildings, the raising of other crops (oats, rye, wheat, potatoes, etc.), domestic duties, and home manufacturing (especially the production of clothes).

The discussion of the structure of slave occupations has thus far been limited to the last thirty years of the antebellum era. How similar or how different was the structure in earlier times? While limitations of data prevent a complete answer to the question, one point seems clear. A substantial share of blacks were artisans throughout the slave experience. So far, the only systematic evidence on the share of craftsmen and other nonagricultural laborers in the slave population during the eighteenth century comes from the analysis of advertisements for runaways. An analysis of the occupations of 1,138 men described in such advertisements over the period from 1736 to 1801, indicates that 22 percent were artisans and craftsmen and 7 percent were house servants. Of course, the runaway slaves listed in these advertisements may well constitute a biased sample, both because the inclination of owners to invest in advertising was probably affected by the value of the slave, and because skilled slaves might have been more likely to run away. Still, the foregoing statistics are in keeping with the sketchy impressions conveyed by the comments of visitors to North America.

Perhaps the most notable change in slave occupations between 1790 and 1860 was the redirection of the labor of field hands. Although cotton was the great agricultural staple of the South on the eve of the Civil War, it was just a minor crop at the end of the eighteenth century. The total production of cotton in 1790 required the full-time labor of about two thousand hands, a mere one half of one percent of the labor required for cotton in 1850. Tobacco was king at the time of Washington's first inauguration. Yet, great as was the redirection of labor from tobacco to cotton, its consequences for the development of slave skills should not be misconstrued. Whether they worked on tobacco or on cotton plantations, field hands spent most of their time raising livestock, grains, and other food crops. The shift in concentration from one staple to another affected the utilization of only a part of the total labor time of field hands. Regardless of the staple in which they specialized, field hands acquired a wide variety of farm skills throughout the slave era.

The Interregional Redistribution of Slaves

The switch from tobacco to cotton was associated with a remarkable change in the geographic location of the slave population. For most of the slave era, the overwhelming majority of blacks was concentrated in a tight area around Chesapeake Bay. In 1690, Maryland and Virginia contained slightly over two thirds of the entire black population. A century later, Virginia and Maryland still held over 56 percent of the slave population. The movement of the slave population away from its concentration near Chesapeake Bay into the south central and southwestern states did not assume large proportions until the beginning of the nineteenth century. By 1820 the share of slaves in Virginia and Maryland had declined to 35 percent. And on the eve of the Civil War these two states held just 15 percent of the nation's bondsmen. After remaining relatively stable for a century and a half, the center of the black population had, within the span of five decades, moved from the neighborhood of Chesapeake Bay to a point somewhere in western Georgia.

Two factors combined to bring about this rapid geographic redistribution of slaves. The first was the spectacular rise in the world's demand for cotton. From a total output of just 3,000 bales in 1790, U.S. cotton production increased to 178,000 bales in 1810, to 732,000 bales in 1830, and to 4,500,000 bales in 1860. Planters eager to respond to the lure of profit rushed westward to lands in Georgia, Alabama, Mississippi, Louisiana, and Texas that were far better suited for cotton production than those of Maryland, Virginia, and the Carolinas. The second factor was the improvement of transportation. The development of river steamers and railroads reduced transportation costs and made it feasible to bring into production lush lands once considered too remote for commercial exploitation.

Figure 11

The Distribution of the Slave Population in 1790 and 1860

Slaves: Number, 1790

Each Dot Represents 200 Slaves

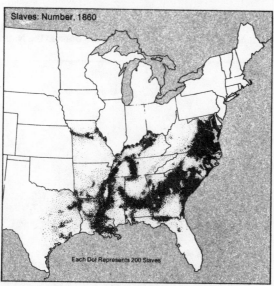

Slaves: Number, 1860

Each Dot Represents 200 Slaves

Figure 12

The Interregional Movement of Slaves, 1790-1860

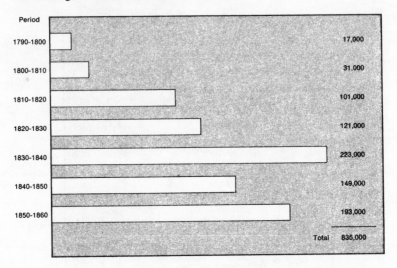

Period	
1790-1800	17,000
1800-1810	31,000
1810-1820	101,000
1820-1830	121,000
1830-1840	223,000
1840-1850	149,000
1850-1860	193,000
Total	835,000

Figure 13

Actual Slave Population of Importing States Compared with Population that Would Have Existed in These States if Growth Had Been at the National Rate

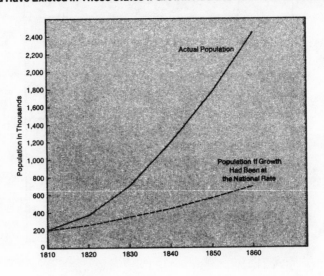

Between 1790 and 1860 a total of 835,000 slaves were moved from the exporting to the importing states. The tempo of migration accelerated with time. The traffic during the last half of the seventy-year period was three times as large as during the first half. The main exporting states were Maryland, Virginia, and the Carolinas. Together they supplied over 85 percent of the migrants. The four largest importers were Alabama, Mississippi, Louisiana, and Texas, which together received about 75 percent of the displaced blacks. The impact of the migration on the rates of growth of the slave populations of the exporting and importing states was quite substantial. By 1860 the exporting states had just 60 percent of the slave population they would have had if they had grown at the national average. On the other hand, migration swelled the slave population of the importing states to 3.6 times the level that would have obtained if these states had grown at the national average.

How were slaves moved from east to west? Were most blacks in the interregional movement sold by owners in the East to slave traders who transported them to western markets where they were resold? Or did most slaves take the interregional journey together with their owners as part of a movement in which whole plantations migrated to the West?

These are crucial questions. Several of the main aspects of the traditional interpretation of the slave economy hinge on the answers. In the traditional view, the inefficient practices of slave plantations led to soil exhaustion in the states of the "Old South." Robbed of their fertility, these soils, it was said, could no longer profitably support agriculture based on slave labor. However, the interregional slave trade gave a new lease on life to slavery in the Old South. In the words of John Elliott Cairnes, an eminent British economist of the mid-nineteenth century and an ardent abolitionist, it was "the profit developed by trading in slaves, and this alone," which "enabled slavery in the older slave states of

North America to survive the consequences of its own ravages." Slavery was saved, he said, by a "vast extension of the territory of the United States," which opened "new soils to Southern enterprise."

The problem of the planter's position was at once solved, and the domestic slave trade commenced. Slavery had robbed Virginia of the best riches of her soil, but she still had. a noble climate — a climate which would fit her admirably for being the breeding place of the South. A division of labour between the old and the new states took place. In the former the soil was extensively exhausted, but the climate was salubrious; in the latter the climate was unfavourable to human life spent in severe toil, but the soil was teeming with riches. The old states, therefore, undertook the part of breeding and rearing slaves till they attained to physical vigour, and the new that of using up in the development of their virgin resources the physical vigour which had been thus obtained.

This frequently repeated characterization of the interregional movement of slaves is without foundation in fact. Available evidence indicates that about 84 percent of the slaves engaged in the westward movement migrated with their owners. Only 127,000 slaves were sold from the east to the west over the fifty years from 1810 to 1860, or an average of a little over 2,500 sales per year. If the planters of the Old South engaged in deliberate breeding for export, it was a minor "crop." The total value of all the slaves sold from east to west in 1860 was about $3,000,000. So small an item, less than one percent of the gross value of agricultural output in the exporting states, could hardly have been the margin between the success or failure of plantation agriculture, especially when it is realized that only one quarter of the price of a prime-aged slave in the typical interregional sale was profit (the other three quarters represented rearing costs). In other words, the average profit per slaveholder in the selling states derived from the interregional slave trade was less than four dollars per year.

Of course, the traditional interpretation of the interregional slave traffic is not confined to economic issues. To many, the most critical aspect of the slave trade was its corrosive effect on the integrity of the slave family. Since most issues regarding the impact of slavery on the black family are considered in a later chapter, the discussion here is confined to an examination of the contention that the interregional slave migration resulted in the widespread division of marriages, with husbands wrung from wives and children from both.

That the interregional slave trade resulted in the destruction of *some* slave marriages is beyond dispute. What is at issue is the extent of the phenomenon. Data contained in sales records in New Orleans, by far the largest market in the interregional trade, sharply contradict the popular view that the destruction of slave marriages was at least a frequent, if not a universal, consequence of the slave trade. These records, which cover thousands of transactions during the years from 1804 to 1862, indicate that more than 84 percent of all sales over the age of fourteen involved unmarried individuals. Of those who were or had been married, 6 percent were sold with their mates; and probably at least one quarter of the remainder were widowed or voluntarily separated. Hence it is likely that 13 percent, or less, of interregional sales resulted in the destruction of marriages. And since sales were only 16 percent of the total interregional movement, it is probable that about 2 percent of the marriages of slaves involved in the westward trek were destroyed by the process of migration. Nor is it by any means clear that the destabilizing effects of the westward migration on marriages was significantly greater among blacks than it was among whites.

The New Orleans records also throw into doubt the claims that sales of single children under thirteen were very frequent and that such children "were hardly less than a staple in the trade." For only 9.3 percent of the New Orleans sales

Figure 14

A Comparison of the Age Distribution of Slaves Sold in New Orleans with the Age Distribution of All Slaves Migrating from East to West

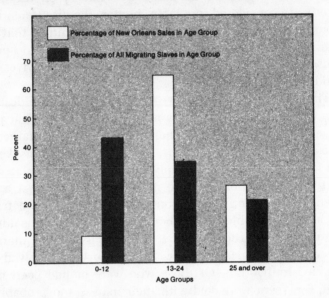

were of children under thirteen. Projected to the national level, this implies that the total interregional sales of children amounted to just 234 per annum. This small number of child sales could easily have been explained by orphans, as U. B. Phillips and other southern historians have claimed. Because of the high death rates of the time, approximately 15.9 percent of children under thirteen were orphans. Thus there were approximately 190,000 orphans in the age category 0–12 in 1850. The interregional sale of just 1 out of every 810 orphans would account for the full extent of the trade in children.

Many readers will, no doubt, consider these findings too far from accepted truth, too much at variance with the mass of evidence compiled by previous scholars, to be believable. Yet close examination reveals that the "mass of evidence" is actually very fragmentary and extremely weak. Frederic Bancroft, whose book *Slave Trading in the Old South* is the most authoritative and scholarly expression of the conventional view, asserts that the great frequency of child sales is an indisputable fact. And he counters U. B. Phillips's claim that "young children . . . were hardly ever sold separately" with what he calls overwhelming evidence to the contrary. However, his "overflowing" measure of "indisputable facts" turns out to be a listing of a little more than a score of isolated transactions involving the sale of approximately fifty children over a span of twenty-six years (from 1834 to 1860).

The prevailing view of the slave trade has been fashioned by historians primarily from the accounts of firsthand observers of the slave South. Since such observers lacked the hard data needed to actually determine the scope and nature of this trade, they could only convey their impressions. Unfortunately these impressions are far from uniform. There were not many detached and objective observers of slavery after 1830. Most so-called observations or travel accounts were actually polemics against or for slavery. In choosing between these conflicting and contradictory tracts, the historians who fashioned the conventional view of the slave trade uniformly rejected the impressions of southern writers as apologetics and accepted the views of northern or European critics as accurate. It is, of course, tempting to believe that truth must be on the side of justice, and that conviction may have guided these scholars, since no objective criteria for the decisions that led them to reject some accounts and accept others is apparent.

If historians have not previously exploited the New Orleans data, it is not because their existence was unknown, but because the volume of data was so massive that it could not be assailed successfully by scholars untrained in modern statistical methods. Nor did these records arise under circumstances or for purposes that were likely to make respondents give false information regarding the age, sex, or place of origin of slaves. The records were created by a law requiring the registration of all slave sales in order to give legal force to an owner's claim to title. Thus the records are quite similar to those maintained today for the clearance of titles to real estate. While it would, of course, be desirable to have similar records from elsewhere in the South, there is no reason to believe that the age and sex structure of interstate sales at New Orleans were markedly different from those of other south central cities. Moreover, New Orleans, more than any other city, dominated the interregional slave trade, receiving annually about one third of the slaves sold between states.

While the New Orleans data show that slaveowners were averse to breaking up black families, they do not tell us about the reasons for their reluctance. Because earlier historians became overly preoccupied with dramatic and poignant but relatively isolated instances of the destruction of black marriages, they failed to grasp the extremely important role that the master class assigned to the family institution, a role that will be examined in chapter 4. Commitment to an exaggerated view of the eagerness of masters to put families on the auction block prevented historians from recognizing the strength and stability that the black family acquired despite the difficult circumstances of slave life.

Markets for Slaves

There were two main types of market for slaves. One was the purchase market. Slaves were generally purchased by individuals who desired to procure labor for long periods of time. However, the labor of a slave was frequently desired for only relatively short periods — a day, a week, a month, or a year. Individuals who desired to employ slave labor for brief spans could do so by entering the hire or rental market. As with other expensive, long-lived assets, there was an extremely active rental market for slaves.

As we have seen, selling in the market was only one means of reallocating slave labor among regions and firms. And in the interregional movements, selling was far less important than the migration of whole farms or plantations. One should not leap from this fact to the conclusion that the role of the market mechanism was inconsequential. For although the east-west trade has, because of its potential for drama, been at the center of the attention of historians, it accounted for only a relatively small fraction of the total domestic sale of slaves. The New Orleans data indicate that only 25 percent of the slaves sold there were from the exporting states. Approximately 68 percent of the slaves marketed in the Crescent City were owned by residents of Louisiana. The other 7 percent belonged to owners who lived in western states which were, like Louisiana, net importers of slaves.

A study of slave trading in Maryland over the decade from 1830 to 1840 revealed that total sales (local and interstate) amounted to 1.92 percent of the slave population each year. If that ratio is projected to the national level, total slave sales over the period 1820–1860 averaged about fifty thousand per year. In other words, on average, only one slaveholder out of every twenty-two sold a slave in any given year, and roughly one third of these were estates of deceased persons.

This low sales rate clashes with the notion that speculative purchases and sales of slaves were common among southern planters, that slaves were frequently bought and sold to take advantage of temporary aberrations of price, in much the same way as planters sought to profit from daily, weekly, or monthly gyrations in the prices of cotton or railroad bonds. The analogy is fallacious. Speculation in ware house receipts on cotton or in railroad bonds did not involve the same type of costs as would have been incurred in the attempt to speculate on slaves. A planter who sold one or more of his slaves merely because prices were temporarily high would have incurred not only the usual brokerage fees, but would have lost the income from the labor of these slaves as well as of the land, buildings, and equipment that would lie idle, or be used less intensively, while he waited for the prices of slaves to fall to a point that warranted repurchase. Week-to-week or month-to-month fluctuations in slave prices were rarely large enough to cover such costs. Moreover, slaves were hardly as homogeneous an asset as "middling" short staple cotton. Even among prime field hands (healthy males in the ages eighteen to thirty), individual variations in strength, intelligence, and energy created spreads in prices of several hundred dollars. Characteristics that made a slave particularly useful to one owner, such as the familiarity with the routine of a given plantation or some personal attachment that affected motivation, might have little value to another owner, and hence were not easy to recover through sales to slave traders.

That slaves were generally purchased for use, rather than speculation, is clearly revealed by the extremely low sales rates of ongoing plantations. Not only was a purchased slave rarely resold, but slaves born on such estates were rarely put on the market. These conclusions have emerged from the analysis of the birth, purchase, and sales records of nineteen plantations with a total population of thirty-nine hundred slaves. Over a period of ninety years ending in 1865, a mere seven slaves were sold from these plantations. Of these, six were born on their plantations and one was purchased. Since a total of thirty-three hundred slaves were born on these nineteen plantations during the years in question, the ratio of sales to births was a mere 0.2 percent. On these plantations, at least, the breeding of slaves for sale in the market simply was not practiced.

How then did most slave sales originate? The Maryland study indicated that approximately one half of all sales were the consequence of the breakup of the estates of deceased planters whose heirs were unable or unwilling to continue the family business. There is little evidence regarding the circumstances which attended the balance of the sales. Some, no doubt, were forced by bankruptcies or other financial distress. However, since the bankruptcy rate was quite low in agriculture, it is unlikely that distressed sales accounted for more than a small fraction of the total. Some slaves were sold because they could not, or would not, adjust to the routine of given plantations. Occasionally sales were initiated by slaves who wished to be reunited with a member of the family, or who, for some reason, were prepared to work harder or better for one planter than another. Some sales were initiated by the government, for it was common to require slaves convicted of crimes to be sold outside of the county or state. This was true even of slaves convicted of capital offenses. Loath to lose the capital value of a slave through execution, the courts frequently commuted the death sentence to a brief (perhaps six months) prison sentence plus whipping, branding, and sale beyond the borders of the state, sometimes outside of the country. Even in such cases as the Nat Turner rebellion, economic motivation led to the transformation of many of the death sentences into deportation orders.

Adjustment to the need for the permanent or long-term reallocations of labor among occupations and regions was achieved through both sales and migration. The response to transient changes in labor requirements was brought about through the hire market. While historians have been well aware of the practice of slave renting, it has received insufficient attention in their writings. Perhaps they have felt that this phase of slavery was not as disruptive as the permanent separations sometimes forced by sales. Moreover, renting was too much like the hiring of free labor and might have seemed too incidental, perhaps even too aberrant, to be treated as a central feature of the system. This was especially true of slave artisans who frequently hired out on their own account. Such slaves operated in virtually the same way as their free counterparts. They advertised their services themselves, negotiated their own contracts, received monies and paid debts themselves, and obtained their own residences and places of business. The primary difference between such slaves and free artisans was that the slaves were required to pay their owners a fixed percentage of their income.

Hiring was not a minor or inconsequential feature of slavery. Through the examination of data in the manuscript schedules of the U.S. census, it has been determined that about 31 percent of urban slave workers were on hire during 1860. In some cities, such as Richmond, the proportion was in excess of 50 percent. The proportion of slave rentals in rural areas was lower, generally running about 6 percent. For the slave labor force as a whole, then, about 7.5 percent were on hire at any moment of time. Since hire contracts rarely ran for more than a year, and many were for substantially shorter periods of time, the ratio of hire transactions to slaves was probably 15 or more percent. Thus hire transactions were probably over five times as frequent as sales.

While many slave hires were negotiated directly between the owner and renter, or by a slave directly with a renter, there were commercial agencies which specialized in the business of providing "temporary employment." Richmond alone had nine such agencies which provided rentals for local residents and for people in the surrounding countryside as well as for those living in neighboring cities.

Renters of slaves included railroads which temporarily needed larger than usual numbers of workers because of construction of new lines, industrial firms which experienced sharp cyclical or seasonal fluctuations in business, and farms during such peak periods of activity as harvesting. Hires were also made by persons who had occasional needs — the homeowner who wanted to repair a roof or the family that needed extra servants for a wedding. The most frequent rental contracts appear to have been yearly ones. In such cases contracts usually were quite detailed in specifying the obligations of the renter. Renters had to provide adequate living quarters, food, clothing, and medical care for the slave. Frequently they also had to provide the slave with a new suit of clothing and a new pair of shoes at the end of the hire period. If the slave ran away or became ill, the burden of the lost time fell on the renter. Renters were liable for the full value of a slave who ran away or who died because of their negligence. That renters took the injunctions of their contracts seriously is suggested by fragmentary evidence on the mortality rates of hires; these rates do not appear to have been above those experienced by all slaves in the appropriate age categories.

Thus the dictum propounded during the nineteenth century, and so widely accepted today, that the ownership of men was incompatible with the shifting labor requirements of capitalist society, is without warrant in fact. The antebellum South successfully adjusted to the rapidly changing labor requirements of various southern firms and localities through a variety of mechanisms. In the one area where a direct comparison is possible, the interregional movement, it appears that the east-west migration rate was slightly higher for slaves than for free men. Nor is it true that ownership by men prevented blacks from acquiring most of the skills required by a relatively modern economy. Because slavery precluded the ownership of property by bondsmen, it drastically reduced the opportunity of blacks to obtain entrepreneurial experience. Slavery also resulted in barring blacks from law, education, and a number of other professions. It is certainly important to probe into the ways in which such restrictions limited opportunity for blacks; but it is also important to know more about the nature of the skills that blacks were able to acquire.

Three.

Profits and Prospects

The Issues

The source and the magnitude of the profit of slaveowners has been something of a mystery. The absence of hard data touched off a debate on these issues among professional historians that has extended for nearly three quarters of a century. Until recently, the debate was dominated by the views of Ulrich B. Phillips. A Southerner by birth, and a professor of history at the Universities of Wisconsin, Michigan, and Yale, Phillips was for many years the doyen of those writing on the antebellum South. His interpretation of the economics of slavery was first set forth in an essay published in 1905 and later elaborated in books published in 1918 and 1929. Phillips scoured southern archives for both quantitative and qualitative information bearing on the operation of slave plantations. His search was more thorough than that of any scholar who preceded him and most of those who followed him. Still, the evidence he turned up was insufficient for the calculation of representative profit margins. In the end, he based his argument largely on data he collected with respect to the prices of slaves and prices of cotton.

In Phillips's view, the inefficiency of slave labor made it a profitable investment only when there was a conjunction of three conditions. These conditions were: 1, an extreme scarcity of, and a high price for, free labor; 2, a system of agricultural organization and a set of crops that permitted the strict supervision of slaves in simple routines; and 3, a low price for slaves. Phillips argued that all of these conditions existed in the southern colonies prior to the American Revolution and that is why slavery took root and prospered there.

He also argued that these propitious conditions for slavery began to give way during the decade following the peace treaty of 1783. In particular, the eroding of world markets for plantation crops undermined the second condition. The price of tobacco, said Phillips, had fallen to such low levels "that the opening of each new tract for its culture was offset by the abandonment of an old one." "Indigo production was decadent," he added, "and rice culture was in painful transition." Without the development of the cotton gin, slavery might have disappeared. However, the rise of the cotton culture gave a new impetus to black bondage. The booming world market for cotton stimulated the domestic demand for slaves and reinvigorated the slave trade.

A new threat to the continuation of slavery arose, said Phillips, when the congressional ban against further importations of Africans was put into force in 1808. It took some time for the effects of this action to be felt in the marketplace. Finally, the low and relatively steady slave prices of earlier years gave way to an era in which slave prices bounded upward. Phillips stressed the fact that the rise in slave prices was far more rapid than the rise in cotton prices. To him, the ratio of cotton to slave prices was as crucial in evaluating the wisdom of an investment in slaves as the price-to-earnings ratio was for evaluating the wisdom of an investment in corporate stocks.

The data assembled by Phillips showed that the ratio of slave to cotton prices rose by over sixfold between 1805 and 1860. A change of this magnitude clearly indicated to Phillips that, by the last decade of the antebellum era, slaves were overvalued — that is, priced too high to permit an investor to earn a normal rate of profit.

What caused the rise in the ratio of slave to cotton prices? According to Phillips, it could not be explained by a decline in the cost of maintaining slaves. Nor could it be explained by an increase in the productivity of slaves since, "in his capacity for work, a prime negro in 1800 was worth nearly or quite as much as a similar slave in 1860."

The rise, Phillips concluded, was primarily the consequence of speculation. The supply of slaves had been "cornered" as a consequence of the closing of the slave trade. Hence "it was unavoidable that the price should be bid up to the point of overvaluation." This speculative pressure was reinforced by two other tendencies. First, there were economies of scale in cotton production. Thus, plantation owners were constantly trying to increase the size of their slave force in order to reap the benefits of large-scale operations. Second, slaves were desired not only for productive purposes but also as symbols of social status and wealth.

It should be stressed that Phillips never provided evidence that speculation, economies of scale, and conspicuous consumption were responsible for the rise in the slave–cotton price ratio. He merely asserted that these were the true explanatory factors.

The proposition that slavery was unprofitable to most planters suggests that the slave system was dying, or at least declining, due to internal economic contradictions. Phillips did not himself propound this thesis, but it was forcefully developed by a number of historians who fall into what might be called, "the Phillips school." These scholars attempted to ferret out the economic forces which would eventually have led to the self-strangulation of slavery. Three features of the slave economy were singled out.

First, it was asserted that southern planters were beset by an irresistible tendency toward the overproduction of cotton. The chief author of this thesis was Charles W. Ramsdell of the University of Texas. Ramsdell argued that the tendency toward overproduction was clearly evident in the rapid expansion of the cotton culture after 1858, and in the subsequent decline in the price of cotton. To support his point he contrasted the last few years of the decade with conditions that prevailed at its start. Ramsdell noted that the fifties began with a high price for cotton and a moderate level of production. The production of cotton increased slowly between 1850 and 1857 and its price remained relatively stable, varying from about ten cents per pound to over thirteen cents. But 1858 began a period of rapid increase in cotton production and a simultaneous decline in price. Ramsdell stressed that the size of the cotton crop doubled between 1850 and 1860. About 70 percent of the increase took place between 1857 and 1860.

What caused this sudden rise in output? It was due, said Ramsdell, "in part to the rapid building of railroads throughout the South toward the end of the decade, which brought new lands within reach of markets and increased the cotton acreage; but part of the increase was due to the new fields in Texas." To Ramsdell, prevailing circumstances clearly indicated that the future course of output was up, while that of prices was down. "Had not the war intervened," he continued, "there is every reason to believe that there would have been a continuous overproduction and very low prices throughout the sixties and seventies."

But what precisely was the "every reason" for Ramsdell's belief? It was merely his conviction that the virgin lands of Texas would have been brought into cotton production and that the increased output of cotton would have led to a decline in its price. Ramsdell presented no evidence to back up his prediction.

The second argument for the economic self-strangulation of slavery has come to be known as the "natural limits" thesis. This thesis was derived from two subsidiary propositions. The first asserts that climate and soil set a limit to the geographic extension of the cotton culture and, hence, of slave agriculture. Charles Ramsdell, who was also one of the principal authors of this view, contended that this natural limit had in fact been reached by 1860. The other proposition asserts that slavery required continuous territorial expansion in order to remain profitable. Since slavery led to rapid soil exhaustion, an adequate level of slave productivity could be maintained only by continuously bringing new land into production. Consequently, if expansion was ruled out by the natural limits of soil and climate, the level of slave productivity would soon have fallen to levels too low to permit the survival of the system.

The third argument for the existence of fatal internal economic contradictions rests on an asserted incompatibility between slavery and urban society. This thesis has been enunciated by a long list of writers including John Cairnes, Frederick Douglass, Charles H. Wesley, Lewis C. Gray, Charles Ramsdell, and Richard C. Wade. Some writers based this view on the racist contention that the slave was "too primitive" to successfully adapt to the complexities of urban production and life. Others saw the threat as arising from the difficulty of controlling slaves in an urban environment. Strikes, attacks on property, other forms of crime, and the greater ease of escape all added greatly to the cost of policing slaves. It has also been asserted that as the density of cities increased, the cost of control rose at a disproportionate rate: the "peculiar institution" was bound to be squeezed between the unprofitability of urban slavery and the relentless tendency toward the urbanization of society.

Some writers found evidence of the corrosive effects of urbanization on slavery in the decennial censuses. Population reports showed a marked and accelerating decline in the proportion of slaves living in the ten largest southern cities between 1820 and 1860. Indeed, during the last decade of the antebellum era the decline was absolute.

Not all members of the Phillips school leaped from the proposition that slavery was unprofitable to the conclusion that slavery was bound to fall of its own weight. The most notable exception is Eugene Genovese. A scholar of Marxist persuasion, Genovese sought to free Phillips's analysis of its racist aspects and bring to the fore what he considered to be the true class relationship implied by Phillips's research and discoveries.

Like other members of the Phillips school, Genovese agreed that slavery was economically inefficient, that it exhausted the soil, that it restricted the development of manufacturing, that it conflicted with urbanization, and that it generated a relentless drive for territorial expansion. He was, however, ambivalent on the issue of profitability, at times agreeing that on a strict commercial basis an investment in slaves may not have been profitable, and at other times arguing that it probably was. Nor did Genovese regard this as a matter that had to be resolved. Quite the contrary — he lashed out against the preoccupation of his predecessors with the issue of profitability, a preoccupation which blinded them to the central, overriding characteristics of the slave system and the slaveowning class.

Planters, said Genovese, were "precapitalist" aristocrats imbued with an "antibourgeois spirit," with values and mores which subordinated the drive for profit to honor, luxury, ease, accomplishment, and family. "Whereas in the North people followed the lure of business and money for their own sake, in the South specific forms of property carried the badges of honor, prestige, and power." Because of these noneconomic objectives, slaveowners were prepared to shun the greater profits of industry, to maintain their wealth in slaves, even though physical capital offered higher rates of return.

Consequently, the notion that planters would have abandoned slavery simply because of declining profits was absurd, said Genovese. While slaveholders were not unconcerned about profit, they were more concerned about maintenance of their power, their moral values, their social milieu. Given such an outlook, there was no reason to assume that planters would "divest themselves of slaves as easily as a northern capitalist sold his holdings of railroad stock or of corporate bonds when the earnings on such securities faltered." Genovese believed that in the face of declining profits slaveholders would seek a political solution to their economic plight. In his view, the Civil War was the solution of the master class to the growing crisis that confronted it toward the end of the antebellum era. The slavocracy hoped in one "bold stroke to complete their political independence and to use it to provide an expansionist solution for their economic and social problems."

In contrast to the formidable legions that made up the Phillips school, those who believed that slaveholders earned high rates of return were until recently a beleaguered minority. This small group of scholars viewed slavery as an economically viable system and rejected the view that economic forces by themselves would have soon undermined the system. Agreement on these points did not, however, lead to a common view on the efficiency of slave labor or on the relative importance of the various sources from which masters derived income from their bondsmen.

Lewis C. Gray, the author of the leading history of southern agriculture, is virtually the only modern student of slavery who rejected the contention that slaves were inefficient and unproductive. He argued that while slaves were an inferior form of labor in manufacturing, they not only "displayed considerable skill" in farming but frequently worked harder and were more responsible than free labor. Gray held that in the production of staple commodities, the slave was clearly more efficient than the free laborer. That superiority, he said, was the explanation for the tendency of slave labor to replace free labor in cotton, sugar, rice, and tobacco. Gray discounted slave breeding as a major source of profit. "[M]erely rearing slaves for sale was not profitable, since [the] increase [in slaves] would constitute by itself only a very moderate interest on capital. . . . Consequently it did not pay to keep a larger force than was needed to cultivate the land."

On the other hand, Kenneth Stampp, the author of the most systematic rebuttal to Phillips, felt that slaves were profitable not because they were more efficient than free labor but because their labor cost less. The lower cost of slaves tended to offset the superior efficiency of free labor. As a consequence, "the slave was earning for his owner a substantial, though varying, surplus above the cost of maintenance." Stampp also placed more emphasis on slave breeding or rearing as a source of income than did Gray. "[N]umerous shreds of evidence . . . ," he said, "indicate that slaves were reared with an eye to their marketability — that the domestic slave trade was not 'purely casual.'" Many masters "calculated the natural increase as part of the profit upon their invested capital. They might realize this profit by putting additional acres under cultivation, or they might realize it by doing business with the slave traders."

Perhaps no member of the anti-Phillips school placed greater emphasis on slave rearing as a source of profit than Frederic Bancroft. "Slave-rearing," he said, "early became the source of the largest and often the only regular profit of nearly all slaveholding farmers and of many planters in the upper South." Bancroft put the "annual value of the natural increase of the slaves on a plantation" at between 4 and 8 percent of the investment in slaves. "It was often several times as much as a planter's profit on his crop. . . . Indeed, the merely agricultural result of planting was more often a loss than a gain."

The Level of Profits and the Capitalist Character of Slavery

Strange as it may seem, the *systematic* investigation of the average rate of profit on investments in slaves did not begin until more than half a century after U. B. Phillips launched the issue. There were some casual attacks on the problem in the 1930s and 1940s, but for various reasons they were wanting. In general, the authors of these early efforts failed to appreciate the complexity of the problem of calculating profit rates. They gave little thought to the nature of the equations to be used in the calculation, failed to take account of the multiplicity of revenues and costs that had to be estimated, and did little to probe the representativeness of the scattered and incomplete records on which their estimates were based.

The study by Alfred H. Conrad and John R. Meyer marked a decisive turning point in the effort to deal with the question of profits. "From the standpoint of the entrepreneur making an investment in slaves," they wrote, "the basic problems involved in determining profitability are analytically the same as those met in determining the returns from any other kind of capital investment." In posing the problem in this way, Conrad and Meyer were, of course, merely taking up one of Phillips's suggestions. For it was Phillips who originally stressed the similarity between the slave and stock markets. However, while Phillips did not know how to pass from his conceptualization of the problem to the measurement of the rate of return on an investment in slaves, these two economists did.

Conrad and Meyer produced separate estimates of the rates of return on males and females. The computation of the return on male slaves was the simpler case. They first derived the average capital cost per slave, including not only the price of a slave, but also the average value of the land, animals, and equipment used by a slave. Estimates of gross annual earnings were then built up from data on the price of cotton and the physical productivity of slaves. The net figure was obtained by subtracting the maintenance and supervisory costs for slaves from gross earnings. The average length of the stream of net earnings was determined from mortality tables. With these estimates Conrad and Meyer computed rates of return on male slaves and found that for the majority of antebellum plantations the return varied between 5 and 8 percent, depending on the physical yield per hand and the prevailing farm price of cotton. On the farms in poor upland pine country or in the exhausted lands of the eastern seaboard, the range of rates was merely 2 to 5 percent. However, in the "best lands of the new Southwest, the Mississippi alluvium, and the better South Carolina and Alabama plantations" rates ran as high as 10 to 13 percent.

The computation of the rate of return on female slaves was somewhat more complicated. Conrad and Meyer had to take account not only of the productivity of a female in the field, but of such additional matters as the productivity of her offspring between their birth and the time of their sale; maternity, nursery, and rearing costs; and the average number of offspring. Contending that very few females produced less than five or more than ten children that survived to be sold, Conrad and Meyer computed lower and upper limits on the rate of return. These turned out to be 7.1 and 8.1 percent respectively. Thus, planters in the exhausted lands of the upper South who earned only 4 or 5 percent on male slaves, still were able to achieve a return on their total operation equal to alternative opportunities. They did so by selling the offspring of females to planters in the West, thus earning rates of 7 to 8 percent on the other half of their slave force. Proof of such a trade was found not only in the descriptions of contemporaries, but also in the age structure of the slave population. The selling states had a significantly larger proportion of persons under fifteen and over fifty, while the buying states predominated in slaves of the prime working ages.

Rather than ending the controversy on profitability, the study of Conrad and Meyer intensified it. However, because of their work, the debate became much more sharply focused than before. They had clearly identified the crucial variables pertinent to the calculation, and the type of equations on which the calculation had to be based. Subsequent work by over a score of scholars was aimed at correcting their estimates of the values of the relevant variables and at refining their computational equations.

It is interesting that the first wave of criticisms of Conrad and Meyer turned up errors running almost exclusively in one direction — errors that made their estimate of the rate of profit too high. Thus, it was pointed out that their assumption that all slaves lived the average length of life biased the estimated rate of profit upward. They also greatly overestimated the number of slave children per female who lived to reach age eighteen. And they underestimated the amount of capital equipment required for slaves, as well as such varied costs as medical care, the employment of managerial personnel, food, and clothing.

As the debate developed, it became clear that Conrad and Meyer had also erred on the other side. They greatly underestimated the average productivity of a prime hand (a healthy slave between the ages of eighteen and thirty) as well as the productivity of females relative to males. At the same time they overestimated such items as maternity costs and the amount of land, equipment, and livestock required for young and old field hands. They also made the erroneous assumption that the land and physical capital employed by each slave died when he or she died.

To trace the twists and turns of this highly technical debate is beyond the scope of this book. Some of the more crucial technical issues are discussed in appendix B. At this point we wish merely to stress that the net result of the various corrections has been to raise, not lower, the Conrad and Meyer estimate of the rate of return. On average, slave-owners earned about 10 percent on the market price of their bondsmen. Rates of return were approximately the same for investments in males and females. They were also approximately the same across geographic regions. There were, of course, fluctuations around the average. But, for reasons considered in detail below, over the period from 1820 through 1860, there was no secular trend in the level of profits away from the average.

The discovery of a high and persistent rate of profit on slaves constitutes a serious, and probably irreparable, blow to the thesis that the price of slaves was largely attributable to conspicuous consumption. If conspicuous consumption had increased the market price of slaves over the level indicated by business considerations alone, the expected rate of return from an investment in slaves would have been below that earned on alternative investments. The corrected computations of Conrad and Meyer revealed no such profit deficit. Quite the contrary — the computations yielded average rates of return equal to, or in excess of, the averages which obtained in a variety of nonagricultural enterprises. For example, the average rate of return earned by nine of the most successful New England textile firms over the period from 1844 through 1853 was 10.1 percent. And a group of twelve southern railroads averaged 8.5 percent for the decade 1850–1860.

The finding that the rate of return on slaves was quite high does not rule out the possibility that some planters were willing to pay a premium to buy slaves, or that some planters held excessive numbers of slaves at prevailing prices. However, it does show that the aggregate demand of this category of slaveowners was too limited to raise the market price of slaves above the level dictated by normal business standards; that is, the demand of those slaveowners who desired to hold slaves for conspicuous consumption was quite small relative to the total demand for slaves.

It should be remembered that the proponents of the thesis that slaves were held widely for reasons of conspicuous consumption never provided conclusive proof of their contention. The thesis did not appear to require a rigorous proof, since the assumption that an investment in slaves was unprofitable made conspicuous consumption a plausible rationalization for the willingness of slaveowners to pay "excessive" prices. In this context it appeared to be sufficient merely to cite evidence which suggested that prestige attached to the ownership of slaves. Yet surely prestige attaches to the ownership of most assets of great value which bring high rates of return to their owners. To show that the ownership of slaves and prestige were positively correlated does not settle the issue of causality. Was the price of slaves high because the ownership of slaves brought prestige, or did the ownership of slaves bring prestige because their price was high? To distinguish between these alternatives one needs to know whether the expected return to slaves was below or above alternative rates. It was precisely on this point that exponents of the thesis of conspicuous consumption erred.

The demonstration that an investment in slaves was highly profitable not only undermines the case for conspicuous consumption; it also throws into doubt the contention that southern slaveholders were a "precapitalist," "uncommercial" class which subordinated profit to considerations of power, life-style, and "patriarchal commitments." The point at issue is not whether the slavocracy valued its power, life-style, and patriarchal commitments, but whether the pur-

Figure 15

The Distribution of Male Slave Prices by Age in the Old South

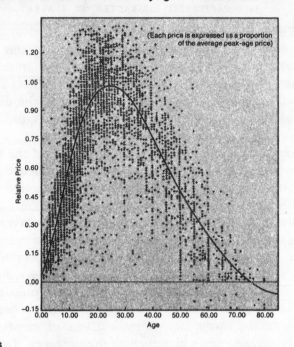

Figure 16

Averages of Price Relatives by Age for Male Slaves in the Old South

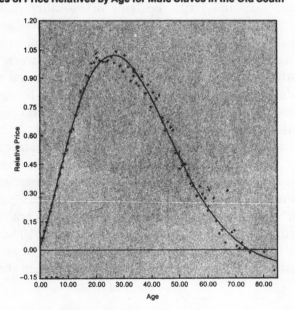

suit of these objectives generally conflicted with, or significantly undermined, the pursuit of profit.

Paternalism is not intrinsically antagonistic to capitalist enterprise. Nor is it necessarily a barrier to profit maximization. Such well-known and spectacularly profitable firms as the International Business Machines Corporation and Eastman Kodak practice paternalism. Their experience suggests that patriarchal commitments may actually raise profits by inducing labor to be more efficient than it would have been under a less benevolent management. There is no reason to rule out the possibility that paternalism operated in this way for slaveowners. No one has shown that masters who practiced paternalism had lower rates of return on the average than those who were unconcerned or heartless with respect to the welfare of their bondsmen.

On the other hand, there is considerable evidence that slaveowners were hard, calculating businessmen who priced slaves, and their other assets, with as much shrewdness as could be expected of any northern capitalist. This point is well illustrated by figure 15, which presents over five thousand prices of male slaves. While there was variation in price at each age (as one would expect of slaves who differed in health, attitudes, and capacities), the distribution displays a quite definite pattern. On average, prices rose until the late twenties and then declined. The decline was slow at first but then became more rapid, until advanced ages were reached. The basic pattern in the movement of prices by age is more clearly displayed in figure 16. Here each observation represents the average of all the prices for a given age. Figures 15 and 16 also display the curve, or profile, that best describes the relationship between price and age.

What explains the age pattern of prices? Conspicuous consumption and other nonpecuniary arguments offered to explain the trend in slave prices over time clearly fail here. It seems hardly likely that twenty-six-year-olds were priced

Figure 17

Annual Net Earnings from Male Slaves by Age about 1850, Old South

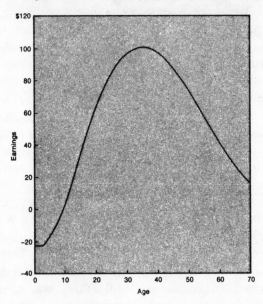

twice as high as ten-year-olds because twice as much honor and prestige were attached to the owners of the older than of the younger slaves.

The age-price profile is better explained by the pattern of earnings over the life cycle of slaves. Indeed, the age-price profile implies a corresponding earnings profile. Figure 17 presents the average net earnings, or profit, from male slaves in the Old South at each age about the year 1850. Net earnings were negative until age eight. Then they became positive and rose to a peak at age thirty-five. It is interesting to note that earnings of sixty-five-year-olds were still positive and, on average, brought an owner as much net income as a slave in the mid-teens. This does not mean that every slave aged

Figure 17

Annual Net Earnings from Male Slaves by Age about 1850, Old South

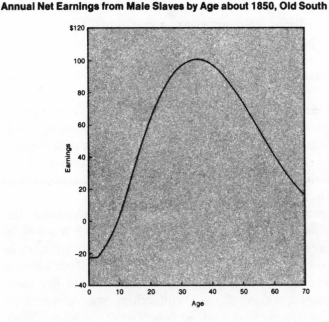

twice as high as ten-year-olds because twice as much honor and prestige were attached to the owners of the older than of the younger slaves.

The age-price profile is better explained by the pattern of earnings over the life cycle of slaves. Indeed, the age-price profile implies a corresponding earnings profile. Figure 17 presents the average net earnings, or profit, from male slaves in the Old South at each age about the year 1850. Net earnings were negative until age eight. Then they became positive and rose to a peak at age thirty-five. It is interesting to note that earnings of sixty-five-year-olds were still positive and, on average, brought an owner as much net income as a slave in the mid-teens. This does not mean that every slave aged suit of these objectives generally conflicted with, or significantly undermined, the pursuit of profit.

Paternalism is not intrinsically antagonistic to capitalist enterprise. Nor is it necessarily a barrier to profit maximization. Such well-known and spectacularly profitable firms as the International Business Machines Corporation and Eastman Kodak practice paternalism. Their experience suggests that patriarchal commitments may actually raise profits by inducing labor to be more efficient than it would have been under a less benevolent management. There is no reason to rule out the possibility that paternalism operated in this way for slaveowners. No one has shown that masters who practiced paternalism had lower rates of return on the average than those who were unconcerned or heartless with respect to the welfare of their bondsmen.

On the other hand, there is considerable evidence that slaveowners were hard, calculating businessmen who priced slaves, and their other assets, with as much shrewdness as could be expected of any northern capitalist. This point is well illustrated by figure 15, which presents over five thousand prices of male slaves. While there was variation in price at each age (as one would expect of slaves who differed in health, attitudes, and capacities), the distribution displays a quite definite pattern. On average, prices rose until the late twenties and then declined. The decline was slow at first but then became more rapid, until advanced ages were reached. The basic pattern in the movement of prices by age is more clearly displayed in figure 16. Here each observation represents the average of all the prices for a given age. Figures 15 and 16 also display the curve, or profile, that best describes the relationship between price and age.

What explains the age pattern of prices? Conspicuous consumption and other nonpecuniary arguments offered to explain the trend in slave prices over time clearly fail here. It seems hardly likely that twenty-six-year-olds were priced sixty-five produced a positive net income for his owner. Some of the elderly were a net loss. However, the income earned by the able-bodied among the elderly was more than enough to compensate for the burden imposed by the incapacitated. The average net income from slaves remained positive until they reached their late seventies. Even after that age the average burden was quite low, since a fair share of the slaves who survived into their eighties still produced positive net incomes.

Thus, the frequent contention that slaveowners preferred to work slaves to death at early ages, in order to avoid the burden of maintenance at late ages, is unfounded. Slaveowners were generally able to employ their bondsmen profitably throughout the life cycle. Planters solved the problem of old age by varying tasks according to the capacities of slaves. There were many occupations on plantations for which the elderly were suited. Women too old to labor in the fields could, for example, be made responsible for the care of slave children or serve as nurses to the sick. They could also be employed as seamstresses, or in spinning cotton and weaving. Elderly men were put in charge of the livestock, or were made responsible for the care of implements. Some became gardeners or household servants. This capacity to utilize the labor of the elderly was probably not so much a feature of slavery *per se* but of the predominantly agrarian nature of slavery. The rise of the problem of what to do with the elderly coincides with the emergence of urbanized, industrial societies. It is a problem that is rarely encountered in the countryside.

Figure 18 compares the prices of males and females. It shows that their prices were virtually identical until age nine, after which female prices rose less rapidly than those of males. At age twenty-seven the female price was about 80 percent of the male price. The ratio fell to 60 percent at age fifty and to less than half at age seventy.

Again, the explanation of this pattern is found in the

Figure 18

Prices of Slaves by Age and Sex about 1850, Old South

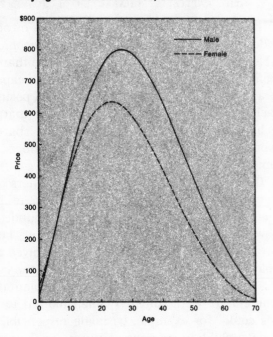

Figure 19

Annual Net Earnings from Slaves by Age and Sex about 1850, Old South

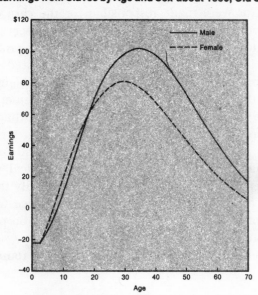

life cycles of the net earnings of males and females, which are shown in figure 19. For most of the years of their lives, female earnings were below those of males by 20 to 40 percent. Interestingly, prior to age eighteen, female earnings exceeded those of males. This differential is not explained by income produced from children borne by teen-age mothers. As will be shown, earnings from childbearing were quite small during these years. The early advantage in female earnings appears to have been due primarily to a more rapid rate of maturity among women than among men.

In the absence of evidence on the market behavior of slaveowners, it was easy for historians inclined to the romantic to postulate a dichotomy between paternalism and profit-seeking. They took evidence of paternalism to imply that slaveowners must have sacrificed profits to other objectives. Now that the profitability of slavery and the overwhelming dominance of business considerations in the market behavior of slaveowners are firmly established, should we assume that paternalism was an invention of apologists for slavery? That conclusion would be as romantic and naïve as the one we have rejected. There is too much evidence of deep personal attachments between owners and their bondsmen to deny that this was a facet of the slave system. "Now my heart is nearly broke," wrote a Louisiana planter on the occasion of the death of the principal slave manager. "I have lost poor *Leven,* one of the most faithful black men [that] ever lived. [H]e was truth and honesty, and without a fault that I ever discovered. He has overseed the plantation nearly three years, and [has] done much better than any white man [had] ever done here, and I lived a quiet life."

Would this expression of affection have been quite so deep if Leven had been inefficient, dishonest, and troublesome? While we do not mean to imply that affection for slaves was purely a function of their earning capacity, we do mean to suggest that it was more usual for affection and productivity to reinforce each other than to conflict with each other. Both cruelty and affection had their place on southern plantations.

The Myth of Slave-Breeding

The thesis that *systematic* breeding of slaves for sale in the *market* accounted for a major share of the net income or profit of slaveholders, especially in the Old South, is espoused in one degree or another by most members of the anti-Phillips school. This proposition was given a considerable fillip by the work of Conrad and Meyer, who found substantially higher returns on women than men in the Old South. "Slavery was profitable to the whole South," they concluded, because "the continuing demand for labor in the Cotton Belt" insured high "returns to the breeding operation on the less productive land in the seaboard and border states."

The words "systematic" and "market" were underlined in the previous paragraph to emphasize that what is implied by the breeding thesis is more than the existence of general incentives for the encouragement of large slave families. *Systematic breeding for the market* involves two interrelated concepts: 1, interference in the normal sexual habits of slaves to maximize female fertility through such devices as mating women with especially potent men, in much the same way as exists in breeding of livestock; 2, the raising of slaves with sale as the main objective, in much the same way as cattle or horses are raised.

The evidence put forward to support the contention of breeding for the market is meager indeed. Aside from the differential in profit rates produced by Conrad and Meyer, the evidence consists largely of unverified charges made by abolitionists, and of certain demographic data. However, subsequent corrections of the work of Conrad and Meyer have shown that rates of return on men and women were approximately the same. And the many thousands of hours of research by professional historians into plantation records have failed to produce a single authenticated case of the "stud" plantations alleged in abolitionist literature.

The demographic argument for the existence of slave breeding is based on two principal observations. First, the slave-exporting states had fewer slaves in the age group fifteen to twenty-nine, and more at very young and old ages, than the slave-importing states. Second, the fertility rate, measured as the ratio of children under one year to women aged fifteen to forty-nine, was slightly higher in the exporting than in the importing states. Neither of these demographic observations is sufficient to establish the existence of breeding for the market. The deviations of the age distribution in importing and exporting states existed not only for slaves but for free men. As such, they are proof that both free men and slaves migrated from east to west. But this point has never been in contention. What is in contention is the claim that the slave migration took place through market trading instead of through the migration of whole plantations.

As was shown in chapter 2, only 16 percent of the interregional movement of slaves took place through market trading. This small movement, an average of about twenty-five hundred persons per year, produced a gross income for the Old South planters in 1860 of just $3,000,000, and a net income only a quarter as high. It is hardly likely that the fate of slavery in the Old South depended on an item which accounted for less than one percent of farm receipts. Indeed, one could more easily make a case for the indispensability of the sweet potato crop, since this item brought in more income to slaveowners than the interregional sale of their bondsmen.

Equally erroneous is the argument that it was only in the

Figure 20

Division of Female Price between the Value of the Childbearing Capacity and the Value of the Field Productive Capacity, New South

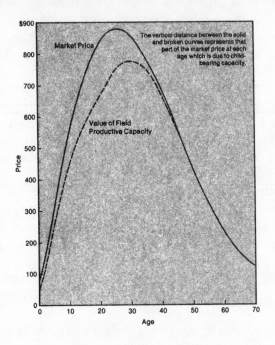

Old South, where land was of poor quality, that planters had an inducement to encourage fertility; while in the New South, where the yield of the soil was high, planters preferred to have "female slaves working in the field than to have them indisposed with pregnancy or occupied with children." Indeed, this is the rationalization put forth to explain why the fertility rate was higher in the Old than the New South.

Figures 20 and 21 contradict this analysis. They show

Figure 21

Division of Female Price between the Value of the Childbearing Capacity and the Value of the Field Productive Capacity, Old South

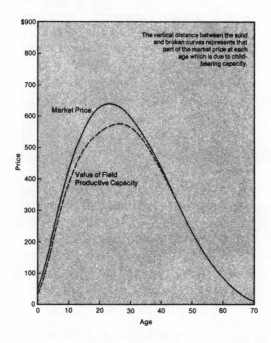

that both in absolute value and as a percentage of total price, the childbearing capacity of a female was more highly valued in the New South than in the Old South. For females aged twenty, for example, the present value of the child-bearing capacity was $170 in Louisiana in 1850 but only $80 in the Old South. Thus, *both* regions of the South had economic motivation to encourage fertility. If anything, the incentive to encourage child rearing was greater in the West than in the East. The economic rationale put forth for a

Figure 22

Division of Annual Net Earnings from Females between Childbearing Capacity and Field Earnings, by Age, Old South

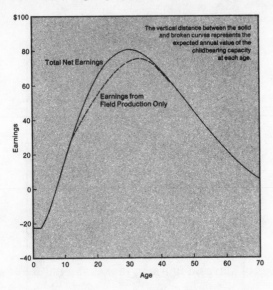

The vertical distance between the solid and broken curves represents the expected annual value of the childbearing capacity at each age.

Total Net Earnings

Earnings from Field Production Only

regional division of labor in which the Old South concentrated on child rearing and the New South on field production is, we submit, without foundation in fact.

How then does one explain the slightly higher fertility rates of the Old South? A fertility rate, it should be remembered, is a ratio. The denominator consists not only of married women but also of single women. Hence the fertility rate will be higher in the Old South if the share of single women without children in the interregional migration was higher than in the population that remained behind. As shown in chapter 2, this was, in fact, the case.

An even more fundamental error of the proponents of the slave-breeding thesis is their assumption that interference with normal family life to increase fertility could have had a large and positive effect on profit. The assumption that practicing selective breeding and fostering promiscuity or polygamy increased the fertility rate has never been supported, and analysis of data in the manuscript schedules of the U.S. census shows just the opposite. Farms with high women-to-men slave ratios exhibit lower fertility rates than farms with equal sex ratios. Moreover, women of a given age paired with men on the same farm had higher fertility rates than women of the same age who lived on farms without mates. For example, pairing of twenty-year-old women increased their fertility by 42 percent over that of unmatched women.

But even if selective breeding was the policy that maximized fertility rates, it does not follow that it would maximize profit. The contention that it would rests on two dubious assumptions: 1, that a large increase in the fertility rate of females would result in a large increase in plantation income; and 2, that there was no cost to interfering in the sexual lives of slaves. Figure 22 makes the nature of the first error apparent. It shows that on average, net income from childbearing was only about 10 percent of the total net income earned by women during their childbearing years. Consequently, even if the fertility rates of females could have been raised by 25 percent, an increase that would have brought slave fertility above the level usually considered to be the biological maximum, the increase in annual net earnings per female slave would have been less than 2.5 percent, since not all income-earning *females* were in the childbearing ages. Furthermore, females accounted for only 40 percent of the net income attributable to slaves. Hence the maximum increase in net income per working slave, through attempts to manipulate fertility rates, would have been below one percent — or less than a dollar per year per slave (in dollars of 1850). This trivial increase in net income could easily have been offset by the effects of selective breeding on worker morale. For example, runaways, slow-downs, or other breaches of slave discipline, equivalent to the loss of three work days per year, would have wiped out the entire potential gain achieved by pushing the fertility rate to the biological maximum.

Proponents of the breeding thesis have been misled by their failure to recognize the difference between human beings and animals. That eugenic manipulation increases the fertility of animals does not mean it would have the same effect on human beings. Not only does promiscuity increase venereal disease (an issue which does not plague animal husbandry) and thereby reduce fertility, but emotional factors are of considerable significance in successful human conception. These emotional factors, of course, also carry over into the work routine. Distraught and disgruntled slaves did not make good field hands.

Consequently, most planters shunned direct interference in the sexual practices of slaves, and attempted to influence fertility patterns through a system of positive economic incentives, incentives that are akin to those practiced by various governments today. The United States, for example, provides tax benefits for marriage and children; France has direct subsidies for childbearing; the Soviet Union combines subsidies with honorific awards — mothers of unusually large families become "Heroes of the Soviet Union." So too on the plantation.

First and foremost, planters promoted family formation both through exhortation and through economic inducements. "Marriage is to be encouraged," wrote James H. Hammond to his overseer, "as it adds to the comfort, happiness and health of those entering upon it, besides insuring a greater increase." The economic inducements for marriage generally included a house, a private plot of land which the family could work on its own, and, frequently, a bounty either in cash or in household goods. The primary inducements for childbearing were the lighter work load and the special care given to expectant and new mothers. The field-work requirement of women after the fifth month of pregnancy was generally reduced by 40 or 50 percent. In the last month they were frequently taken off fieldwork altogether and assigned such light tasks as sewing or spinning. Nursing mothers were permitted to leave for work at a later hour than others and were also allowed three to four hours during the day for the feeding of their infants. There were, of course, more long-range benefits, too. Women who bore unusually large numbers of children became "heroes of the plantation" and were relieved from all fieldwork.

The point of the preceding argument is neither to establish the total absence of attempts at eugenic manipulation nor to deny the existence of masters who used slaves to give vent to their lust, of overseers who treated slave women under their control as if they were members of a harem, and of sons of slaveowners who seduced girls at extremely tender ages. No doubt such sexual abuses were encouraged by a legal system which not only deprived slave women of the right to legal remedy but sanctioned the right of slaveholders to manipulate the private lives of their chattel.

But the question here is not the impact of the legal system; it is the impact of economic forces. While there were circumstances under which the economics of slavery encouraged widespread promiscuity and concubinage, circumstances which are described in chapter 4, the main thrust of the economic incentives generated by the American slave system operated against eugenic manipulation and against sexual abuse. Those who engaged in such acts did so, not because of their economic interests, but despite them. Instructions from slaveowners to their overseers frequently gave recognition to this conflict. They contain explicit caveats against "undue familiarity" which might undermine slave morale and discipline. "Having connection with any of my female servants," wrote a leading Louisiana planter, "will most certainly be visited with a dismissal from my employment, and no excuse can or will be taken." No set of instructions to overseers has been uncovered which explicitly or implicitly encouraged selective breeding or promiscuity.

The Economic Viability of Slavery After the Revolution and on the Eve of the Civil War

Two episodes during the antebellum era have been singled out as proof that underlying economic forces were working toward the destruction of the slave system. Phillips located one of these episodes in the decade following the close of the American Revolution. Ramsdell located the other in the decade preceding the Civil War.

Phillips based his case on scattered reports by planters who spoke of hard times. "Slave prices everywhere . . . ," he wrote, "were declining in so disquieting a manner that as late as the end of 1794 George Washington advised a friend to convert his slaves into other forms of property. . . ." However, Phillips was not able to use the series on slave prices that he so laboriously constructed to test these assertions, since his series only extended back to 1795. He simply accepted the scattered reports of distress as proof that "the peace of 1783 brought depression in all the plantation districts," which lasted for more than a decade and which converted the previously profitable investment in slaves into a heavy burden.

As it turns out, slave prices showed some weakness after the Revolution, but there was not a sustained, severe depression. While slave prices were acutely depressed during the last years of the Revolution, they rebounded to roughly the pre-Revolutionary level by the mid-1780s and remained on a

Figure 23

An Index of Real Slave Prices in the United States, 1772-1810

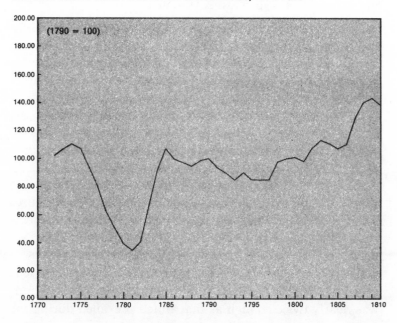

Figure 24

An Index of the Course of the Demand for Slaves, 1772-1810

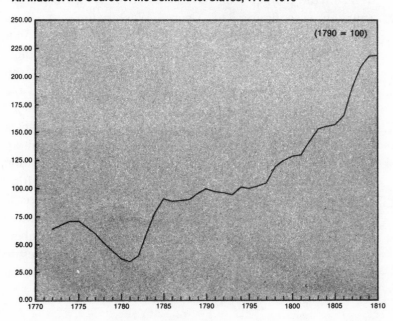

fairly high plateau for the rest of that decade. Between 1784 and 1794 slave prices averaged 89 percent of their pre-Revolutionary level. There was an additional drop of about 5 percent between 1794 and 1795. But this slide was abruptly reversed in 1798.

Furthermore, neither the softening of prices during the early 1790s nor the brief plunge later in the decade necessarily implies that the demand for slaves was declining. It may only show that the supply of slaves was increasing more rapidly than the demand for them. This appears to have been the case. As was shown in chapter 1 (see figures 6 and 7) the decade of the 1790s was marked by an unprecedented increase in the size of the slave population. Not only was the natural increase large, but slave imports — which exceeded 79,000 — were greater than in any previous decade. Indeed, the decade rate of imports during the 1790s was nearly twice as high as that which prevailed during the previous half century.

Despite the post-Revolutionary softness in prices, the trend in the demand for slaves was strongly upward from 1781 on (see figure 24). George Washington's apparent gloom was not generally shared by other slaveowners. As a group, slaveowners wanted to increase, not reduce, their holdings of slaves. Even in 1796, when prices were at the lowest point of the post-Revolutionary era, the demand for slaves was over 50 percent higher than it had been in 1772.

The hesitation in the growth of demand for a few years after 1791 may have been due to fear created by the Haitian slave revolt, as well as reactions to the various emancipation laws in northern states. On the other hand, the Haitian revolution could have been responsible for a sudden increase in the supply of slaves in the United States during these years. There are reports which indicate that large numbers of slaveowners from the West Indies sold their slaves to American buyers or fled with them to establish new plantations on the mainland. Southern supply may have been swelled also by the attempt of northern slaveowners to avoid the consequences of emancipation.

In any case, the heavy flow of slaves into the United States clearly contradicts the thesis that slavery was rescued from its deathbed by the rise of the cotton culture. If slavery had become generally unprofitable during the 1780s and 1790s, one would have observed a cessation of slave imports. If the crises had been of substantial proportions, the flow of slaves would have reversed. The United States would have turned from a net importer to a net exporter of slaves, as American planters strove to limit their losses by selling their chattel to areas where slavery was still profitable.

The episode singled out by Ramsdell turns, not on the movement of slave prices, but on the movement of cotton production and cotton prices. He knew very well that slave prices were rising throughout the 1850s. Nevertheless, Ramsdell believed that planters were being irresistibly driven toward the overproduction of cotton and that this undefinable force was tolling the death knell of slavery. He saw clear evidence of the tendency to overproduction in the unprecedented rise in the output of cotton between 1850 and 1860. The increase in production during this decade was greater than the increase over the entire previous century. Moreover, the rate of increase in cotton production accelerated as the decade wore on. Between 1857 and 1860 alone, cotton production increased by 1,500,000 bales. This spectacular rise was more than had been achieved during the four decades stretching from the invention of the cotton gin to the close of the Jacksonian administration.

To Ramsdell, the implication of this compulsion to shift resources into cotton was obvious. The price of cotton was bound to decline — would, indeed, eventually decline to levels so low that slavery would become unprofitable. The

Figure 25

The Course of Cotton Production, 1791-1861

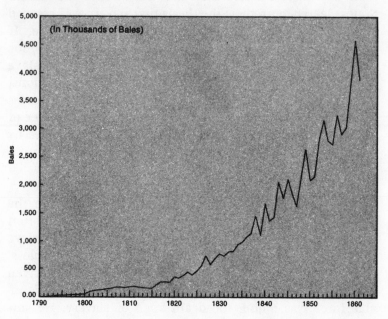

signs of the future were already evident, for the leap in
output between 1858 and 1860 had initiated the predicted
decline in prices. Thus "those who wished it [slavery]
destroyed," concluded Ramsdell, "had only to wait a little
while — perhaps a generation, probably less."

While one cannot deny that the rise in cotton production
during the decade of the 1850s was spectacular, the conclusion that this increase reflected irrational, uncommercial
behavior *is* disputable. Neither an extremely rapid growth
in output, nor a fall in price are *per se* evidence of overproduction. The output of cotton *cloth*, for example, tripled
between 1822 and 1827. At the same time the price of

Figure 26

The Course of Cotton Prices, 1802-1861

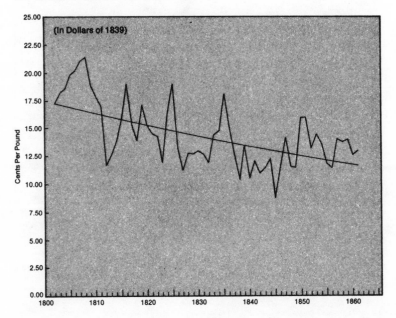

cloth declined by 35 percent. Yet no one has ever accused these northern cloth manufacturers of an irresistible tendency to overproduction. Quite the contrary, their dynamism in responding to the booming market for cloth has been celebrated far and wide. And the capacity of cloth manufacturers to bring down their prices has been taken as a mark of the vitality of the factory system.

There was nothing unusual about the slight decline in cotton prices that occurred between 1857 and 1860. The fact is that the general trend of raw cotton prices was downward from 1802 on (see figure 26). Although there were fluctuations about this trend, the average annual rate

Figure 27

The Deviation of Cotton Prices from Their Trend Values, 1802-1861

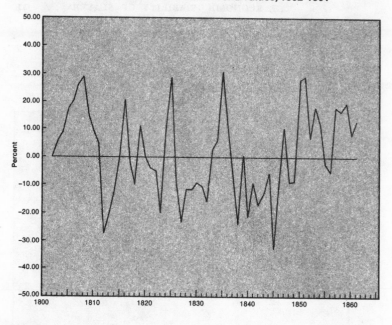

Figure 28

A Comparison between Indexes of Cotton Demanded and Supplied, 1829-1861

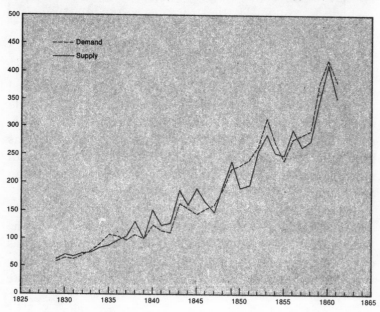

of decrease was 0.7 percent. The basic cause of this long-term decline was the steady increase in productivity. Among the developments which made cotton farming increasingly more efficient were the improvements in the varieties of cottonseeds, the introduction of the cotton gin, the reduction in transportation and other marketing costs, and the relocation of cotton production in the more fertile lands of the New South.

It was, therefore, to be expected that increases in production would generally be associated with declining prices. Since advances in productivity caused costs to fall, profits of planters may have been rising despite declining cotton prices. What is crucial, then, is not the absolute level of prices, but the level of profits. An approximation to the movement of profits may be obtained by examining the deviation of cotton prices from their long-term trend. When cotton prices were above their long-term trend value, profits of planters were likely to have been above normal. When prices were below their trend values, profits on cotton production were likely to have been below normal.

Figure 27 indicates that the 1850s constituted a period of sustained boom in profits for cotton planters. It was an era that outstripped even the fabled prosperity of the 1830s. Nearly every year of the decade was one of above-normal profit. What is more, profits remained high during the last four years of the decade, with prices averaging about 15 percent above their trend values. No wonder cotton production doubled between 1850 and 1860. It was clearly a rational economic response to increase cotton production by over 50 percent between 1857 and 1860. If planters erred, it was not in expanding cotton production by too much. Quite the contrary — they were too conservative. Their expansion had not been adequate to bring prices down to their trend values and profits back to normal (equilibrium) levels.

What was responsible for making the 1850s so prosperous for cotton planters? An answer is provided by figure 28.

It shows that the worldwide demand for cotton began to increase rapidly beginning in 1846. Over the next fifteen years, the average annual rate of change in demand was about 7 percent per annum. Figure 28 also shows that changes in the supply of cotton generally lagged behind changes in demand. As a consequence, prices and profits tended to be above normal in periods when demand was increasing, and below normal when demand was decreasing or stagnating.

To summarize: The unprecedented increase in cotton production after 1857 was due to a rapid advance in the world demand for U.S. cotton. The lag of cotton supply behind demand caused the price of cotton to rise well above normal levels, creating unusually large profits for planters. While planters responded to this incentive, they did not increase output rapidly enough to return cotton prices and profits to a normal level.

Thus, the tale about the uncommercial planter who was gripped by an irresistible tendency to the overproduction of cotton is sheer fantasy. It is to those who romanticize the antebellum South what the story of the slave-breeding planter was to abolitionist critics — a convenient invention.

Slavery in the Cities and the "Natural Limits" Thesis

Many writers have been convinced that slavery would have been extinguished even in the absence of a Civil War because of the natural geographic limits to which the cotton culture was confined, and because of the pressure generated by rising urbanization. These two barriers were like the jaws of a vise that would, perhaps within a decade or two after 1860, have crushed the life out of the slave system. The "natural limits" thesis holds that the rise in ratio of slave labor to land eventually would have reduced the value of a slave to less than his subsistence cost. The rise in the labor-to-land ratio seemed assured, since the land suitable for cotton was limited while the supply of slave labor was bound to grow with the growth of the slave population. The cities would not have provided an outlet for this excess because the cities were a hostile environment, an environment in which slavery could not persist.

One might be inclined to dismiss the natural limits thesis out of hand. It appears to depend on the assumption that slaves could be used only in the production of cotton. Aside from the slur that slaves could not be taught other occupations, the assumption obviously exaggerates the identity between the cotton culture and slavery. As pointed out in chapter 2, about 6 percent of slaves worked in towns, and 20 percent of those living on plantations were employed as artisans and semiskilled workers of various sorts. Still, close to 60 percent of slaves were involved in one or another aspect of cotton production. Although the cotton culture was not identical with slavery, it was one of the most important occupations of slaves. The crude form of the natural limits thesis can be modified by arguing, not that all slaves had to be employed in the cotton culture, but that the proportion of slaves employed in cotton had to remain at about the antebellum level. The justification for limiting the flow of slaves into other areas of production need not imply a calumny against Negroes. It could be based on the argument that the slave system of labor organization was too rigid to permit the efficient involvement of a larger percentage of slaves in nonagricultural activity than had been achieved during the antebellum era. In any case, there is a sufficiently large group of adherents to the natural limits thesis to warrant an objective test of it.

Appendix B presents an equation that makes such a test possible. This equation enables one to predict the change in slave prices, given information on the cotton prices, the output of cotton, the size of the labor force employed in cotton farming, the cost of slave maintenance, and the market rate of interest. The values of all these variables for the post–Civil War era are known — except the rate of growth of the slave labor force that would have been employed in cotton production and the cost of slave maintenance. However, the unknown values are supplied by the natural limits thesis itself. Given the requirement that the proportion of the labor force devoted to cotton remain constant, and given the constancy in the labor-force participation rate, the rate of growth of slave labor devoted to cotton would have been equal to the rate of growth of the Negro population. Moreover, the natural limits thesis implicitly accepts the relative constancy, if not of the absolute standard of living, of at least the relative income shares of slaves. Hence, maintenance costs would have moved with gross earnings.

The results of the test are presented in figure 29. It shows that far from falling, the prices of slaves would have risen. Indeed the average annual rate of increase between 1860 and 1890 would have been 1.4 percent, a figure slightly lower than the prewar trend of growth. In other words, prime hands in 1890 would have sold at 52 percent more than they did in 1860. This startling conclusion was completely unanticipated by the proponents of the natural limits thesis. It rests on two solid facts. The first is that the demand for American cotton grew a little more rapidly than the supply, not only until 1890 but right up to World War I. Hence the real price of cotton was higher in 1890 than in 1860. Second, the quantity of land devoted to cotton did not remain constant at the 1859 level. Quite the contrary, it grew at a rate (2.06 percent per annum) which was in excess of the growth rate of the black labor force. In other words, the assumption that the quantity of additional land available for use in cotton was almost exhausted by 1860

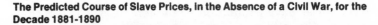

Figure 29

The Predicted Course of Slave Prices, in the Absence of a Civil War, for the Decade 1881-1890

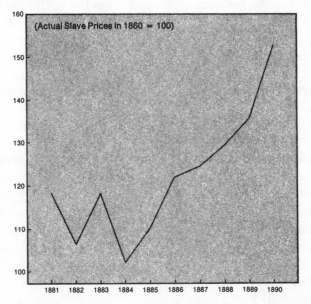

(Actual Slave Prices in 1860 = 100)

is false. The land devoted to cotton nearly doubled between 1860 and 1890; it more than doubled between 1890 and 1925.

The irony of the widespread acceptance of the natural limits hypothesis is that it was refuted by the man who is usually cited as its chief architect. For, as noted above, Ramsdell's principal basis for predicting the demise of slavery was his belief that the land-to-labor ratio in cotton would grow rather than decline.

There still remains the argument that slavery could not have persisted in an urban environment. On a superficial level, the census statistics on the slave population of the ten largest southern cities appear to buttress the conventional view. While there was an increase of 160 percent in the total slave population between 1820 and 1860, the increase in the slave population of the ten cities was less than half that rate. Between 1850 and 1860 the decline was not just relative. During the decade preceding the Civil War, the slave population of the ten cities dropped by nine thousand, or 12 percent. For some cities the absolute decline was not just limited to the 1850s. Baltimore, St. Louis, and Washington all had smaller slave populations in 1860 than in 1820.

These figures certainly appear to justify the statement that "slavery was disintegrating in Southern cities," and that "wherever" slavery "touched urban conditions it was in deep trouble." They also appear to back up the various arguments advanced to explain the inhospitality of the urban environment, such as the incongruity between slavery and the factory method of production, the high and increasing costs of controlling slaves in the cities, the hostility of free urban workers to competition from slaves, and the increasing fear of slave rebellions.

Yet when one probes somewhat more deeply, the case begins to weaken. There was something less than a pell-mell rush of slaves out of the cities. For example, the slave population of the second set of ten southern cities did not decline between 1850 and 1860; it grew moderately. Nor did all cities within the first set lose slaves. Four of the first ten cities experienced vigorous growth over the entire four-decade period. The rate of increase in the slave population of this subgroup not only matched the national average but exceeded it by 50 percent.

How does one square the contention that in "the border cities the institution [of slavery] had nearly disappeared," with the more than 200 percent growth of the slave population of Louisville, or the fact that the total slave population of the four leading border cities actually exhibited a moder-

Figure 30

Decade Rates of Change in the Slave Populations of Three Southern Cities and in Slave Prices

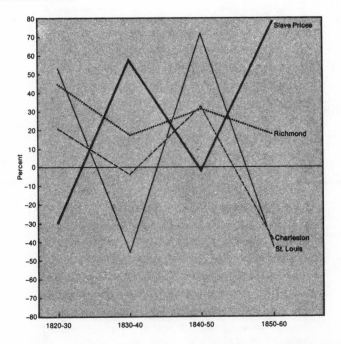

ate increase between 1820 and 1860? Again, the assertion that elsewhere in the South urban slavery had generally "diminished in extent and vitality" is hardly a fitting description for such cities as Mobile, Savannah, Richmond, Montgomery, or Memphis, which all exhibited vigorous increases in their slave populations.

There are also certain nagging details that have been overlooked in the traditional treatment of the decline of urban slavery. For example, the change in the population of the cities displayed a distinctive wavelike pattern, rising in some decades and falling in others. This same wavelike movement is evident in slave prices. However, the pattern in prices is *exactly the reverse* of the pattern exhibited by

Figure 31

Indexes of the Demand for Slaves in the Cities and the Countryside

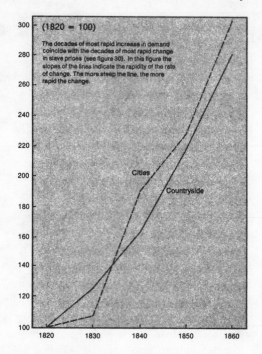

(1820 = 100)

The decades of most rapid increase in demand coincide with the decades of most rapid change in slave prices (see figure 30). In this figure the slopes of the lines indicate the rapidity of the rate of change. The more steep the line, the more rapid the change.

the slave population. In other words, the urban slave population increased most rapidly when slave prices were increasing most slowly; and the slave population decreased (or increased most slowly) when slave prices were increasing most rapidly.

Another neglected detail is that the cities which experienced the largest losses in slave population had the largest influxes of white immigrant labor. As a group, the cities of declining slave population also had a higher proportion of skilled workers, older slaves, and female slaves than did the cities of increasing slave population.

Thus, the pattern in which the slave population changed in the urban areas was more complex than is suggested by the conventional view. The theory that slavery and urbanization became increasingly more incompatible as the century wore on cannot account for the remarkable rate of growth of the slave population in nearly half of the main urban centers. The forces invoked to explain why slaves were driven from the cities do not explain why a larger percentage of unskilled than skilled slaves left for the countryside. Nor do these forces explain the wavelike pattern in the outflow. These undulations in population cannot be related to fluctuations in the rate of rebellion, or to changes in special urban taxes, or to cycles in the restrictions on slave movements in the cities.

Translated into the language of economists, the traditional view that slaves were being driven from the cities is a theory of a declining urban demand for slaves. The main factors cited to explain the "disintegration" of urban slavery — the increasing cost of control, the hostility of white workers, the fear of rebellion on the part of slaveowners — would all have worked to reduce the level of demand in the cities. Yet the measurement of the course of demand indicates no such downward trend. Quite the contrary, the total urban demand for slaves rose in every decade between 1820 and 1860. Declines in the urban demand for slaves were rare events. In the case of the top ten cities, they occurred in only four instances: in St. Louis during the decade of the 1830s, in New Orleans during the decade of the 1840s, and in Baltimore and Charleston during the 1850s. In all other decades these four cities experienced an increasing demand for slaves; the remaining six cities increased their demand for slaves throughout the decades which elapsed between 1820 and 1860.

What proponents of the conventional theory have failed to realize is that the factors impinging on demand were quite diverse. Some conditions, such as the increasing competition from white immigrant labor, served to reduce the urban demand for slaves. Other forces worked in the opposite direction. Both the rapid rise in the free population of southern cities and the rise in income per capita swelled the urban demand for slaves. On balance, the factors that increased the demand for slaves in the cities proved to be substantially stronger than those which served to depress it.

Why then did the slave population of the cities decline? Because the cities had to compete with the countryside for a supply of slaves whose growth was limited to the rate of natural increase. During those decades in which the combined rural and urban demand was growing more rapidly than the supply of slaves, prices of slaves were forced up. Both the city and the countryside reacted to the rise in price, but in substantially different ways. In the rural areas there were no close substitutes for slave labor. In the language of economists, the rural demand for slaves was highly "inelastic." In the cities, however, free labor, particularly immigrant labor, proved to be a very effective substitute. This made the urban demand for slaves quite "elastic." Consequently, as the competition of the cities and the countryside forced the price of slaves up relative to the price of free labor, the cities shifted toward the relatively cheaper form of labor. In other words, slaves were shifted from the cities to the countryside not because the cities didn't want slaves, but because as slave prices rose, it was easier for the cities than the countryside to find acceptable, lower-cost alternatives to slave labor.

That the demand for slaves was much more "inelastic" in the countryside than in the cities, is, we believe, a discovery of major importance. This information not only provides the solution to the mysterious decline in the urban population of slaves but, as will be shown in chapter 6, it is central to the resolution of the paradox of forced labor.

The Sanguinity of the Slaveholding Class on Economic Prospects

For many historical questions, the expectations of slave-holders with respect to their economic prospects is as important as the reality that they experienced. Did their expectations diverge from economic reality? It has been argued that "there was great fear about economic prospects in the 1850s" among slaveholders. Despite the booming market in cotton, slaveholders were supposed to have been deeply perturbed about long-run economic conditions. Among the long-run issues which are said to have made them pessimistic were the prospects of a rapid exhaustion of existing cotton lands and the need to obtain new reserves, the unstable state of the international cotton market, and the fear that the northern and British interests were conspiring to manipulate the international market to the disadvantage of the South.

It is possible to test the contention that slaveholders were pessimistic about the future by constructing an "index of sanguinity." The equation from which the index is constructed is set forth in appendix B. The index turns primarily on the ratio of the average purchase price of slaves to their average annual hire rate. The annual hire rate reflected the market's appraisal of the productive value of slaves over the ensuing year. The purchase price reflected the market's appraisal of the productive value of slaves, not only during the next year but over the balance of their lives. Hence, when investors thought the future was going to be more lucrative than the present, the purchase price of slaves rose relative to the annual hire rate. When they expected the economic situation to deteriorate in the future, the purchase price fell relative to the annual hire rate.

Indexes of the sanguinity of slaveholders are presented for the Old and New South in figure 32. Several features

Figure 32

An Index of the Sanguinity of Slaveholders, 1830-1860

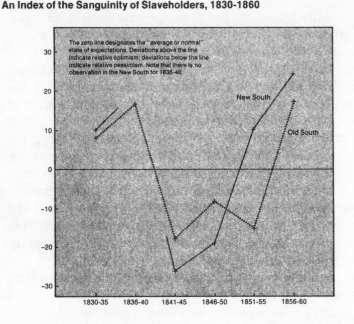

of these indexes are noteworthy. First, slaveholders were not consistently sanguine. There were periods during which slaveholders were more optimistic than was justified by the movement of current earnings; but there also were periods during which their pessimism depressed slave prices more rapidly than earnings. Pessimism ruled the behavior of slaveholders in the Old South during the 1840s and the first half of the 1850s. Over 60 percent of the precipitous fall in the average slave price which took place in the Old South between 1836–40 and 1841–45 was due to the fact that slaveholders expected earnings to decline more rapidly than they actually did.

Second, for the whole period, expected earnings grew

only slightly more rapidly than actual earnings. That the overall rate of change in the sanguinity index is positive, is due largely to the buoyancy of expectations during the last half of the 1850s. Between 1830–35 and 1851–55, the sanguinity index declined for both the Old and New South. Third, expectations tended to be more volatile in the New South than in the older area. Expectations in the newer region declined more rapidly during periods of falling earnings and rose more rapidly during periods of rising earnings.

Finally, slaveholders in neither region expected to see their peculiar institution abolished by an impending political catastrophe. During the decade of the fifties sanguinity was increasing quite rapidly, accounting for 40 percent of the rise in slave prices in the Old South and 75 percent of the rise in the New South. Slaveholders not only expected their social order to endure but foresaw an era of prosperity.

That investors went through periods of pessimism and optimism should not be interpreted as supporting the claim that the price of slaves was determined by wild speculation. Pessimism and optimism were generally rooted in experience. The pessimism of the early 1840s was brought on by a decade of faltering demand during which the price of cotton dropped by nearly 70 percent — to an all-time low of 5.6 cents per pound. Similarly, the optimism of the late 1850s reflected the booming demand for cotton which maintained the price of that commodity at a high level despite a record expansion in the cotton crop. Such behavior is more characteristic of sober businessmen doing their best to perceive an uncertain future. It contradicts rather than supports the stereotype of the reckless speculator, which has tended to dominate some historical portraits.

It should not be assumed that the optimism of slaveholders with respect to economic issues means that they were oblivious to the rapidly developing political crises which marked the end of the 1850s. A political crisis does not, however, necessarily imply an economic crisis. Stock prices, for example, frequently rise with political tensions as investors contemplate the possible effects of a war on profits. The indexes portrayed in figure 32 suggest that in the late 1850s slaveholders expected the political policies pursued by their leaders, including the possibility of war, to lead to an improvement of their economic position. The South, of course, had its Cassandras. But during 1855–60, slaveholders as a group did not anticipate the complete collapse of their peculiar institution that was to follow from the Civil War.

Four.

The Anatomy of Exploitation

Webster's Third New International Dictionary gives two definitions of personal exploitation. These are:

1. an unjust or improper use of another person for one's own profit or advantage;
2. utilization of the labor power of another person without giving a just or equivalent return.

Slaves were exploited in both of these senses. For the advantage of their masters, they were whipped, sold on the auction block, separated from loved ones, deprived of education, terrorized, raped, forced into prostitution, and worked beyond limits of human endurance. The labor power of slaves was also utilized without giving slaves an equivalent return. This aspect of their exploitation was most apparent in the case of hires. The man who rented a slave paid the full market value of the slave's services, but the slave received only part of that payment. The slave's income was the expenditure of the renter on his maintenance; the balance of the value produced by the slave went to the owner of the slave in the form of a rental fee.

While the existence of exploitation is beyond question, the extent of that exploitation is less clear. How frequent was the mean and improper use of slaves and how far did meanness go? How much of the income produced by slaves was expropriated from them?

The posing of these questions may seem irrelevant, even malicious. For many, it is enough merely to recognize the existence of 250 years of exploitation under slavery and to stress its horror. To haggle over the extent of the exploitation suggests callousness to the agony of human bondage, and appears to diminish the significance of the moral issue.

If all that was at stake was the refinement of the historical image of the slaveholding class, the issue of the extent of exploitation could be disregarded. Slaveholders have long been driven from the stage of American life, and the descendants of slaveholders generally do not wish to dwell on the meaner aspects of their ancestry. It is the need to arrive at an accurate historical image of the black man that gives urgency to the issue.

For it is widely assumed that the plantation regime under which most slaves lived was so cruel, the exploitation so severe, the repression so complete, that blacks were thoroughly demoralized by it. In this view, blacks were virtually cultural ciphers until they obtained their freedom in 1865. Little positive development of black culture or personality was possible under the unbridled exploitation of slavery; those developments which did take place were largely negative. Under the regime of the lash the blacks had little incentive to improve themselves and "got into very bad habits of doing as little as possible." Undernourished, if not starved, they lacked both the physical capacity and the mental stamina to tackle any but the most routine tasks, and even these were poorly carried out. Forced or encouraged into promiscuity, blacks became extremely casual in their sexual relations: sexual rivalries threw "many slave quarters in constant turmoil"; "[c]hastity was 'out of the question' " and many girls became pregnant· at twelve, thirteen, and fourteen years of age. Sexual laxity on the part of the slaves, combined with a wide array of policies pursued by masters, reduced the black family to "cultural chaos." Bereft of "deep and enduring affection," fathers and mothers not only came to regard their children with "indifference" but often neglected them in sickness and even practiced infanticide.

No one's personality could, according to this view, fail to be affected by a regime so brutal that some have compared plantations to concentration camps and others have compared them to prisons. In the daily fire of such "total" exploitation, masters and overseers fashioned a distinctive type of "slavish personality" that Stanley M. Elkins identified as "Sambo."

Sambo, the typical plantation slave, was docile but irresponsible, loyal but lazy, humble but chronically given to lying and stealing; his behavior was full of infantile silliness and his talk was inflated by childish exaggeration. His relationship with his master was one of utter dependence and childlike attachment: it was indeed this childlike quality that was the very key to his being.

This, then, is the portrait contained in many current histories of the antebellum South. Both masters and slaves are painted as degraded brutes. Masters are vile because they are the perpetrators of unbridled exploitation; slaves are vile because they are the victims of it. How true to life is the portrait?

Food, Shelter, and Clothing

The belief that the typical slave was poorly fed is without foundation in fact. This mistaken view may have arisen from a misinterpretation of the instructions of masters to their overseers. For these documents often mention only corn and pork in outlining the rations that were to be distributed to Negroes. The typical daily ration described was two pounds of corn and one half pound of pork per adult. The misinterpretation stems from the incorrect assumption that the lack of reference to other foods meant that the slave diet was restricted largely to corn and pork.

Overseers' instructions, however, were not book-length manuals. They usually occupied just a few handwritten pages (generally ranging between one thousand and three thousand words in total) and were confined to outlining the major features of the routine the master wished to be pursued. They were not meant to be exhaustive documents, but to underscore those aspects of plantation management that particular owners held to be especially important. The incomplete nature of these widely quoted instructions is seen by the frequent omission of such important matters as rations for children, the disposition of wheat and other grain crops besides corn, the care of chickens and other small livestock, the production and disposition of dairy products, and the different feeds to be used for the various categories of livestock. The instructions to overseers are useful not because they contain a complete description of the plantation routine but because they reveal which aspects of that routine were uppermost in the minds of plantation owners.

The rationing of corn and pork to slaves was emphasized by slaveholders for two reasons. First, while corn and pork did not constitute the totality of the slave diet, they were the core of the diet on most plantations. Unlike other foods such as fruit and vegetables which were fed to slaves only in certain seasons, daily, weekly, or monthly rations of corn and pork were distributed throughout the year. Secondly, while beef, chickens, dairy products, and Irish potatoes had to be consumed soon after they were slaughtered or harvested (because they were difficult to preserve for later use), pork and corn were kept in store for the full year. Winter, especially January and February, was the season for killing, curing, and smoking pork, which could then be kept under lock and key in smoke houses until it was needed. Ensuring that the store of pork and corn was sufficient to last the entire year was one of the principal duties of the overseer, which is why explicit instructions on the disbursement of these two staples were common. The overseer, wrote one master, "must himself keep the keys of the [corn] cribs, smokehouses and all other buildings in which any property belonging to me is stored and must himself see to the giving out of food." Feed everyone "plentifully," wrote another, "but waste nothing."

More careful reading of plantation documents shows that the slave diet included many foods in addition to corn and pork. Among the other plantation products which slaves consumed were beef, mutton, chickens, milk, turnips, peas, squashes, sweet potatoes, apples, plums, oranges, pumpkins, and peaches. Certain foods not produced on most plantations were frequently purchased for slave consumption, including salt, sugar, and molasses. Less frequent, but not uncommon, purchases for slaves included fish, coffee, and whiskey. In addition to food distributed to them, slaves supplemented their diet, in varying degrees, through hunting and fishing as well as with vegetables grown in the garden plots assigned to them.

Unfortunately, surviving plantation records are not complete enough to permit determination of the average amounts of each of the foods purchased for slaves or of the quantities of meats and fish that slaves obtained through hunting and fishing. However, on the basis of data obtained from the manuscript schedules of the 1860 census, it has been possible to compute the average amounts of eleven of the principal foods consumed by slaves who lived on the large plantations of the cotton belt. These eleven foods are

Figure 33

A Comparison of the Average Daily Food Consumption of Slaves in 1860 with the Average Daily Food Consumption of the Entire Population in 1879

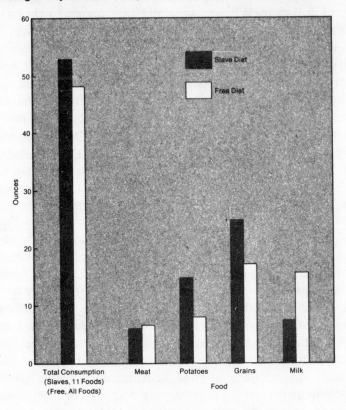

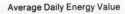

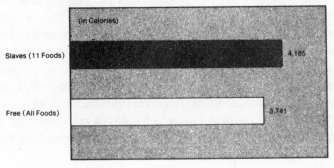

beef, pork, mutton, milk, butter, sweet potatoes, white potatoes, peas, corn, wheat, and minor grains. While this list is short, it probably accounts for 80 percent of the caloric intake of slaves. Fish, fowl, game, sugar, as well as the various omitted vegetables and fruits, were choice items; but they did not constitute a large part of the diet for either whites or blacks during the middle of the nineteenth century. Figure 33 shows that the average daily diet of slaves was quite substantial. The energy value of their diet exceeded that of free men in 1879 by more than 10 percent. There was no deficiency in the amount of meat allotted to slaves. On average, they consumed six ounces of meat per day, just an ounce lower than the average quantity of meat consumed by the free population. While pork was more important in the slave than in the free diet, the difference was not as large as is usually presumed. Slaves averaged 70 percent of the free population's consumption of beef. The milk consumption was low by free standards, but still amounted to about one glass per day for each slave.

By weight, grains and potatoes dominated the diet of both the free and slave population. Much has been made of the fact that corn was the principal grain consumed by slaves, while wheat was the principal grain in the free diet. Yet from a nutritional standpoint, both are excellent foods, high in energy value and with substantial protein content. Wheat is richer in calcium and iron, but corn has more vitamin A. What has completely escaped attention is the fact that while both slaves and free men ate large quantities of potatoes, slaves consumed virtually nothing but sweet potatoes, although most of the potatoes consumed by free men were white. The significance of this dichotomy is that sweet potatoes are a much better food than white potatoes. Sweet potatoes are especially rich in vitamins A and C and are also fairly high in calcium.

The high slave consumption of meat, sweet potatoes, and peas goes a long way toward explaining the astounding

Figure 34

The Nutritional Value of the Slave Diet: Average Slave Consumption of Various Nutrients in 1860 as a Percentage of Modern Recommended Daily Allowances

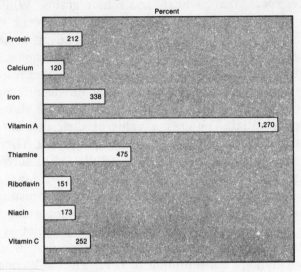

Percent

Protein	212
Calcium	120
Iron	338
Vitamin A	1,270
Thiamine	475
Riboflavin	151
Niacin	173
Vitamin C	252

Figure 35

The Distribution of Slaves on Large Plantations, by Persons per Slave House, 1860

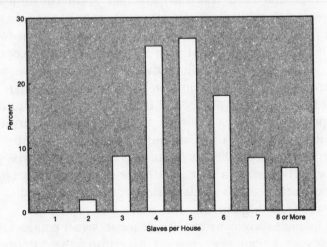

results shown in figure 34. The slave diet was not only adequate, it actually exceeded modern (1964) recommended daily levels of the chief nutrients. On average, slaves exceeded the daily recommended level of proteins by 110 percent, calcium by 20 percent, and iron by 230 percent. Surprisingly, despite the absence of citrus fruits, slaves consumed two and one half times the recommended level of vitamin C. Indeed, because of the large consumption of sweet potatoes, their intake of vitamin A was at the therapeutic level and vitamin C was almost at that level. Of course, the fact that the *average* daily nutrient content of the slave diet was good does not mean that it was good for all slaves. And even the best-fed slaves experienced seasonal variation in the quality of their diet, due to the limitations in the technology of food preservation during the antebellum era.

Data on slave housing are much more sparse than on slave diets. The most systematic housing information comes from the census of 1860, which included a count of slave houses. These census data show that on average there were 5.2 slaves per house on large plantations. The number of persons per free household in 1860 was 5.3. Thus, like free men, most slaves lived in single-family households. The sharing of houses by several families of slaves was uncommon. Occasionally, on very large plantations, there were dormitories for unmarried men and women. But these were exceptional. The single-family household was the rule.

Unfortunately, the census did not collect information on the size or the quality of slave houses. Descriptions in plantation records and in travelers' accounts are fragmentary. They suggest a considerable range in the quality of housing. The best were three- or four-room cottages, of wood frame, brick, or stone construction, with up to eight hundred square feet of space on the inside, and large porches on the outside. Such cottages had brick or stone chimneys and glazed windows. At the other pole were single-room log cabins without windows. Chimneys were constructed of twigs and clay; floors were either earthen or made of planks resting directly on the earth.

Comments of observers suggest that the most typical slave houses of the late antebellum period were cabins about eighteen by twenty feet. They usually had one or two rooms. Lofts, on which the children slept, were also quite common. Windows were not glazed, but closed by wooden shutters. Some houses also had rear doors. Chimneys were usually constructed of brick or stone. The building material was usually logs or wood. Seams in the log cabins were sealed by wooden splints and mud. Floors were usually planked and raised off the ground.

While such housing is quite mean by modern standards, the houses of slaves compared well with the housing of free workers in the antebellum era. It must be remembered that much of rural America still lived in log cabins in the 1850s. And urban workers lived in crowded, filthy tenements. One should not be misled by the relatively spacious accommodations in which U.S. working-class families live today. That is an achievement of very recent times. As late as 1893, a survey of the housing of workers in New York City revealed that the median number of square feet of sleeping space per person was just thirty-five. In other words, the "typical" slave cabin of the late antebellum era probably contained more sleeping space per person than was available to most of New York City's workers half a century later.

The best information on clothing comes from the records of large plantations. These indicate that a fairly standard annual issue for adult males was four shirts (of cotton), four pairs of pants (two of cotton and two of wool), and one or two pairs of shoes. Adult women were issued four dresses per year, or the material needed to make four dresses. Hats were also typically issued annually (women received headkerchiefs). Blankets were issued once every two or three years. There seems to have been much more variability in the issue of socks and underclothes. Issues of petticoats to women are mentioned in a few records, but not in most. Mention of socks and underwear for men is also irregular. For winter months men had jackets, sometimes overcoats, although the frequency of their issue is unclear. Clothing for children showed some variation from estate to estate, but by far the most common issue was a one-piece garment which looked like an extra-long shirt.

Slave clothing was usually made of a coarse but durable cloth. The leather in slave shoes was of a high grade, but little attention was devoted to matters of fashion. Finer clothes were supplied to house servants and other favored slaves. Slaves also supplemented the standard issue by their own purchases. As indicated below, many slaves were able to earn substantial sums of money. Much of this was spent on such items of clothing as headkerchiefs and brightly colored cloth for dressmaking.

Medical Care

While the quality of slave medical care was poor by modern standards, there is no evidence of exploitation in the medical care typically provided for plantation slaves. The inadequacy of the care arose not from intent or lack of effort on the part of masters, but from the primitive nature of medical knowledge and practices in the antebellum era.

That adequate maintenance of the health of their slaves was a central objective of most planters is repeatedly emphasized in instructions to overseers and in other records and correspondence of planters. "The preservation of the health of the negroes," wrote J. A. S. Acklen to his overseer, "and the care of them when sick, will require your best attention; and to be ignorant of the best mode of discharging your duties in these particulars, is to be unfit for the responsible station you hold." P. C. Weston charged his

Table 2

Clothing Recommended for an Adult Worker by Social-work Agencies in New York City in 1907 Compared with the "Typical" Clothing Allotment for an Adult Male Slave

NEW YORK WORKER	"TYPICAL" SLAVE ISSUE
2 hats or caps	1 hat
1 overcoat (every 2 or 3 years)	? overcoat
1 suit	1 jacket
1 pair pantaloons	4 pair pants
2 pair overalls	
5 shirts	4 shirts
6 collars	
4 ties	
4 handkerchiefs	
summer and winter underwear	? underwear
6 pair hose	? hose
2 pair shoes	1½ pair shoes
repair of shoes	
gloves or mittens	

The "typical" slave issue does not include purchases of clothing by slaves. The New York study in which the above list was published reported that the average expenditure of New York workers on clothes was below the recommended level.

overseer "most distinctly to understand that his first object is to be, under all circumstances, the care and well being of the negroes." Consequently,

All sick persons are to stay in the hospital night and day, from the time they first complain to the time they are able to work again. The nurses are to be responsible for the sick not leaving the house, and for the cleanliness of the bedding, utensils, &c. The nurses are never to be allowed to give any medicine without the orders of the Overseer or Doctor. A woman, beside the plantation nurse, must be put to nurse all persons seriously ill. In all cases at all serious the Doctor is to be sent for, and his orders are to be strictly attended to; no alteration is to be made in the treatment he directs.

While planters worried about slaves who feigned illness to get out of work, they were generally more concerned about losing slaves or impairing their health through the neglect of real illness. Thus Bennet H. Barrow, owner of one of the largest Louisiana plantations, treated slaves as though they were sick even when he thought they were pretending. Nor was Barrow alone in this attitude. In their sick records planters sometimes described the malady which had removed a slave from production as "nothing," "complaining," and "more lazy and mad than sick." James Hammond insisted that, "[e]very reasonable complaint must be promptly attended to; and with any marked or general symptom of sickness, however trivial, a negro may lie up a day or so at least." "Unless it is a clear case of imposition," wrote still another planter, "a negro had better be allowed a day's rest when he lays up. A little rest often saves much by preventing serious illness."

Facilities for the treatment of the sick generally varied with the size of the plantations. The larger plantations maintained substantial hospitals. On one plantation with 168 slaves, for example, the hospital was a two-story brick building which had eight large rooms. Such hospitals usually contained separate rooms for men and women. A special room was often set aside for confinement cases. One or more of the rooms were "clinics" for the treatment of "outpatients." These rooms contained a pharmacy as well as other equipment needed for ministering to the sick. On smaller planta-tions, the "hospital" was merely an ordinary cabin reserved for the sick. In some instances, masters set aside several rooms in their own houses for use as a hospital. The ra-tionale for hospitalizing slaves was twofold: it permitted the sick to receive special care including not only rest and medication but also special diets; it also isolated the sick slaves from the healthy ones and thus minimized the danger of contagion. Many planters insisted that slaves be removed from their cabins to hospitals as soon as their ill-ness was made known.

Few plantations were large enough to justify the ex-clusive retention of a full-time physician. However, virtually all plantations of moderate or large size had at least one full-time nurse, usually an elderly slave, and many also had experienced midwives. The nurses and midwives worked under the direct supervision of the planter or his overseer. Planters sought to be, and overseers were expected to be, knowledgeable about current medical procedures and about drugs and their administration. Physicians were regularly brought onto the plantations to care for slaves whose health problems could not be treated adequately by the nurses, midwives, overseers, or planters. Some planters contracted for the physicians' services for a year at a time, paying a flat fee that was usually proportional to the number of persons covered by the contract. Others paid for services as rendered. In either case, the doctor attending to the slaves was usually the same doctor who ministered to the planter's family. Bills submitted by these physicians indicate, time after time, that they treated both slaves and members of the master's family during the same visit.

That it was generally the intent of planters to supply slaves with medical care of a relatively high quality does not imply that the objective was usually realized. Not only was the state of medical knowledge and arts quite primi-tive during the antebellum era, but the prevailing theory of disease frequently led to treatments which were inimical to the recovery of patients. Disease was assumed to be caused by "poisons emanating from decaying animal and vegetable matter," which were transmitted to human beings by "impure airs and waters." To rid the body of these poisons, doctors resorted to bleeding, blistering, and purging. Bleeding and purging were a standard treatment for such diseases as dysentery, cholera, and pleurisy. In each case, of course, the prescribed treatment removed from the body fluids that were vital to recovery. The therapy, no doubt, hurried to their graves many patients who might have survived if they were spared the services of doctors.

For many of the illnesses that afflicted slaves, especially pneumonia and diseases of the gastrointestinal tract, which were the greatest killers of blacks, the services of doctors were either useless or harmful. It was only in limited cases, such as smallpox and malaria (after the 1820s when sulphate of quinine became generally known), that doctors possessed effective pharmaceutical weapons. Beyond these, the useful medicines contained in the chests of doctors were primarily anodynes such as opium, paregoric, Dover's powder, and laudanum which, although they did not cure, at least served to relieve severe distress. Doctors were effective in cases requiring minor surgery, such as opening abscesses, removing teeth, and the setting of broken bones. They were also helpful in dealing with hernias, which were quite common among slaves. Although they lacked the surgical knowledge needed to repair the rupture, they did prescribe the use of trusses.

The prevailing theory of disease did have one quite salutary effect. It led many planters to adhere to a hygienic regimen. Few matters were more frequently emphasized in the instructions to overseers than the need to insure not only the personal cleanliness of slaves but also the cleanliness of their clothes, their bedding, and their cabins. Instructions required overseers "personally" to see that they keep their clothing mended and clean, and that they wash their clothes as often as once a week, for which purpose time must be regularly set apart the latter end of the week. He must see that they are clean on Sundays and not straggling about the country dirty and ragged, and he must see that they appear clean every Monday morning in the year, without any failure whatever.

He must see that they keep their houses clean and their yards free from weeds and filth.

Some planters went even further. Hammond required a complete cleaning of slave cabins twice a year. During these spring and fall cleanings, all contents of the cabin were to be removed and sunned, all walls were to be washed, mattresses were to be restuffed, and the grounds under the houses were to be sprinkled with lime. Once a year every house was to be "whitewashed inside and out." The punishment for slaves who failed to keep themselves personally clean was a forced scrubbing by the driver and two other blacks. Another planter required the ground under the cabins to be swept every month and had cabins whitewashed twice a year. Charles Tait, a leading planter in Alabama, required the cabins of his slaves to be moved to new ground every fourth year "to prevent filth accumulations and cholera or diphtheria."

Slave health care was at its best for pregnant women. "Pregnant women," wrote one planter, "must be treated with great tenderness, worked near home and lightly." "Light work" was generally interpreted as 50 to 60 percent of normal effort and was to exclude activity which required heavy physical effort. During the last month of pregnancy work was further reduced, although various planters felt, as did P. C. Weston, that "pregnant women are always to do some work up to the time of their confinement, if it is only walking into the field and staying there." On large estates, women were usually confined in the "lying-in" ward of the plantation hospital. In normal cases the delivery was usually handled by a midwife. But if some difficulty in the delivery was anticipated, a doctor was called in. The period of confinement generally lasted about four weeks, during part of which time mothers were attended to by a midwife or a nurse. There frequently followed another two weeks of light work in the vicinity of the slave quarters. Women were expected to nurse their children, and hence were kept on relatively light work schedules for the balance of the year. Until the sixth or eighth month after birth, nursing took place four times per day during working hours, and nursing mothers were expected to work at only 50 to 60 percent of normal levels. For the balance of the first year infants were usually nursed twice a day during hours of work.

Demographic evidence gives strong support to descriptions of pre- and post-natal care contained in plantation rules, letters, and diaries. Computations based on data from the 1850 census indicate that the average death rate due to pregnancy among slave women in the prime childbearing ages, twenty to twenty-nine, was just one per thousand. This means that out of every 167 women in this age category who gave birth, only one died. The slave mortality rate in childbearing was not only low on an absolute scale, it was also lower than the maternal death rate experienced by southern white women.

The mortality rate for infants was less favorable than that of their mothers. Of every thousand slaves born in 1850, an average of 183 died before their first birthday. The death rate for white infants in the same year was 146 per thousand. In other words, the infant death rate for slaves was 25 percent higher than for whites. This finding appears to give credence to charges that mean treatment of infant slaves was widespread. In so doing it raises the strange paradox of planters who treated pregnant women and new mothers quite well while abusing their offspring.

Work on the demographic data for 1850 and 1860 has not

proceeded far enough to permit a full resolution of this paradox. Definitive answers to many of the questions posed by the relatively high infant death rates experienced by slaves are at least several years off. The work thus far, however, has revealed little evidence to support the charge that masters neglected the care of infants. Most of the difference between the infant death rates of slaves and free persons appears to have been due to the fact that the South was less healthy than the North. The infant death rate of southern whites in 1850 was 177 per thousand — virtually the same as the infant death rate of slaves. Along this dimension, then, exploitation of blacks arose because slavery was confined to the South and because slaves were not free to choose where to live.

By and large, slave deaths during the first year of life, like those of free infants, were due to diseases such as whooping cough, croup, pneumonia, cholera, and various maladies of the gastrointestinal system — diseases about which the men of the antebellum era had little understanding and over which they had little control. Of those causes of death that apparently could be controlled, suffocation was most significant. About 9.3 percent of the slave infants who died in 1850 were reported to have succumbed from this cause. Among whites, only 1.2 percent of infants were reported to have died from suffocation. The excess of the slave suffocation rate over the white suffocation rate accounted for nearly fifteen deaths out of every thousand slave births.

There has been much debate among historians as to the causes of infant suffocations. Some have attributed them to infanticide, arguing that life was so unbearable for slaves that many mothers preferred to kill their young rather than to rear them in bondage. This argument is undermined by the extremely low suicide rate among slaves. Less than one slave in every ten thousand committed suicide in 1850. That was only one third of the suicide rate among the

Figure 36

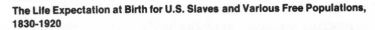

The Life Expectation at Birth for U.S. Slaves and Various Free Populations, 1830-1920

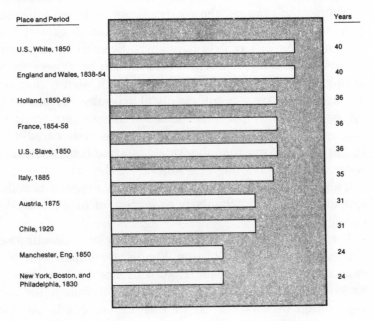

Place and Period	Years
U.S., White, 1850	40
England and Wales, 1838-54	40
Holland, 1850-59	36
France, 1854-58	36
U.S., Slave, 1850	36
Italy, 1885	35
Austria, 1875	31
Chile, 1920	31
Manchester, Eng. 1850	24
New York, Boston, and Philadelphia, 1830	24

white population. Others have used suffocation as evidence that neglect of children by slave mothers was widespread. While one cannot rule out the possibility that deaths due to suffocation reflected neglect on the part of the mothers involved, the fact remains that out of every one hundred slaves born, less than two infants died of this cause. The mortality statistics, therefore, leave plenty of room for slave mothers who gave their children tender care.

Nor should one necessarily accept the statistics on slave suffocations at face value. Many deaths that were interpreted as suffocation because of the absence of a prior fever or other then-accepted symptoms of illness could have been caused by undisclosed infections. That more such deaths were reported as suffocation for slaves than for free men might have been due to the jaundiced view of the overseers who reported the death statistics to the census takers.

Neither the 1850 nor the 1860 censuses collected information on morbidity. The only currently available data comes from a sample of 545 field hands who lived on fifteen plantations. This sample provides information on illness rates during 2,274 man years of labor time. It shows that on average each slave was sufficiently ill to be absent from work for just 12.0 days per year. This low illness rate tends to support the impression that slaves were well cared for. It also calls into question the widely asserted contention that slaves were always feigning illness. At the very least, the low absence rate shows that if pretense of illness was widespread, slaves were singularly unsuccessful in their deceptions.

For many, statistics on life expectancy are the ultimate measure of physical well-being. Figure 36 compares the life expectancy of U.S. slaves in 1850 with those of free men in various places between 1830 and 1920. Although the life expectation of slaves in 1850 was 12 percent below the average of white Americans, it was well within the range experienced by free men during the nineteenth century. It was, for example, nearly identical with the life expectation of countries as advanced as France and Holland. Moreover, U.S. slaves had much longer life expectations than free urban industrial workers in both the United States and Europe.

The Family

The administration of most large plantations was based on two organizations. Fieldwork revolved around gangs.

They were the vehicles through which planters were able to achieve a degree of specialization and efficiency that was unmatched elsewhere in agriculture. This aspect of plantation organization is considered in chapter 6.

The other organization of central importance was the family. Planters assigned three functions to the slave family. First, it was the administrative unit for the distribution of food and clothing and for the provision of shelter. As we have already seen, the single-family house, not the dormitory, was almost the universal form of shelter on larger plantations. The records of planters also indicate that whether food was cooked in a common kitchen or in the house of individual families, allotments of rations were generally made by family. The same was true for clothing.

The family was also an important instrument for maintaining labor discipline. By encouraging strong family attachments, slaveowners reduced the danger that individual slaves would run away. By permitting families to have *de facto* ownership of houses, furniture, clothing, garden plots, and small livestock, planters created an economic stake for slaves in the system. Moreover, the size of the stake was variable. It was possible for some families to achieve substantially higher levels of income and of *de facto* wealth ownership than others. The size and quality of houses and the allotments of clothes as well as the size of the garden plots differed from family to family.

Third, the family was also the main instrument for promoting the increase of the slave population. Not only did planters believe that fertility rates would be highest when the family was strongest, but they relied on the family for the rearing of children. Although infants and very young children were kept in nurseries while mothers labored in the field, these supplemented rather than replaced the family. The central importance of the family in the rearing of slaves is revealed by the narratives of former slaves collected by the

W.P.A. in the 1930s. In discussing their early upbringing and the influences on them, the former slaves frequently refer to what their parents taught them but rarely, if ever, invoke the names of women who ran the nurseries.

To promote the stability of slave families, planters often combined exhortations with a system of rewards and sanctions. The rewards included such subsidies as separate houses for married couples, gifts of household goods, and cash bonuses. They often sought to make the marriage a solemn event by embedding it in a well-defined ritual. Some marriage ceremonies were performed in churches, others by the planter in the "big house." In either case, marriages were often accompanied by feasts and sometimes made the occasion for a general holiday. The sanctions were directed against adultery and divorce. For many planters, adultery was an offense which required whippings for the guilty parties. Some planters also used the threat of the whip to discourage divorce.

Thus, while the existence of slave marriages was explicitly denied under the legal codes of the states, they were not only recognized but actively promoted under plantation codes. That the legal basis for slave marriage was derived from codes which held sway within the jurisdiction of the plantation, points to a much neglected feature of legal structure of the antebellum South. Within fairly wide limits the state, in effect, turned the definition of the codes of legal behavior of slaves, and of the punishment for infractions of these codes, over to planters. Such duality of the legal structure was not unique to the antebellum South. It existed in medieval Europe in the duality between the law of the manor and of the crown; it was a characteristic of the regimes under which the American colonies were governed; and in lesser degree, it exists with respect to certain large institutions today (for example, with respect to university regulations).

The importance of the dual legal structure of the antebellum South is that the latitude which the state yielded to the planter was quite wide. For most slaves it was the law of the plantation, not of the state, that was relevant. Only a small proportion of the slaves ever had to deal with the law-enforcement mechanism of the state. Their daily lives were governed by plantation law. Consequently, the emphasis put on the sanctity of the slave family by many planters, and the legal status given to the slave family under plantation law, cannot be lightly dismissed.

Recognition of the dualistic nature of the southern legal structure puts into a different perspective the emphasis which some historians have placed on the "pre-bourgeois" character of antebellum society. What made that society pre-bourgeois was not the absence of a commercial spirit among planters, but the wide area of legal authority which the state yielded to them. In Europe, the rise of capitalism was accompanied by a determined struggle to weaken the authority of the manor and to transfer its powers to the centralized state. This process was sharply curtailed in the South. While the South developed a highly capitalistic form of agriculture, and while its economic behavior was as strongly ruled by profit maximization as that of the North, the relationship between its ruling and its servile class was marked by patriarchal features which were strongly reminis-cent of medieval life. Unlike the northern manufacturer, the authority of the planter extended not only to the con-duct of business but to the regulation of the family lives of slaves, the control of their public behavior, the provision of their food and shelter, the care of their health, and the protection of their souls.

We do not mean to suggest that planters viewed the slave family purely as a business instrument. Victorian attitudes predominated in the planting class. The emphasis on strong, stable families, and on the limitation of sexual ac-tivity to the family, followed naturally from such attitudes. That morality and good business practice should coincide created neither surprise nor consternation among most planters.

Of course not all planters, and not all of their overseers, were men who lived by the moral codes of their day. That many of these men sought sex outside of the confines of their wives' beds is beyond question. To satisfy their desires they took on mistresses and concubines, seduced girls of tender ages, and patronized prostitutes. Such sexual exploitation was not limited to the South. And within the South, sexual exploitation by white men was not limited to black women.

The point at issue here is not whether the sexual exploitation of slave women by masters and overseers existed, but whether it was so frequent that it undermined or destroyed the black family. Let us pose the question somewhat more sharply: Are there reasons to believe that the degree of sexual exploitation which white men imposed on black women was greater than that imposed on white women? We put the issue in this way because while the sexual exploitation of white women was rife, few have gone so far as to claim that such exploitation destroyed the family institution among whites. Is the asymmetry in the presumed effects of sexual exploitation on the families of blacks and whites justified by available evidence?

Antebellum critics of slavery answered these questions in the affirmative. They accused slaveowners and overseers of turning plantations into personal harems. They assumed that because the law permitted slaveowners to ravish black women, the practice must have been extremely common. They also assumed that black women were, if not more licentious, at least more promiscuous than white women, and hence less likely to resist sexual advances by men, whether black or white. Moreover, the ravishing of black women by white men was not the only aspect of sexual exploitation which devastated the slave family. There was also the policy of deliberate slave-breeding, under which planters encouraged promiscuous relationships among blacks. Thus, economic greed and lust on the part of the planters, and submissiveness on the part of the slaves, combined to make the sexual exploitation of black women so extreme as to be beyond comparison with the situation of white women.

The evidence on which these assumptions and conclusions were based was extremely limited. While none of the various travelers through the South had seen deliberate slave-breeding practiced, they had all heard reports of it. Some travelers published conversations with men who admitted to fathering a large number of the slaves on their plantations. Others wrote of the special solicitude shown by one or another master to mulatto offspring, a solicitude which in their minds strongly implied parenthood. There were also the descriptions of the treatment of especially pretty slave women on the auction block and of the high prices at which such women sold, prices too high to be warranted by field labor and which could be explained only by their value as concubines or as prostitutes.

Even if all these reports were true, they constituted at most a few hundred cases. By themselves, such a small number of observations out of a population of millions, could just as easily be used as proof of the infrequency of the sexual exploitation of black women as of its frequency. The real question is whether such cases were common events that were rarely reported, or whether they were rare events that were frequently reported. The prevalence of mulattoes convinced not only the northern public of the antebellum era, but historians of today, that for each case of exploitation identified, there were thousands which had escaped discovery. For travelers to the South reported that a large proportion of the slaves were not the deep black of Africans from the Guinea coast but tawny, golden, and white or nearly white. Here was proof beyond denial of either the ubiquity of the exploitation of black women by white men, or of the promiscuity of black women, or of both. But this seemingly irrefutable evidence is far from conclusive. It is not the eyesight of these travelers to the South which is questionable, but their statistical sense. For mulattoes were not distributed evenly through the Negro population. They were concentrated in the cities and especially among freedmen. According to the 1860 census, 39 percent of freedmen in southern cities were mulattoes. Among urban slaves the proportion of mulattoes was 20 percent. In other words, one out of every four Negroes living in a southern city was a mulatto. But among rural slaves, who constituted 95 percent of the slave population, only 9.9 percent were mulatto in 1860. For the slave population as a whole, therefore, the proportion of mulattoes was just 10.4 percent in 1860 and 7.7 percent in 1850. Thus it appears that travelers to the South greatly exaggerated the extent of miscegenation because they came into contact with unrepresentative samples of the Negro population. They appear to have had much more contact with the freedmen and slaves of the urban areas than with slaves living in the relative isolation of the countryside. Far from proving that the exploitation of black women was ubiquitous, the available data on mulattoes strongly militates against that contention.

The fact that during the twenty-three decades of contact between slaves and whites which elapsed between 1620 and 1850, only 7.7 percent of the slaves were mulattoes suggests that on average only a very small percentage of the slaves born in any given year were fathered by white men. This inference is not contradicted by the fact that the percentage of mulattoes increased by one third during the last decade of the antebellum era, rising from 7.7 to 10.4 percent. For it must be remembered that mulattoes were the progeny not just of unions between whites and pure blacks but also of unions between mulattoes and blacks. Under common definition, a person with one-eighth ancestry of another race was a mulatto. Consequently, the offspring of two slaves who were each one-eighth white was to be classified as a mulatto, as was the offspring of any slave, regardless of the ancestry of his or her mate, whose grandfather was a white. A demographic model of the slave population, which is presented in the technical appendix, shows that the census data on mulattoes alone cannot be used to sustain the contention that a large proportion of slave children must have been fathered by white men. And other available bodies of evidence, such as the W.P.A. survey of former slaves, throw such claims into doubt. Of those in the survey who identified parentage, only 4.5 percent indicated that one of their parents had been white. But the work of geneticists on gene pools has revealed that even the last figure may be too high. Measurements of the admixture of "Caucasian" and "Negro" genes among southern rural blacks today indicate that the share of Negro children fathered by whites on slave plantations probably averaged between 1 and 2 percent.

That these findings seem startling is due in large measure to the widespread assumption that because the law permitted masters to ravish their slave women, they must have exercised that right. As one scholar recently put it, "Almost every [white] mother and wife connected with the institution [of slavery] either actually or potentially shared the males in her family with slave women." The trouble with this view is that it recognizes no forces operating on human behavior other than the force of statute law. Yet many rights permitted by legal statutes and judicial decisions are not widely exercised, because economic and social forces militate against them.

To put the issue somewhat differently, it has been presumed that masters and overseers must have ravished black women frequently because their demand for such sexual pleasures was high and because the cost of satisfying that demand was low. Such arguments overlook the real and potentially large costs that confronted masters and overseers who sought sexual pleasures in the slave quarters. The seduction of the daughter or wife of a slave could undermine the discipline that planters so assiduously strove to attain. Not only would it stir anger and discontent in the families affected, but it would undermine the air of mystery and distinction on which so much of the authority of large planters rested. Nor was it just a planter's reputation in the slave quarter of his plantation that would be at stake. While he might be able to prevent news of his nocturnal adventure from being broadcast in his own house, it would be more difficult to prevent his slaves from gossiping to slaves on other plantations.

Owners of large plantations who desired illicit sexual relationships were by no means confined to slave quarters in their quest. Those who owned fifty or more slaves were very rich men by the standards of their day. The average annual net income in this class was in excess of $7,500. That amount was more than sixty times per capita income in 1860. To have a comparable income today, a person would need an after-tax income of about $240,000 or a before-tax income of about $600,000. So rich a man could easily have afforded to maintain a mistress in town where his relationship could have been not only more discreet than in the crowded slave quarters of his own plantation, but far less likely to upset the labor discipline on which economic success depended.

For the overseer, the cost of sexual episodes in the slave quarter, once discovered, was often his job. Nor would he find it easy to obtain employment elsewhere as an overseer, since not many masters would be willing to employ as their manager a man who was known to lack self-control on so vital an issue. "Never employ an overseer who will equalize himself with the negro women," wrote Charles Tait to his children. "Besides the morality of it, there are evils too numerous to be now mentioned."

Nor should one underestimate the effect of racism on the

demand of white males for black sexual partners. While some white men might have been tempted by the myth of black sexuality, a myth that may be stronger today than it was in the antebellum South, it is likely that far larger numbers were put off by racist aversions. Data on prostitution supports this conjecture. Nashville is the only southern city for which a count of prostitutes is available. The 1860 census showed that just 4.3 percent of the prostitutes in that city were Negroes, although a fifth of the population of Nashville was Negro. Moreover, all of the Negro prostitutes were free and light-skinned. There were no pure blacks who were prostitutes; nor were any slaves prostitutes. The substantial underrepresentation of Negroes, as well as the complete absence of dark-skinned Negroes, indicates that white men who desired illicit sex had a strong preference for white women.

The failure of Nashville's brothels to employ slave women is of special interest. For it indicates that supply as well as demand considerations served to limit the use of slaves as prostitutes. The census revealed that half of Nashville's prostitutes were illiterate — not functionally illiterate, but completely lacking in either the capacity to read, or to write, or both. In other words, the supply of prostitutes was drawn from poor, uneducated girls who could only command the wages of unskilled labor. Given such a supply, a slaveholder did not have to be imbued with Victorian morals to demur from sending his chattel into prostitution. He could clearly earn more on his slave women by working them in the fields where they would not be subject to the high morbidity and mortality rates which accompany the "world's oldest profession."

The contention that the slave family was undermined by the widespread promiscuity of blacks is as poorly founded as the thesis that masters were uninhibited in their sexual exploitation of slave women. Indeed, virtually no evidence, other than the allegations of white observers, has ever been presented which sustains the charge that promiscuity among slaves was greater than that found among whites. The question then arises, "Do the allegations reflect the reality of black behavior or are they merely reflections of the preconceptions of the observers?"

The allegations appeared creditable because they emanated not only from southern defenders of slavery but also from critics of the system. While the charges of Southerners could be set down as apologetics, one could not so easily dismiss the words of the abolitionists and other enemies of slavery. On the issue of promiscuity the antislavery forces differed from the apologists not in denying its existence but in the explanation of its extent. Slavery, the critics believed, worked to exacerbate rather than to hold in check the carnal instincts of blacks.

Unfortunately, abolitionists and other antislavery writers were not free of racism merely because they carried the banner of a moral struggle. With their greater physical separation from blacks, these writers were often more gullible and more quick in their acceptance of certain racial stereotypes than slaveholders. This, as we shall see, was a key factor in their underestimation of the efficiency of slave labor. Moreover, coming from the upper classes, as many of these writers did, they shared with slaveholders certain common conceptions regarding the behavior of all laboring folk. Thus, Fanny Kemble, whose descriptions of the family life of slaves is often quoted by historians, saw Irish peasants, English manufacturing workers, and American Negroes as all exhibiting the same "recklessness" toward human propagation.

The available demographic evidence on slaves suggests a picture of their sexual lives and family behavior that has little in common with that conveyed by the allegations. One of the most revealing pieces of information is the pattern of child spacing among mothers between the ages of eighteen and thirty. For those whose children were stillborn or who died within the first three months, the average elapsed time until the birth of the next child was slightly more than one year. However, for those mothers whose children survived the first year of life, the elapsed time before the birth of the next child was somewhat over two years. This is the pattern of child spacing that one would expect to find in a noncontraceptive population in which mothers engaged in breast feeding for the first year of their children's lives. For one of the effects of breast feeding is to reduce the likelihood of conception. In other words, the pattern of child spacing among slaves suggests that the nursing of infants by their mothers was widespread.

This finding hardly supports the charge that slave mothers were indifferent to their children, generally neglected them, and were widely engaged in infanticide. Quite the contrary, the ubiquity of the year-long pattern of breast feeding, combined with the nearly identical rate of infant mortality among slaves and southern whites, and with the rare occurrences of suffocation and other accidents as the cause of death of infant slaves, suggests that for the most part, black mothers cared quite well for their children.

An even more telling piece of information is the distribution of the ages of mothers at the time of the birth of their first surviving child. This distribution, which is shown in figure 37, contradicts the charge that black girls were frequently turned into mothers at such tender ages as twelve, thirteen, and fourteen. Not only was motherhood at age twelve virtually unknown, and motherhood in the early teens quite uncommon, but the average age at first birth was 22.5 (the median age was 20.8). Thus the high fertility rate of slave women was not the consequence of the wanton impregnation of very young unmarried women by either white or black men, but of the frequency of conception after the first birth. By far the great majority of slave children were borne by women who were not only quite mature, but who were already married.

Figure 37

The Distribution of First Births, by the Ages of Slave Mothers

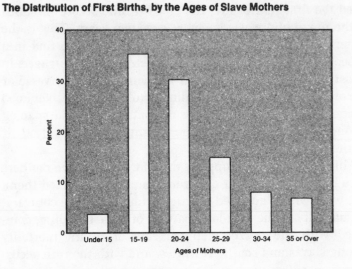

The high average age of mothers at first birth also suggests that slave parents closely guarded their daughters from sexual contact with men. For in a well-fed, noncontraceptive population in which women are quite fecund after marriage, only abstinence would explain the relative shortage of births in the late-teen ages. In other words, the demographic evidence suggests that the prevailing sexual mores of slaves were not promiscuous but prudish — the very reverse of the stereotype published by many in both the abolitionist and slaveholding camps and accepted in traditional historiography. Narratives collected from ex-slaves provide support for the prevalence of prudishness in the conduct of family life. "Dem's moral times," recollected Amos Lincoln, who was reared on a plantation in Louisiana. "A gal's twenty-one 'fore she marry. They didn't go wanderin' 'round all hours. They mammies knowed where they was. Folks nowadays is wild and weak."

That marriage altered the sexual behavior of slaves is clearly indicated by the difference between the seasonal pattern of first births and that of second and subsequent births (see figure 38). Data culled from plantation records indicate that for second and subsequent births, roughly equal percentages of infants were born during every quarter of the year. But the seasonal pattern of first births shows a definite peak during the last quarter of the year — precisely the pattern to be expected in an agrarian society in which a large proportion of marriages took place soon after the harvest. Over twice as many first births took place during the last quarter of the year — roughly nine to thirteen months after the end of the harvest, depending on the region and crop — as took place during the first quarter of the year. This pattern cannot be attributed merely to the fact that slaves had more leisure time during the winter interstice, and hence, more opportunity for sexual intercourse. If that was all that had been involved, the peaking of births during the last quarter of the year would have occurred not only for first children but for subsequent children as well.

Also fallacious is the contention that slave marriages, since they were arbitrarily dictated by masters, frequently produced odd age combinations — young men married to old women and vice versa. Figure 39 shows that most marriages were contracted among partners quite close in age. The average age difference between husband and wife was just three years. In almost all cases, the man was the same age or older than the woman. Reversals in this pattern were quite uncommon.

That slave life pivoted around stable, nuclear families does not mean that the black family was merely a copy of the white family. No doubt the African heritage of blacks, as well as their particular socioeconomic circumstances, re-

Figure 38

A Comparison of the Seasonal Distribution of First Births with that of All Other Births

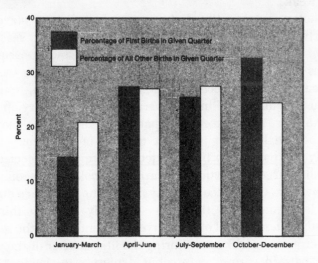

Figure 39

The Distribution of Age Differences between Slave Husbands and Wives

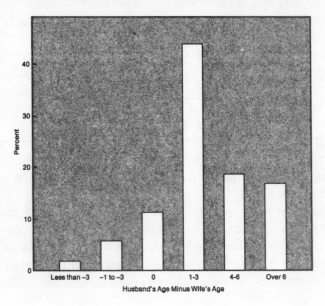

sulted in various characteristics which were, if not restricted to, at least more frequent among black than white families. For example, various bits of evidence suggest that wives tended to play a stronger role in black than in white families. Careful delineation of such special characteristics and the determination of their incidence is a task which has not yet been adequately essayed. The evidence already in hand, however, clearly invalidates many of the generalizations that now permeate history books.

It is not true that "the typical slave family was matriarchal in form" and that the "husband was at most his wife's assistant." Nor is it true that the "male slave's only crucial function within the family was that of siring offspring." For better or worse, the dominant role in slave society was played by men, not women. It was men who occupied virtually all of the managerial slots available to slaves. There were very few female overseers or drivers. Men occupied nearly all the artisan crafts; among them were carpentry, coopering and blacksmithing. In the city of Charleston in 1848, for example, all of the 706 slave artisans were male.

While females worked along with males in the field, their role was strictly delimited. Much has been made of the women who worked in plow gangs. But such participation was quite uncommon. Plow gangs were confined almost exclusively to men, and predominantly to young men. During the period of cultivation, women worked along with older men and children in the hoe gangs, where strength was not so important a factor. Only at harvesttime were women the equal of "any man" since dexterity, not strength, was the crucial characteristic of successful cotton picking. Just as some jobs on the plantation were confined strictly to men, others were confined strictly to women. Men were virtually never spinners, weavers, seamstresses, or nurses. The differentiation between male and female roles continued into the domestic staffs of plantations, although the division was somewhat less sharp. Gardeners and coachmen were jobs for males; laundresses and cooks, female jobs.

There was also a division of labor within the slave family, a division that began with courtship. It was the male who, at least on the surface, initiated the period of courtship. And it was the man who secured the permission of the planter to marry. After marriage, the tasks of cooking, ordinary household cleaning, laundering, and care of the children fell to the mother. Work in the garden patches of the slave household, hunting and fishing for extra food, and chopping wood were among the tasks of the father.

Planters recognized husbands as the head of the family. Slave families were listed in their record books with the husband at the top of the list. Houses were assigned by the names of husbands and the semiannual issues of clothing to families were made in the name of the husband. Garden patches were assigned to the husbands and the money earned from the sale of crops from these patches was held in his name. When slaves wanted advances of cash from these accounts, they were made to the men. Slave purchases of cloth and apparel (whether intended for men, women, or children) were charged against the names of the husbands, as were purchases of such other items as pails, pots, and special foods.

While both moral convictions and good business practice generally led planters to encourage the development of stable nuclear families, it would be a mistake to assume that the black family was purely, or even predominantly, the creation of white masters. The exact interplay of external and internal forces in shaping the black family is still unknown. But there is considerable evidence that the nuclear form was not merely imposed on slaves. Slaves apparently abandoned the African family forms because they did not satisfy the needs of blacks who lived and worked under conditions and in a society much different from those which their ancestors experienced. The nuclear family took root among blacks because it did satisfy those needs. Witness to the meaning which the family held for slaves is given by the deep anguish which they usually expressed on those occasions when their families were rent apart on the auction block. "Well, dey took us on up dere to Memphis and we was sold jest like cattle," said Nancy Gardner, a former slave who lived in Oklahoma. "Dey sold me and ma together and dey sold pa and de boys together. Dey was sent to Mississippi and we was sent to Alabama. My pa, O how my ma was grieved to death about him! She didn't live long after dat."

During the relatively infrequent instances when economic forces led the planter to destroy, rather than to maintain slave families, the *independent* striving of slaves to maintain their families came into sharp focus. Mrs. Josie Jordan, an ex-slave from Tennessee, reported that her mother "had two children while belonging to Mister Clark and he wouldn't let them go with mammy and pappy. That's what caused her misery. Pappy tried to ease her mind but she jest kept a'crying for her babies, Ann and Reuban, till Mister Lowery got Clark to leave them visit with her once a month." Further testimony to this striving is given by the ads which planters placed in newspapers advertising for the capture of runaways. These ads frequently indicate the planter's belief that his slave was attempting to reunite with the family from which the slave had recently been removed.

The abolitionist position on the black family, which has been accepted so uncritically by historians, was strikingly inconsistent. To arouse sentiment against the slave system they accurately portrayed the deep anguish which was caused by the forced breakup of slave families while simultaneously arguing that slavery had robbed black families of all meaning. This latter view was given vivid expression in Fanny Kemble's journal. The relationship between slave parents and children, she wrote, was reduced to the "connection between the animal and its young." In her view black families were stripped of "all the unspeakable tenderness and solemnity, all the rational, and all the spiritual grace and glory" which she associated with parenthood in upper-class English families. Under slavery, she concluded, parenthood became "mere breeding, bearing, suckling, and there an end." The anguish on the auction block as well as the struggle of blacks to reunite their severed families, both during and immediately after slavery, suggests that the love that permeated slave families eluded Fanny Kemble and most other white observers — perhaps because of a veil of racial and class biases which obscured their vision and prevented them from seeing the real content of black family life.

Punishment, Rewards, and Expropriation

The exploitative nature of slavery is most apparent in its system of punishment and rewards. Whipping was probably the most common punishment meted out against errant slaves. Other forms of punishment included the deprivation of various privileges (such as visits to town), confinement in stocks, incarceration, sale, branding, and the death penalty.

Whipping could be either a mild or a severe punishment, depending on how it was administered. Some whippings were so severe that they resulted in death. Indeed, in cases such as murder, the sentences of slaves who would otherwise have been executed were frequently converted to severe whipping, coupled with exportation to another state or a foreign country. For, as indicated in chapter 2, by converting the death penalty to whipping and exportation, the state could recover a substantial part of the value of a slave that

Figure 40

The Distribution of Whippings on the Bennet H. Barrow Plantation during a Two-Year Period Beginning in December, 1840

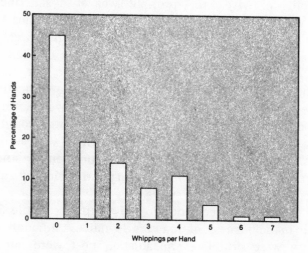

would have been lost through his execution. In other instances, whipping was as mildly applied as the corporal punishment normally practiced within families today.

Reliable data on the frequency of whipping is extremely sparse. The only systematic record of whipping now available for an extended period comes from the diary of Bennet Barrow, a Louisiana planter who believed that to spare the rod was to spoil the slave. His plantation numbered about 200 slaves, of whom about 120 were in the labor force. The record shows that over the course of two years a total of 160 whippings were administered, an average of 0.7 whippings per hand per year. About half the hands were not whipped at all during the period.

There was nothing exceptional about the use of whipping to enforce discipline among slaves until the beginning of the nineteenth century. It must be remembered that through the centuries whipping was considered a fully acceptable form of punishment, not merely for criminals but also for honest men or women who in some way shirked their duties. Whipping of wives, for example, was even sanctified in some versions of the Scripture. The Matthew's Bible, which preceded the King James version, told the husband, in a note at 1 Pet. 3, that if his wife was "not obedient and healpfull vnto hym endeuoureth to beate the feare of God into her heade, and that therby she maye be compelled to learne her duitie and do it." During the seventeenth and most of the eighteenth centuries whipping was commonly employed as a punishment in the North as well as in the South. Not until the end of the eighteenth century and the beginning of the nineteenth century did whipping rapidly fall from favor in the free states.

To attribute the continuation of whipping in the South to the maliciousness of masters is naïve. Although some masters were brutal, even sadistic, most were not. The overwhelming majority of the ex-slaves in the W.P.A. narratives who expressed themselves on the issue reported that their masters were good men. Such men worried about the proper role of whipping in a system of punishment and rewards. Some excluded it altogether. Most accepted it, but recognized that to be effective whipping had to be used with restraint and in a coolly calculated manner. Weston, for example, admonished his overseer not to impose punishment of any sort until twenty-four hours after the offense had been discovered. William J. Minor, a sugar planter, instructed his managers "not [to] cut the skin when punishing, nor punish in a passion." Many planters forbade the whipping of slaves except by them or in their presence. Others limited the number of lashes that could be administered without their permission.

The decline of whipping as an instrument of labor discipline outside of the South appears to have been heavily influenced by economic considerations. With the rise of capitalism, impersonal and indirect sanctions were increasingly substituted for direct, personal ones. The hiring of free workers in the marketplace provided managers of labor with a powerful new disciplinary weapon. Workers who were lazy, indifferent, or who otherwise shirked their duties could be fired — left to starve beyond the eyesight or expense of the employer. Interestingly enough, denial of food was rarely used to enforce discipline on slaves. For the illness and lethargy caused by malnutrition reduced the capacity of the slave to labor in the fields. Planters preferred whipping to incarceration because the lash did not generally lead to an extended loss of the slave's labor time. In other words, whipping persisted in the South because the cost of substituting hunger and incarceration for the lash was greater for the slaveowner than for the northern employer of free labor. When the laborer owns his own human capital, forms of punishment which impair or diminish the value of that capital are borne exclusively by him. Under slavery, the master desired forms of punishment which, while they imposed costs on the slave, did so with minimum impairment to the human capital which the master owned. Whipping generally fulfilled these conditions.

While whipping was an integral part of the system of punishment and rewards, it was not the totality of the system. What planters wanted was not sullen and discontented slaves who did just enough to keep from getting whipped. They wanted devoted, hard-working, responsible slaves who identified their fortunes with the fortunes of their masters. Planters sought to imbue slaves with a "Protestant" work ethic and to transform that ethic from a state of mind into a high level of production. "My negros have their name up in the neighbourhood," wrote Bennet Barrow, "for making more than any one else & they think Whatever they do is better than any body Else." Such an attitude could not be beaten into slaves. It had to be elicited.

Much of the managerial attention of planters was focused on the problem of motivating their hands. To achieve the desired response they developed a wide-ranging system of rewards. Some rewards were directed toward improving short-run performance. Included in this category were prizes for the individual or the gang with the best picking record on a given day or during a given week. The prizes were such items as clothing, tobacco, and whiskey; sometimes the prize was cash. Good immediate performance was also rewarded with unscheduled holidays or with trips to town on weekends. When slaves worked at times normally set aside for rest, they received extra pay — usually in cash and at the rate prevailing in the region for hired labor. Slaves who were performing well were permitted to work on their own account after normal hours at such tasks as making shingles or weaving baskets, articles which they could sell either to their masters or to farmers in the neighborhood.

Some rewards were directed at influencing behavior over periods of intermediate duration. The rewards in this category were usually paid at the end of the year. Year-end bonuses, given either in goods or cash, were frequently quite substantial. Bennet Barrow, for example, distributed gifts averaging between $15 and $20 per slave family in both 1839 and 1840. The amounts received by particular slaves were proportional to their performance. It should be noted that $20 was about a fifth of national per capita income in 1840. A bonus of the same relative magnitude today would be in the neighborhood of $1,000.

Masters also rewarded slaves who performed well with patches of land ranging up to a few acres for each family. Slaves grew marketable crops on these lands, the proceeds of which accrued to them. On the Texas plantation of Julian S. Devereux, slaves operating such land produced as much as two bales of cotton per patch. Devereux marketed their crop along with his own. In a good year some of the slaves earned in excess of $100 per annum for their families. Devereux set up accounts to which he credited the proceeds of the sales. Slaves drew on these accounts when they wanted cash or when they wanted Devereux to purchase clothing, pots, pans, tobacco, or similar goods for them.

Occasionally planters even devised elaborate schemes for profit sharing with their slaves. William Jemison, an Alabama planter, entered into the following agreement with his bondsmen.

[Y]ou shall have two thirds of the corn and cotton made on the plantation and as much of the wheat as will reward you for the sowing it. I also furnish you with provisions for this year. When your crop is gathered, one third is to be set aside for me. You are then to pay your overseer his part and pay me what I furnish, clothe yourselves, pay your own taxes and doctor's fee with all expenses of the farm. You are to be no expense to me, but render to me one third of the produce and what I have loaned you. You have the use of the stock and plantation tools. You are to return them as good as they are and the plantation to be kept in good repair, and what clear money you make shall be divided equally amongst you in a fair proportion agreeable to the services rendered by each hand. There will be an account of all lost time kept, and those that earn most shall have most.

There was a third category of rewards. These were of a long-term nature, often requiring the lapse of a decade or more before they paid off. Thus, slaves had the opportunity to rise within the social and economic hierarchy that existed under bondage. Field hands could become artisans or drivers. Artisans could be allowed to move from the plantation to town where they would hire themselves out. Drivers could move up to the position of head driver or overseer. Climbing the economic ladder brought not only social status, and sometimes more freedom; it also had significant payoffs in better housing, better clothing, and cash bonuses.

Little attention has hitherto been paid to the manner in which planters selected the slaves who were to become the artisans and managers. In some cases boys were apprenticed to carpenters, blacksmiths, or some similar craftsmen when they were in their early teens, as was typically done with whites. For slaves, this appears to have been the exception rather than the rule. Analysis of occupational data derived from probate and plantation records reveals an unusual distribution of ages among slave artisans. Slaves in their twenties were substantially underrepresented, while slaves in their forties and fifties were overrepresented. This age pattern suggests that the selection of slaves for training in the crafts was frequently delayed until slaves reached their late twenties, or perhaps even into the thirties.

Normally this would be an uneconomical policy, since the earlier an investment is made in occupational training, the more years there are to reap the returns on that investment. Slavery altered this pattern by shifting the authority to determine occupational investments from the parents to the masters. In free societies, kinship is usually the primary basis for determining which members of the new generation are trained in skilled occupations. But the slaveholder lacked the vested interests of a parent. He could, therefore, treat entry into the skilled occupations as a prize that was to be claimed by the most deserving, regardless of family background. The extra effort put forth by young field hands who competed for these jobs appears to have more than offset the loss in returns due to the curtailed period over which the occupational investment was amortized. We do not mean to suggest that kinship played no role in the intergenerational transfer of skills among slaves. We merely wish to stress that its role was significantly reduced as compared with free society.

Another long-run reward was freedom through manumission. The chance of achieving this reward was, of course, quite low. Census data indicate that in 1850 the manumission rate was just 0.45 per thousand slaves. Manumission could be achieved either through the philanthropy of a master or through an agreement which permitted a slave to buy himself out. Sometimes gifts of freedom were bestowed while the master was still alive. More often it was a bequest set forth in a will. Self-purchase involved arrangements under which slaves were permitted to purchase themselves with money that they earned from work on their own account, or in the case of skilled urban slaves, by increasing the share of income which the artisan paid to his master. Some skilled slaves were able to accumulate enough capital to purchase their freedom within a decade. For others the period extended to two decades or more. Little information is currently available on the prices at which such transactions were concluded. It is not known whether slaves involved in self-purchase were generally forced to pay a price in excess of their market value.

From the foregoing it is clear that slaves did not all live at a uniform level of income. The elaborate system of rewards erected by planters introduced substantial variation in the slave standard of living. Much work remains to be done before it will be possible to reconstruct with reasonable accuracy the full range of the slave income distribution. It has been possible, however, to estimate the "basic income" of slaves in 1850. This, together with some fragmentary evidence on the higher incomes of slaves, will at least suggest the range of income variation that prevailed.

By "basic income" we mean the value of the food, clothing, shelter, and medical care furnished to slaves. The average value of the expenditure on these items for an adult male in 1850 was about $48.00. The most complete information on the extra earnings of field hands comes from several Texas plantations. The leading hands on these estates frequently earned between $40 and $110 per year above basic income through the sale of cotton and other products raised on their patches. This experience was not unique to Texas. On one Alabama plantation, eight hands produced cotton that earned them an average of $71 each, with the high man collecting $96. On still another plantation the average extra earnings of the thirteen top hands was $77. These scattered cases suggest that the ratio of high earnings to basic earnings among field hands was in the neighborhood of 2.5.

When the incomes of artisans are taken into account, the spread in slave earnings became still wider. The top incomes earned by craftsmen must have been several times basic income. This is implied by the high prices which artisans had to pay to buy themselves out. The average price of a prime-aged blacksmith was about $1,700 in 1850. Thus, a thirty-year-old man who was able to buy himself out in a decade probably earned in the neighborhood of $170 per year over subsistence. This suggests a ratio of artisan to basic income of about 4.5.

The highest annual figure we have been able to uncover for extra earnings by a field hand in a single year is $309. Aham, the Alabama slave whose sales of peaches, apples, and cotton yielded this sum, had accumulated enough capital over the years so that in 1860 he held notes on loans totaling over $2,400. The ratio of Aham's agricultural income to basic income is 7.4. If we assume that Aham earned 6 percent, or $144, on the loans, the ratio would rise to 10.4. The highest income above maintenance that we have found for an artisan is $500. In this case the ratio of earned to basic income is 11.4.

While the reward structure created much more room for upward mobility within the slave system than is usually supposed, the scope of opportunity should not be exaggerated. The highest levels of attainment were irrevocably foreclosed to slaves. The entrepreneurial talent obviously possessed by bondsmen such as Aham could not be used to catapult them into the stewardship of great businesses as long as they remained slaves. No slave, regardless of his gifts, could aspire to political position. No man of letters — there were slaves who acquired considerable erudition — could ever hold an appointment in the faculty of a southern university as long as he was a bondsman. The entrepreneurial genius had to settle for lingering in the shadow of the master on whose protection he was dependent. The man of letters could go no further than the position of tutor to the children of a benevolent and enlightened planter. It was on the talented, the upper crust of slave society, that deprivations of the peculiar institution hung most heavy. This, perhaps, explains why it was that the first to flee to northern lines as Yankee advances corroded the Rebel positions were not the ordinary field hands, but the drivers and the artisans.

As previously noted, a part of the income that slaves produced was expropriated from them. Determination of the average annual amount of this expropriation over the life cycle of the entire slave population is an extremely complex matter. For the rate of expropriation differed from slave to slave, as well as from year to year for particular slaves. The issues involved in the computation and the procedures employed are discussed in appendix B. The results of the computation are displayed in figure 41. This figure presents the average accumulated value or, in the language of economists, the "expected present value" of the income that was expropriated at each age of the life cycle. Prior to age twenty-six, the accumulated expenditures by planters on slaves were greater than the average accumulated income which they took from them. After that age the reverse was true. Planters broke even early in the twenty-seventh year. Over the balance of the life cycle the accumulated or present value of the expropriation mounted, on average, to a total of $32. This last figure is 12 percent of the average present value of the income earned by slaves over their lifetimes. In other words, on average, 12 percent of the value of the income produced by slaves was expropriated by their masters.

The relatively late age at which planters broke even is of great significance and requires further discussion. Two factors are responsible for this lateness. The first is that the

Figure 41

The Average Accumulated Value (Expected Present Value) of the Income Expropriated from Slaves over the Course of the Life Cycle

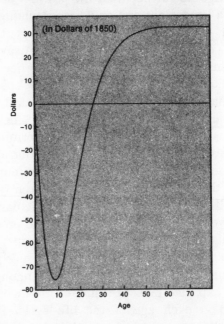

cost of capital was high in the South, and planters had to advance capital to cover the expense of rearing slaves for many years before they received a return from the labor of slaves. Second, because of the high mortality rates which prevailed for both black and white in the antebellum era, less than half the slaves lived to the break-even age. Fully 40 percent of the slaves died before age nineteen. Thus, a substantial part of the income taken from those slaves who survived into the later years was not an act of expropriation, but a payment required to cover the expenses of rearing children who failed to reach later ages. An additional part of the income taken from productive slaves, much smaller than that taken to cover child rearing, was used to sustain unproductive elderly slaves, as well as the incapacitated at all ages.

These intergenerational transfers of income were not, of course, limited to slave society. They took place among free men as well. For free men must also bear the cost of rearing the young, including those who fail to survive, as well as of supporting the sick and the aged. But among free men, the decision regarding the pattern of intergenerational transfers is made by parents rather than masters. The question thus arises, "How did masters alter the pattern of intergenerational transfers as compared to what it would have been if slaves had been free?" It is much easier to pose the question than to provide an answer. We do not yet have an answer to this question. We would, however, caution against two assumptions. It is not necessarily true that the substitution of planters for parents as decision makers on this issue had a large effect on the pattern of intergenerational transfers. Nor is it necessarily true that readers would consider all changes in the pattern of transfers made by the planters to have been negative. For example, planters spent more (a larger share of earnings) on the medical care of slave children than did the parents of freedmen during the decades following the Civil War.

The high break-even age also helps to explain why U.S. planters encouraged the fertility of slave women, while slaveowners in other parts of the hemisphere appear to have discouraged it. The crux of the matter is that child rearing was profitable only if the expected life of slaves at birth was greater than the break-even age. In the U.S., the life expectation of slaves exceeded the break-even age by more than a half decade. But in colonies such as Jamaica, available evidence suggests that life expectation fell below the break-even age, probably by at least a half decade.

Consequently, during most of the eighteenth century, masters in colonies such as Jamaica discouraged family formation and high fertility rates, preferring to buy adult slaves in Africa rather than to rear them. It was general policy to maintain an imbalance between the sexes with men outnumbering women by a ratio of 4 to 3. To further reduce the basis for stable families, planters encouraged polygamy among slaves by rewarding favored men with second and third wives. Thus, for the remainder of the population, the male-female ratio was about 13 to 8. So large a disproportion between the sexes was bound to encourage sexual activity outside of the family and to reduce fertility. The care given to infants was quite poor compared with the South. Mothers were not encouraged to nurse their children; the southern practice of a 40 to 50 percent reduction of the workload of nursing mothers was not imitated in Jamaica. Further evidence of the neglect of pregnant women is to be found in the high rate of stillbirths. On one of the leading Jamaican plantations, 75 out of 345 births over a four-year period were stillborn. It has also been charged that abortion was both encouraged and widely practiced.

The 12 percent rate of expropriation reported on slave income falls well within the modern tax rate on workers. It has been estimated that about 30 percent of the income of workers at the poverty level is taken from them through sales, real estate, and income taxes. On the other hand, such workers, on average, receive payments and various services from the government which more than offset the tax burden. Were there any services received by slaves which offset the income expropriated from them? The answer is yes, but they cannot be quantified reliably at present. Slaves shared in the benefits of large-scale purchases made by the planter. Their clothing, for example, would have been more costly if purchased individually. Perhaps an even more important benefit was the saving on interest charges. Through the intervention of their masters slaves, in effect, were able to borrow at prime rates. Given the high interest charges which black sharecroppers suffered in the post–Civil War era, and the debt-peonage which enmeshed so many of them, the level of interest rates is not a small issue. Pending a more precise measurement of offsetting services, it seems warranted to place the average net rate of the expropriation of slave income at about 10 percent.

Expropriation is not, however, the only form of exploitation. As is shown in chapter 6, the *economic* burden imposed on slaves by other forms of exploitation probably exceeded that due to expropriation by a considerable margin.

Five.

The Origins of the Economic Indictment of Slavery

From Morality to Economics

In the beginning, crusaders against slavery based their attack on moral grounds. Since "God had made all nations of one blood," slavery was not just a "Hellish Practice," not just a "filthy sin," not just a "Capital Sin," but "the greatest Sin in the World, of the very Nature of Hell itself"; indeed, it was the very "Belly of Hell." With such burning conviction, the radical Quakers who led the onslaught against human bondage felt no hesitation in calling on their brethren to subordinate material considerations to Christian principle. Though their efforts were sharply resisted at first, the radical view eventually prevailed. "To live in ease and plenty by the toil of those whom violence and cruelty have put in our power," said the 1754 epistle of the Philadelphia Yearly Meeting, "is neither consistent with Christianity nor common justice, and we have good reason to believe draws down the displeasure of Heaven."

The abolitionist attack never lost its moral fervor. But as the antebellum era wore on, the ideological campaign against slavery became more elaborate and many-sided. It became no longer sufficient to state that the great power that slavery gave one group of men over another was, in and of itself, sinful. The emphasis shifted to the contention that those who held such power were bound to misuse it. From 1830 on, much of the abolitionist literature was aimed at documenting the abuses which arose from the arbitrary authority exercised by slaveholders. Antislavery periodicals told and retold of instances of degrading sale on the auction block, of broken families, of ill-fed and neglected children, of seduction and rape, and of torture and murder.

Beginning in the late 1820s, still another theme began to achieve prominence. Some critics took up the argument that slavery had hurt rather than profited the economy of the South — hurt not just the blacks but the whites as well; not just nonslaveholders but also the slaveholders. Thus the attack on human bondage was no longer limited to a demand for equity. It was not "just" that slavery was immoral. Slavery was also an inefficient and wasteful economic system which degraded labor, led to misallocations of investment, stifled technological progress, inhibited industrialization, and thwarted urbanization. By the 1840s, these scattered economic criticisms began to assume the proportions of a full-scale indictment.

Cassius Marcellus Clay was one of the early architects of the economic indictment of slavery. Clay, a cousin of Senator Henry Clay, was a prominent antislavery politician, and the editor of a newspaper in Lexington, Kentucky, called the *True American*. His views were given more than local significance when Horace Greeley printed them in the New York *Tribune*. Clay's economic critique of slavery was cogently set forth in a letter which was first published by the *Tribune* in 1843 and then republished by Greeley as a brief pamphlet entitled, "Slavery: The Evil — The Remedy."

There were two main elements in Clay's economic indictment. Slavery, he asserted, was an inefficient form of economic organization. It was inefficient because slavery "impoverishes the soil," because, in comparison with whites, slaves were "not so skilful, so energetic, and above all, have not the stimulus of self-interest"; because three million slaves performed "only about one-half of the effective work of the same number of whites in the North"; because slaves not only "produce less than freemen" but also "consume more"; because slavery was "the source of indolence, and destructive of all industry"; and because slavery caused the "poor" to "despise labor" by "degrading" it, while simultaneously turning the "mass of slaveholders" into "idlers." The other element in Clay's indictment concerned the effect of slavery on economic growth. Clay asserted that slavery retarded economic growth and development by restricting education, by diverting capital into the purchase of slaves where it became "a dead loss," by discouraging the development of "mechanical" skills, and by retarding the growth of manufacturing.

Clay set forth this characterization almost as briefly as we have here. What he propounded was a set of theses. He never provided evidence to support his theses. Clay was neither an economist nor a scholar; he was a politician, a polemicist, and an ideologist. His aim was not to discover the behavioral models which best characterized the operation of the slave economy, but to rally public opinion to the antislavery banner.

Of those who attempted to fill the evidential void, the two who were most influential were Hinton Rowan Helper and Frederick Law Olmsted. Both men had far-reaching impact on the thought of their times. Neither deviated very far from the theses set out by Clay, although they elaborated several variations and appeared to provide proof that the theses were valid. Olmsted's evidence was drawn from direct observations of individual farms, and hence was of a microscopic nature. Helper's evidence, which was derived from the aggregative data published in the federal census of 1850, in various state documents, and in leading journals, was of a macroscopic nature. That evidence of both types led to the same conclusions regarding the inefficiency of slavery and its detrimental effects on economic growth served to enhance the credibility of the separate findings. The influence of Helper and Olmsted did not end with the closing of the antebellum era. Their writings have had a profound effect on the thought of historians down to the present day and have been instrumental in shaping the traditional interpretation of the slave economy. For this reason the arguments and evidence which Helper and Olmsted advanced need to be considered in some detail.

Hinton Rowan Helper:
The Macro Evidence

Helper was the son of a poor white farmer from the Yadkin Valley of western North Carolina. He had been a store clerk, an unsuccessful gold prospector, and the author of a minor book before he wrote the volume that brought him fame. *The Impending Crisis of the South* was first published in 1857. An eight-column review of the book in Greeley's New York *Tribune* contributed to a first-year sale of thirteen thousand copies. Then in 1859 the Republican party converted Helper's book into a major ideological weapon of its presidential campaign. Condensed editions were published and a hundred thousand copies were distributed by the Republican party. *The Impending Crisis* became the center of a series of bitter political battles, including a congressional debate that delayed the election of the Speaker of the House for two months.

To prove that slavery had retarded southern economic growth, Helper compared the growth of three pairs of states over the period between 1790 and 1850. At the outset, he argued, Virginia was the nation's chief commercial state, outranking not only New York but "all the New England States combined." By 1850, New York had twice as large a population as Virginia, 30 times her exports, 45 times her imports, and eight times her manufacturing output. He then turned to Massachusetts and North Carolina which, he said, began with "about equal capacities and advantages for commercial and manufacturing enterprise." By 1850, Boston was the nation's second commercial city. Beaufort had a harbor comparable to Boston's but, "Has anybody ever heard of her?" In 1850, Massachusetts had nine times North Carolina's manufacturing output and twice as much personal property. Even Massachusetts farms exceeded the total value of those in North Carolina by 50 percent. A comparison between Pennsylvania and South Carolina revealed that Pennsylvania dominated South Carolina in imports by thirteen times, in manufacturing by twenty-two times, in value of farms by five times, in value of real and personal property by 2.5 times, in public libraries by fifteen times, and in newspaper circulation by twelve times.

Helper went on from these paired comparisons to a comparison between the aggregates of free and slave states. While the contrasts were not quite so dramatic, they still showed that the free states led the slave states by substantial margins in such matters as total wealth, manufacturing production, investment in railroads and canals, issues of patents on new inventions, and even in the value of agricultural production.

Helper attributed the poor performance of the South to economic inefficiency, an inefficiency that was due entirely to the existence of slavery. The "causes which have impeded the progress and prosperity of the South," he wrote, "may all be traced to one common source . . . *Slavery!*" Helper found evidence of the inefficiency of slavery in the low rates of return which planters earned on their capital. He told of a South Carolinian who reported that many cotton planters were earning less than one percent on their investment. But if this were mere hearsay evidence, there was unimpeachable testimony to southern inefficiency in the census statistics. The northern hay crop of 1850 alone, which he valued at $11.20 per ton, exceeded in value the entire southern output of cotton, tobacco, rice, hay, hemp, and sugar.

Further proof was to be found in the low value of southern land relative to northern land. Helper put the average value of an acre of northern land in 1850 at $28.07, while the average value of a southern acre was $5.34. What explained the difference of $22.73? Since southern land was equal to, or better than, northern land in "greater mildness of climate, richness of soil, deposits of precious metals, abundance and spaciousness of harbors, and super excellence of waterpower," he contended that "had it not been for slavery, the average value of land in all the Southern and Southwestern States, would have been *at least* equal to the average value of the same in the Northern States." If slaves were emancipated "on Wednesday morning," predicted Helper, then, "on the Thursday following," southern lands "will have increased to an average of at least $28.07 per acre." From this point Helper drew the further conclusion that even uncompensated emancipation of slaves would improve the economic position of slaveholders. For the capital gain on their lands would be twice as great as the loss on the capital value of slaves.

Helper's book was hailed by abolitionists as a "most compact and irresistible array of facts and arguments." This judgment has been widely accepted by historians. However, neither Helper's facts nor his logic are beyond challenge. It is not true that the 1850 value of the hay crop exceeded the value of the chief southern staples. His estimate of the value of the northern hay crop was 48 percent too high and his estimate of the value of the cotton crop was 34 percent too low. Unfamiliar with the national income accounting techniques worked out by George Tucker in 1843 and by

Ezra Seaman in 1848 and 1852, Helper also added the value of feed grains to the value of the inventory of livestock. As a consequence he exaggerated the annual production of meat and double-counted the feed grains. He also confused the concept of the annual product of agriculture with the value of agricultural capital, incorrectly adding the two together. Helper's contention that the agricultural production of the free states far exceeded that of the slave states was, therefore, based on a series of errors all of which served to exaggerate the North's agricultural position. Modern estimates show that the agricultural production of the slave states in 1850 actually exceeded that of the free states by a few percentage points.

Helper's other indexes of the relative performance of the northern and southern economy are also open to question. The principal measures of overall economic performance used by economists today are "real national income" and "real national income per capita." National income is the dollar value of all the final goods and services produced by an economy during a given year. This index can be computed not only for nations, but also for given regions of a nation, or for given industries to obtain such measures as "southern income," "New York income," "income originating in trade," or "income originating in agriculture." When economists compare the productive performance of an economy, or of a sector of an economy, in two different years, they adjust their measure of income for changes in the price level — in effect, hold prices constant. An index of national income with prices held constant is called "real national income." This index measures the change in the output of goods and services over time.

"Real national income per capita" (or simply "real per capita income") is real national income in a given year divided by the population in that year. Economists generally prefer per capita income to total income in measuring the economic growth of nations, since per capita income is a better index of the ability of an economy to satisfy economic welfare. For example, the real national income of the United States rose during the Great Depression of the 1930s even though per capita income declined. This was because the population rose. Thus it is possible for a nation's total income to increase even though each person in the nation is worse off economically. Per capita income is preferred also because it permits comparisons between the economic performance of large and small countries. India, for example, had three times as large a total income as Denmark in 1968. But economists obviously consider the economic performance of Denmark to be better than that of India, since Denmark produced $2,500 of income per capita while the per capita income of India was just $80. Denmark is a small rich country; India is a large poor country.

One cannot really expect Helper to have based his comparison of northern and southern economic performance on measures of regional per capita income, although, as previously noted, Ezra Seaman had published quite good income estimates by states in 1848, nearly a decade before the appearance of Helper's book. Were the indicators which Helper chose as the basis for his comparison reasonably good proxies or substitutes for state and regional income measures?

Of the various indicators used by Helper, those that were potentially most useful related to agriculture, to manufacturing, to urbanization, and to total wealth. Unfortunately, in each case Helper mishandled the data. He double-counted (as in agriculture), used absolute levels when shares were relevant (as in the discussion of urbanization), or used state and regional totals when he should have used per capita figures (as in the comparison of the regional wealth).

But even if Helper had done all of the right things with the data he collected, the types of statements he made about the relative levels of the overall economic performance of the two regions and their relative rates of growth would have been unwarranted. While the share of the population which is urbanized and the share of the labor force in manufacturing are both reasonably well correlated with the level of per capita income, the correlation is not so close as to permit much more than the establishment of quite wide bounds. In other words, the values of these variables for 1850 clearly did not preclude either the North having a higher per capita income than the South or the opposite relationship. In any case, the *rates* of the economic growth of the two regions cannot be inferred merely from the *level,* in a given year, of urbanization, of manufacturing, or even of per capita income. Even if the 1850 per capita income of the North was greater than that of the South, it would not necessarily follow that northern per capita income was growing more rapidly than the per capita income of the South between, say, 1840 and 1860 or between 1790 and 1850, the dates singled out by Helper.

The fact is that Helper presented virtually no evidence bearing on the relative rates of growth in the two regions during the years between 1790 and 1850. The only statistics he presented for 1790 were those on population. The only other economic data that he cited for the pre-1850 period were those on the value of exports from New York and Virginia in 1791 and on estimates of imports into Charleston in 1760. All of his other economic statistics pertained to 1850 or a later year. Helper also misinterpreted the meaning of the export statistics. He failed to realize that each custom district reported only the direct exports from that district to a foreign port. Not only did Helper omit southern exports shipped through northern ports, but he also failed to report on the traffic of the South's principal direct exporter, New Orleans. Available data clearly indicate that the South was well represented in U.S. exports. Cotton alone accounted for 50 percent of all U.S. exports in 1850. Indeed, the dominating role of southern products in U.S. exports was the basis for Senator James H. Hammond's defiant boast that "Cotton is King."

"It thus appears," wrote Helper, "in view of the preceding statistical facts and arguments, that the South, at one time the superior of the North in almost all the ennobling pursuits and conditions of life, has fallen far behind her competitor, and now ranks more as the dependency of a mother country than as the equal confederate of free and independent States." That conclusion followed not from his "statistical facts," but from his unverified assumption that in 1790, states below the Mason-Dixon line enjoyed higher levels of income than those above it, and from the various errors he committed in his effort to arrive at something approximating regional income accounts for 1850.

Helper's arguments on efficiency were as flawed as those on levels of income and rates of growth. He believed that income in the South should have been at least as high as in the North, since the South had the advantage "in soil, climate, rivers, harbors, minerals, forests, and, indeed, almost every other natural resource." Helper attached crucial importance to the fact that southern land values were far below those in the North. "In soil," he wrote, "in climate, in minerals, in water-power for manufactural purposes, and in area of territory, North Carolina has the advantage of New York, and, with the exception of slavery, no plausible reason can possibly be assigned why land should not be *at least* as valuable in the valley of the Yadkin as it is along the banks of the Genesee."

The assumption that the South had a better resource endowment than the North was false. The South was hopelessly outmatched by the North in mineral resources. It had nothing to compare with the iron deposits of Pennsylvania, Minnesota, and Wisconsin, the lead deposits of Illinois, and the coal deposits of Pennsylvania. It was the Northeast, not the South, which had the advantage of "super-excellence of water-power" for manufacturing. The rivers of the South provided excellent avenues of transportation. But navigable rivers were poor sources of water power. In the technology that prevailed before the Civil War, water power could be more cheaply harnessed from the smaller streams of New England, which were well endowed with natural falls in regions that were accessible to existing markets.

Helper stumbled most badly in his discussion of land values. For one thing, the figures he abstracted from the census gave not the value of *land* but the value of land plus buildings, fences, and other improvements. Much of the difference in what Helper called "land values" was thus due to more expensive buildings and to higher ratios of improved to unimproved land in the Northeast than in the South. Nor were the differences in the rate of investment on land between the South and the Northeast necessarily irrational or inefficient. The farms of the north central states also had lower rates of investment on land improvements and buildings than those of the Northeast. For in both the north central states and the South, land was cheap relative to labor and capital. In such a situation, efficiency dictates land-intensive methods of agriculture, such as grazing and mast feeding, rather than capital-intensive or labor-intensive methods such as grain feeding.

Helper also failed to consider the effect on land values of the location of farms with respect to ultimate markets. Even if the natural fertility of the land in the Yadkin Valley matched that of the Genesee Valley, easier access to markets would have made the land in western New York more valuable than the land in western North Carolina. The Genesee Valley was relatively close to the nation's largest market for grains — New York City, the agricultural gateway to Europe — and was connected to it by the Erie Canal and the Hudson River — among the most advantageous means of bulk transport in the antebellum era. The farms of the Yadkin Valley were not only more remote from the major seaport markets, but had to ship their surplus grains by relatively expensive railroads, since the Yadkin River was unnavigable, except by rafts and small boats.

Nor was it true that southern soils and climate were *generally* better for agricultural purposes than northern land and climates. No doubt *some* southern soils were better for agriculture than *some* northern ones. But on average southern soils were inferior to those of the North. The soils of the Cotton Belt, as well as of the subtropic coastal regions, are more sandy than those of the north central states and hence have only quite limited capacity to retain the minerals on which fertility depends. This situation is further aggravated by leaching of the soil due to heavy rainfalls, and by the absence of winter freezes which retain water and minerals in the soil. The climatic factor not only worked to reduce the fertility of soils but, in the technology of the antebellum era, made agriculture more vulnerable to insects in the South than the North. For one advantage of the winter freeze was that it killed off the various pests and disease carriers which affected crops, livestock, and man. High southern humidity also prevented the satisfactory curing of hay in this region before the advent of silos, and hence made livestock rearing relatively less advantageous than in the northern states. Other crops that suffered in the southern climate included oats and some types of wheat. On the other hand, the subtropical climate was not quite warm enough to make sugar more than a marginal product.

Helper's prediction that southern land values would rise fourfold the day after slavery ended, of course, proved to be false. In fact the opposite was true. The collapse of slavery led to a fall in agricultural land values.

Frederick Law Olmsted: The Micro Evidence

Unlike Clay and Helper, who were militant southern abolitionists, Frederick Law Olmsted was neither a Southerner nor a political figure. He was a New York farmer and an author who had won a reputation for himself as an energetic traveler and a keen observer. While Olmsted was stoutly opposed to slavery, he also "opposed instant emancipation by federal edict, not only on constitutional grounds but also because he doubted that it would accomplish what was expected." In 1852 the editor of the New York *Times* hired Olmsted to prepare a series of articles about the slave South based on firsthand observation. Olmsted made three trips to the South in pursuit of this mandate. The first was for a three-month period beginning on December 11, 1852. The second extended from November 10, 1853, to May of 1854. The third ran from May to August of 1854. Altogether, Olmsted spent a total of thirteen months traveling from one end of the South to the other. He wrote a total of seventy-five articles for the *Times*. The articles later formed the basis for four books, of which the last and most famous — *The Cotton Kingdom* — was written shortly after the outbreak of the Civil War.

Olmsted's essays dealt with all aspects of southern culture. He commented incisively on such matters as the manners, dress, housing, diet, education, religion, marriage, family, morals, literature, amusements, and health of both blacks and whites, of lower as well as upper classes. Tribute to his skillfulness as an observer has been paid by virtually every historian of the South. Among those whose conceptions of slavery were influenced by Olmsted were John Cairnes, Karl Marx, W. E. B. Du Bois, U. B. Phillips, W. E. Dodd, Lewis C. Gray, Charles Sydnor, E. Franklin Frazier, Avery O. Craven, Richard Hofstadter, John Hope Franklin, and Kenneth M. Stampp.

It was more than Olmsted's vivid writing style and his flair for detail which led scholars of such diverse viewpoints to draw heavily on his books. Olmsted dealt with both the positive and negative aspects of economic life under the peculiar institution. He reported not just on the destitute white farmers who lived on the border of starvation, but also on the very prosperous small farmers; not just on the badly neglected slaves but also on slaves whose food, clothing, and shelter compared with the best found among the laboring classes of the North; not just on the idle, absentee planters who turned the management of their estates over to "the nearly unlimited government of hireling overseers" but also on the planters of exceptional skill and knowledge in farming whose estates were veritable "show plantations"; not just on wornout lands and abandoned farms of the upper South but also on the newly established and thriving operations of the Southwest; not just on lethargic slaves who performed at extremely low levels, or neglected their duties altogether, unless constantly threatened by the whip, but also on slaves who worked hard and steadily at their tasks and whose product was large by any standard.

Olmsted's ability to see both sides of many issues did not prevent him from coming to an extremely negative overall judgment regarding the economic performance of the slave system. He concluded that the peculiar institution kept not just slaves but virtually the entire free population in deep poverty. The deeply impoverished included not just landless free farmers but even those owning substantial land and as many as five slaves. In Olmsted's words, the "majority of those who sell the cotton crop," were "poorer than the majority of our day-labourers at the North." Planters with as many as thirty-five slaves still could barely eke out a living, earning on average "hardly more than that of a private of the New York Metropolitan Police Force." To live "in a moderately comfortable way," a planter had to own at least fifty slaves. Thus, slavery was a boon only for those at the very top of the southern economic pyramid — for just the top 2 percent of the slaveholders.

Olmsted attributed this poor performance directly to the institution of slavery. The most serious defect of the system was that the labor of slaves was typically of a very low level of productivity. As a result of his investigations of the situation in Virginia, he concluded that it took at least twice as many slaves as free northern laborers to accomplish any given task. This was true both of labor in the field and of domestic labor. In the case of wheat production, he reported that "four Virginia slaves do not, when engaged in ordinary agricultural operations, accomplish as much, on an average, as one ordinary free farm labourer in New Jersey." In the case of domestics, he estimated that a slave accomplished one third to one half as much work as did "the commonest, stupidest Irish domestic drudges at the North."

In Olmsted's view, the low productivity of slaves ramified into every aspect of the economic life of the South. It degraded the entire standard of labor. Because of this low standard, white workers were "driven to indolence, carelessness, indifference to the results of skill, heedlessness, inconstancy of purpose, improvidence, and extravagance." Thus, white southern labor was even less efficient than slave labor, on average accomplishing only about two thirds as much as slave labor. The poor quality of all southern labor resulted in the wasting of resources: the natural fertility of land was rapidly undermined; tools were frequently broken; livestock was neglected; labor skills were allowed to decay; managerial skill was scorned.

Low-quality labor, poor use of resources, and indifferent management all combined, said Olmsted, to make southern agriculture far less efficient than northern agriculture. While a given number of New York farm laborers reaped twenty to forty bushels of wheat per acre, he stated, eight times as much slave labor in Virginia brought forth just six bushels per acre from land of fertility equal to that in

New York. Olmsted doubted that the southern agriculturalists made good use overall of their resources even in the production of cotton. It was only the advantage of climate that made the South, rather than the North, the leading producer of cotton. Far from being an advantage in cotton production, slave labor was a hindrance in this activity, too. Free German laborers who were employed in some Texas cotton fields, said Olmsted, not only picked more cotton per hand than slaves but "the cotton picked by the free labour of the Germans was worth from one to two cents a pound more than that picked by slaves in the same township, by reason of its greater cleanliness."

Olmsted concluded that slave plantations were really relatively inefficient even in cotton production. There was, he said

no physical obstacle in the way of our country's supplying ten bales of cotton where it now does one. . . . Give the South a people moderately close settled, moderately well-informed, moderately ambitious and moderately industrious, somewhat approaching that of Ohio, for instance, and what a business it would have! Twenty double-track railroads from the Gulf to the lakes, and twenty lines of ocean steamers, would not sufficiently meet its requirements. Who doubts, let him study the present business of Ohio, and ask upon what, in the natural resources of Ohio, or its position, could forty years ago, a prediction of its present wealth and business have been made, of its present supply and its present demand have been made, which would compare in value with the commercial resources and advantages of position possessed to-day by any one of the Western cotton States?

What forces, then, permitted the slave system to continue? If slave labor was unremunerative to slaveowners, why didn't competitive forces act to substitute more efficient free labor for costly, inefficient slave labor? Why wasn't slave labor driven from the southern scene by the pressures of the market? Olmsted's answers were both economic and sociological. The law of supply and demand, he said, was indeed operative against slavery and was "a constant counter-acting influence to its evils." What rescued the system from oblivion was the internal slave trade "which makes slaves valuable property, otherwise than for labor." For even if slave labor could not produce a surplus over that required for its own subsistence, slavery persisted because the increasing value of the stock of slaves made slave rearing a profitable venture. Moreover, sociological factors served "to qualify the action of the laws of demand and supply." White workers in the South had been demoralized by the slave system. Whites coming to the South "soon learn to hate labor, give as little of it for [their] hire as [they] can, become base, cowardly, faithless — 'worse than a nigger.' " Thus, employers could only obtain free labor of a superior quality by paying more for it than it was worth.

Despite appearances to the contrary, the main elements of Olmsted's economic critique did not stem from firsthand observation of the actual operation of slave agriculture. For, as Olmsted noted, he reached the conclusion that slave labor was far less efficient, and more costly, in agricultural production than northern free labor during his first visit to Virginia. But his first visit to Virginia took place during the slack season. He arrived in Virginia on December 16, after the harvest of the 1853 crop was completed. He left Virginia in January, well before the period for the cultivation of the new crop had begun. He could not possibly have seen, to any significant extent, the actual operation of slaves in plantation agriculture. Indeed, all of his firsthand reports on the quality of the work of slaves during his first visit pertain to servants, most of whom were either quite young or quite old, or to other nonagricultural labor. By far the greatest space is devoted to recounting what others had told him regarding the quality of slave labor.

The spectrum of opinion contained in these reports was quite wide. Most slaveowners believed that properly supervised slave labor was clearly superior to free labor. Others reported that free labor was, under virtually any circumstance, superior to slave labor. Some said that only public spirit and philanthropic motives caused them to continue to use slave labor. Given such a diversity of opinion, Olmsted could, in good conscience, take up practically any opinion within this spectrum. As it turns out, he adopted the view of a northerner who had come South and was convinced that slave labor was far inferior to northern labor. It was to explain why free labor did not, under such circumstances, drive out slave labor, that Olmsted developed his thesis that white southern labor was generally inferior to slave labor.

The basic problems that confronted Olmsted in Virginia remained with him during the rest of his thirteen months in the South. Approximately 50 percent of his journey in the South took place after the completion of the harvest but before the onset of the period of intensive cultivation. Much of the remainder of his time was spent in cities or in transit. Even when he visited plantations, he spent more time in the homes of planters or overseers than in the fields. Consequently, what he had to report were not mainly his own observations but the opinions of others — opinions which continued to show considerable diversity, although a majority of slaveholders proclaimed the superior efficiency of their system of labor. The few direct observations of field labor made and reported by Olmsted were only of fleeting experiences, since Olmsted spent, at most, only a few days on any given plantation. These, like the opinions he collected from others, were mixed.

The central issue which Olmsted faced in arriving at a judgment of the overall economic effectiveness of the slave system was the frequency distribution of efficient and inefficient plantations. For Olmsted had encountered large, well-managed plantations which produced ten or more bales of cotton per prime hand. He had also encountered, or read of, small, badly run plantations with yields of less than half a bale per person. What relative weights should be assigned

to these extremes as well as to all of the intermediate grada-
tions of productivity? Olmsted sought to resolve the problem by turning to aggregate statistics published in the 1850
census. From this source he deduced that the average South-
wide yield of cotton was a mere 1.3 bales per slave. Assuming that plantations of fifty or more slaves produced at least
2.5 bales per head, Olmsted concluded that the average yield
on all smaller plantations was just "seven-eighths of a bale
per head. . . . Those who plant cotton in this small way
usually raise a crop of corn, and some little else, not enough,
take the country through, one year with another, to supply
themselves and their slaves with food; certainly not more
than enough to do so, on an average." This, then, was the
ultimate evidence on which Olmsted relied to sustain his
case for the general inefficiency of slave labor and to support
his judgment that most slaveowners "must be miserably
poor — poorer than the majority of our day-labourers at the
North."

As with Helper, Olmsted's attempt to make use of census
data to evaluate the performance of the slave economy was
deeply flawed. His computation of the income of slaveowners was based on the false assumption that plantations produced no surpluses for sale in the market other
than cotton. He neglected not only such obvious money
crops as sugar, rice, and tobacco, but also various food
crops and meat which, while mainly consumed by their
producers, were nevertheless in surplus production in the
slave sector of agriculture.

Olmsted's aggregate measure of labor efficiency was even
more erroneous than his calculation of slaveholders' income.
In addition to underestimating the value of output, he
greatly overestimated the labor input. Olmsted included in
his denominator the entire slave population, thus neglecting
to note that close to half the population was either too young
or too old to work or else was engaged in nonagricultural
occupations. Olmsted also failed to take account of the fact

that the proportion of women and children in the slave labor force was much greater than in the free labor force. This error also biased his measure of the efficiency of slave labor downward.

Equally serious errors were committed in Olmsted's analysis of micro data. He badly misused the information on slave hiring rates, for example. While Olmsted correctly recognized that the hire rate measured the value of a slave's labor to planters, he fell into mutually inconsistent arguments in attempting to show that the high rentals paid for slaves meant that the labor cost of a given operation was actually greater to slaveholders than to northern farmers. He derived this conclusion from the contention that while slaves were only half as productive as northern laborers, the hire rate for slaves was 25 percent greater than the wage of northern farm laborers. But clearly, if the rental price of slaves was higher than the wage of northern farm laborers, and if the rental price reflected the value of the slaves' labor to the slaveowner, then slaves could not have been half as productive as free northern laborers.

If, as Olmsted also argued, nearly all of the product and income of plantations was spent on slaves, and if slaves received nearly 25 percent more than northern laborers while producing only half as much as northern laborers, then not only did slaves receive a higher income than northern laborers but slaves were exploiting slaveowners, rather than slaveowners exploiting slaves.

The Fundamental Assumption of Clay, Helper, and Olmsted

Of course, not all of the foregoing criticisms of the works of Helper and Olmsted are new. Some of the same issues were raised by their contemporaries. Gilbert J. Beebe, editor of *The Banner of Liberty*, one of the most widely circulated of the Democratic newspapers in the North during the 1850s, and Elias Peissner of Union College in Schenectady, New York, among others, announced Helper's errors in computing the value of the hay crop, in double-counting, and in mishandling the issue of land values. Although the attacks of such men could be put aside as mere apologetics, Daniel R. Goodloe's criticisms of Olmsted could not. For Goodloe was the abolitionist and journalist chosen by Olmsted to condense his previous works into what was to become *The Cotton Kingdom*. In the course of exercising his assigned task, Goodloe told Olmsted that he underestimated the income of planters from crops other than cotton, that his use of census data to estimate an average yield of 1.3 bales of cotton per slave was inconsistent with his statement that on large plantations the yield was 10 bales per hand, and that he had failed to note the substantial improvement in economic conditions in Virginia and North Carolina after the spurt of railroad construction in 1853 and 1854.

If such criticisms were brushed aside, it was not merely because of the emotional climate of the times or because of imperfections in the counterarguments. Those who fashioned the economic indictment of slavery could hardly be persuaded by attacks which focused on the "details" of their indictment, on "minor" errors in their use or interpretation of census and other data. None of their critics had provided evidence which undermined the fundamental proposition on which that indictment rested: that black slave labor was inherently inferior to white free labor. Nor was it likely that this axiom would have become the center of debate between the contending ideologies. For with very few exceptions, both those in the anti- and in the proslavery camps shared the conviction that blacks were, for racial reasons, generally inferior to whites both as laborers and as human beings.

Strangely enough, the various debates spawned by the economic indictment of the slave system have led few historians into a serious consideration of the racist foundations of that indictment. Yet racism runs through the words of the architects of the indictment like a red line. It is most glaring in the writings of Clay and Helper. "I have studied the Negro character," said Clay. "They lack self reliance — we can make nothing of them. God has made them for the sun and the banana." Helper was even more extreme in his views. Every feature of the Negro, he wrote, "however large, or however small, whether internal or external, whether physical or mental, or moral, loses in comparison with the white, much in the same ratio or proportion as darkness loses in comparison with light, or as evil loses in comparison with good."

To Olmsted, the contrast between black and white was much less intense. Nevertheless, his view of Negroes was clearly biased. He described them as habitual shirkers, habitual pilferers, and habitual liars. "They will lie in their very prayers to God," he wrote, quoting an unnamed source. To a greater extent than the other architects of the economic indictment, Olmsted mixed pseudosociological with purely racial explanations for the "defects" in Negro character and ability. He thought that by eliminating slavery, Negroes could "become thoroughly civilized, thoroughly independent individuals, and thus of tenfold more value in the commonwealth" as free men than they were as slaves. Still, he did not think that "in one generation or two the effects of centuries of barbarism and slavery are to be extinguished," or that Negroes "are ever to become Teutons or Celts."

In Olmsted's view, even if sociological influences could be altered, the racial "limitations" of Negroes would remain. "The African races," Olmsted asserted, "compared with the white, at least with the Teutonic, have greater vanity or love of approbation, a stronger dramatic and demonstrative character, more excitability, less exact or analytic minds, and a nature more sensuous, though (perhaps from want of cultivation) less refined." Africans, he continued, were "far less adapted for steady, uninterrupted labor than we are, but excel us in feats demanding agility and tempestuous energy. A Mississippi steamboat manned by negro deck-hands will wood up a third quicker than one manned by the same number of whites; but white labourers of equal intelligence and under equal stimulus will cut twice as much wood, split twice as many rails, and hoe a third more corn in a day than negroes."

Olmsted's view of Negroes should not be confused with those of Helper and Clay. Helper and Clay were extremely hostile toward Negroes. Helper, in fact, devoted much effort to campaigns aimed at expelling all Negroes from the United States. Olmsted, on the other hand, was a man of intense goodwill toward Negroes. Deeply concerned with their plight, he was convinced that, freed from the fetters of slavery, they could improve "tenfold." Olmsted specifically rejected the proposition that the racial limitations of Negroes were of such a nature that they should be permanently maintained in an inferior social position. There was, he said, no "good reason to consider the negro, naturally and essentially, the moral inferior of the white; or, that if he is so, it is in those elements of character which should for ever prevent us from trusting him with equal social munities with ourselves."

These words clearly differentiate Olmsted from Clay and Helper and, indeed, from most other whites of his time. In his sympathy for Negroes and optimism about them, Olmsted was obviously well ahead of his time. If our objective were to evaluate the man, his enlightenment would certainly deserve more emphasis than his biases.

We, however, must consider another issue — an issue that, as far as the man is concerned, is quite narrow and of small moment. Yet the issue is of overriding importance in appraising the traditional interpretation of slavery. How reliable was Olmsted's assessment of the quality of black labor (not the potential but the actual achievement)? As is shown in chapter 6, certain of his judgments were far off the mark, disastrously so. On this question his enlightenment was simply not strong enough to overcome his biases. Ironically, Olmsted's obvious goodwill toward Negroes has served to distract attention from the extent to which his biases led him to belittle the quality of black labor. Even more, it has lent substantial but, as we shall see, unwarranted credence to his contention that slave labor was at best only half as productive as northern white labor.

John Elliott Cairnes: An Economist's Reformulation

The last of the principal architects of the economic indictment of slavery was John Elliott Cairnes. One of the most eminent British economists of the mid-nineteenth century, he held chairs first at the University of Dublin, then at Queens University, Galway, and finally at University College, London. His volume on *The Slave Power* was originally published in 1862 and republished in 1863 with a new preface, a set of appendixes, and some revisions. The subtitle of *The Slave Power* reveals the polemical nature of the work: "Being an Attempt to Explain the Real Issues Involved in the American Contest." Cairnes, alarmed at the widespread sympathy among Englishmen for the southern struggle for "self-determination," sought in this volume to demonstrate that both morality and economic self-interest dictated that Great Britain should refrain from intervening in the Civil War on behalf of the Confederacy. Toward this end he presented his analysis of the "Character, Career, and Probable Designs" of *The Slave Power*.

Since Cairnes never visited the slave states, he was dependent on others for evidence regarding the actual operation of the slave system. He leaned most heavily on the first two of Olmsted's four volumes, quoting or citing them repeatedly. While Cairnes also relied on such other works as Robert Russell's *North America, Its Agriculture and Climate*, Alexis de Tocqueville's *Democracy in America*, Hinton Helper's *The Impending Crisis*, and J. D. B. DeBow's *The Industrial Resources, etc., of the Southern and Western States*, his main arguments were clearly derived from Olmsted. Indeed, insofar as it deals with the economic characteristics of the slave system, *The Slave Power* is largely a pithy and elegant restatement of the main themes enunciated by Olmsted — largely, but not completely. For Cairnes amended Olmsted's central themes and added to them in a number of important respects. It is these amendments and additions that served to complete the economic indictment of slavery.

Cairnes accepted without question Olmsted's contention that slave labor was very low-quality labor. The "economical defects of slave labour," he said, "may be summed up under the three following heads: — it is given reluctantly; it is unskilful; it is wanting in versatility." Unlike Olmsted, however, Cairnes did not embrace racial explanations of the inferiority of slave labor. He rejected the "calumny of the incorrigible indolence of the negro," arguing "that the negro in freedom is amenable to the same influences as the white man." It was slavery, not race, that made the Negro "evade his task by every means in his power," made him "unsuited for all branches of industry which require the slightest care, forethought, or dexterity," made him "incapable of all but the rudest forms of labour." Indeed, the "difficulty of teaching the slave anything is so great, that the only chance of turning his labour to profit is, when he has once learned a lesson, to keep him to that lesson for life. Where slaves, therefore, are employed there can be no variety of production."

Cairnes also accepted without question Olmsted's contention that southern white labor was inferior in quality to slave labor. In the first edition of his book he stated that virtually all nonslaveholding southern whites were a "promiscuous horde" who were "little removed from savage life, eking out a wretched subsistence by hunting, by fishing, by hiring themselves out for occasional jobs, by plunder." In the revised edition, Cairnes reduced the number of these "mean whites" to 70 percent of the white population. The other 30 percent were "a hardy and industrious" class of free peasants who were able to remain in that condition only because they were isolated from, and formed no part of, the slave economy. This class was found mostly in the border states. The rest of the nonslaveholding whites were so demoralized and degraded that they could not even compete with slave labor. "It is universally agreed," said Cairnes, "that the labour of the 'mean whites' is more inefficient, more unreliable, more unmanageable than even the crude efforts of the slaves."

Like Olmsted, Cairnes made the low quality of slave labor the cornerstone of his argument for the inefficiency of the slave system. But whereas Olmsted cited the tendency of slave agriculture to reduce the fertility of land as one of the many shortcomings of the peculiar institution, Cairnes elevated this feature to central importance, making the degradation of land an inescapable consequence of the employment of slave labor. Slave labor, he argued, was so inept that planters were "obliged to employ their negroes exclusively in the production" of a single crop.

Whatever crop may be best suited to the character of the soil and the nature of slave industry, whether cotton, tobacco, sugar, or rice, that crop is cultivated, and that alone. Rotation of crops is thus precluded by the conditions of the case. The soil is tasked again and again to yield the same product, and the inevitable result follows. After a short series of years its fertility is completely exhausted, the planter — "land-killer" he is called in the picturesque nomenclature of the South — abandons the ground which he has rendered worthless, and passes on to seek in new soils for that fertility under which alone the agencies at his disposal can be profitably employed.

It was on the issue of the general profitability of slavery that Cairnes made his furthest departure from the arguments of Olmsted. The contention that slaves were unprofitable to all except 2 percent of their owners was unacceptable to Cairnes. This argument led to unanswerable conundrums. Why did the system take root in the first place and why did it persist in the South for more than two hundred years? And, if the system was generally unprofitable, why shouldn't opponents of slavery merely wait for the operation of the market to force the system out of existence? Hence, Cairnes sought a reformulation of Olmsted's basic economic critique which did not involve the proposition that planters generally failed to earn profits on their investment in slaves. Cairnes did so by arguing that while slavery was beset by a tendency toward unprofitability, that tendency could be thwarted under certain special circumstances, circumstances that happened to prevail in the South. In this connection Cairnes stressed four conditions that were required for slavery to be profitable.

(1.) *There had to be a demand for crops which could be more efficiently produced on a large rather than on a small scale.* Economies of large-scale production were necessary, said Cairnes, because the only advantage of slave labor over free labor was "that the employer of slaves has absolute power over his workmen." Thus, when large-scale operations are advantageous, slave labor "admits the most complete organization, that is to say, it may be combined on an extensive scale, and directed by a controlling mind to a single end."

(2.) *The method of cultivation of these crops had to require large amounts of labor per unit of land.* Such territorial concentration of labor was necessary in order to keep the cost of supervising slaves low.

(3.) *Soils had to be of a high fertility and practically unlimited in extent.* Only "where the natural fertility of the soil is so great as to compensate for the inferiority of the cultivation, where nature does so much as to leave little for art," only then, said Cairnes, can slave labor "be turned to profitable account." Such land had to be unlimited in extent in order to prevent the butchering of land inherent in slave labor from reducing the amount of high-quality land below the minimum needed to sustain the system.

(4.) *There had to be a substantial interregional slave trade.* Such a trade was necessary in order to permit slaveowners on old, worn-out land to continue to earn profits on their slaves. For "when trading in human beings is once introduced, a new source of profit is developed for the system, which renders it in a great degree independent of the resources of the soil. It is this, the profit developed by trading in slaves, and this alone, which has enabled slavery in the older slave states of North America to survive the consequences of its own ravages."

These four propositions permitted Cairnes to discard Olmsted's contention that slavery was generally unprofitable, while still maintaining that it was an inefficient system which retarded the growth of the South. Moreover, Cairnes's reformulation removed the unanswerable conundrums. Slavery took root on southern soil because economies of large scale and ease of supervision in the production of sugar, tobacco, rice, and cotton — together with the existence of fertile virgin lands — made the crude labor of slaves profitable. Once in operation for any length of time, slavery did, indeed, generate a tendency toward its own destruction. The inefficiency of slave labor, especially the inevitable degradation of the soil that resulted from the employment of such labor, worked in that direction. But the inevitable day of doom could be put off almost indefinitely, through the operation of an interregional slave trade, as long as there was a nearly unlimited supply of virgin land of high fertility. The slave South had, in fact, turned in this direction. It had developed a system of regional specialization under which territories with wornout land specialized in rearing slaves, while the territories of virgin land specialized in using up this slave labor in the production of staple crops.

Cairnes did not completely rule out the possibility that in its late phase southern slavery had actually ceased being profitable in the production of staple crops, even in the Southwest. To some extent, he conceded, slavery was being maintained by a desire for conspicuous consumption. Slavery had "entered into the soul of the people" of the South, engendering "a fashionable taste, a social passion" for bondsmen. "Slaves have thus in the South acquired a factitious value, and are coveted with an eagerness far beyond what the intrinsic utility of their services would explain." Cairnes found some basis for this view in Olmsted's report that even the lands of Texas were being rapidly depleted. Thus it was possible that the rate at which soil was being degraded had become so rapid, that slavery might actually be pressing on the limits of the land needed to maintain the general profitability of the system.

Cairnes responded to this possibility by arguing that while profit had been a necessary condition for the establishment of the system and for its maintenance in the past, profit might have ceased being a necessary condition for its continuation.

It was "idle to argue this question" of the viability of slavery "on purely economic grounds."

It is not simply as a productive instrument that slavery is valued by its supporters. It is far rather for its social and political results — as the means of upholding a form of society in which slaveholders are the sole depositaries of social prestige and political power, as the "corner stone" of an edifice of which they are the builders — that the system is prized. Abolish slavery, and you introduce a new order of things, in which the ascendancy of the men who now rule in the South would be at an end. An immigration of new men would set in rapidly from various quarters. The planters and their adherents would soon be placed in a hopeless minority in their old dominions. New interests would take root and grow; new social ideas would germinate; new political combinations would be formed; and the power and hopes of the party which has long swayed the politics of the Union, and which now seeks to break loose from that Union in order to secure a free career for the accomplishment of bolder designs, would be gone for ever. It is this which constitutes the real strength of slavery in the Southern States, and which precludes even the momentary admission by the dominant party there of any proposition which has abolition for its object.

Cairnes emphasized that the general profitability of slavery to planters did not imply that slavery advanced the material well-being of the South. Slavery had in fact diminished the "gross revenue" of the South and was an obstacle to the economic growth of the region. According to Cairnes, slavery stifled the development of both manufacturing and commerce. Manufacturing was held back because the labor of a slave was so crude, so unskilled, that it was "quite impossible that he should take part with efficiency in the difficult and delicate operations which most manufacturing and mechanical processes involve." Commerce was stifled because "the soul of commerce is the spirit of enterprise, and this is ever found wanting in communities where slavery exists: their prevailing characteristics are subjection to routine and contempt for money-making pursuits." Manufacturing and commerce required "the congregation in towns of large masses of workmen." But "where the workmen are slaves," such congregation in

cities "could only be carried on at the constant risk of insurrection, and this must effectually prevent" the growth
of manufacturing and commerce in slave societies.
Consequently, slavery effectively excluded the South from
these fields of enterprise and kept the South confined to
agriculture. "Slavery," said Cairnes, "finds its natural career
in agriculture." But the nature of slave agriculture implied
that per capita production must eventually decline in this
sector, too. Because of the tendency of slavery to degrade
land, the original level of per capita production in agriculture could only be maintained on virgin soil. And from the
moment such soil began to be exploited by slave labor, the
course of per capita production would be downward. In the
older slave states the process of declining output had gone
so far that normal enterprise could barely yield enough product to meet the maintenance requirements of slaves. As a
consequence the sole, or the main, source of profit to planters
in the slave-selling states was the income earned through the
interregional slave trade. Thus, "Slavery in its simple and
primitive form is developed into slavery supported by a
slave trade — into slavery expansive, aggressive, destructive of human life, regardless of human ties, — into slavery
in its most dangerous and atrocious form. . . ."

While Cairnes's reformulations permitted him to extricate
Olmsted's arguments from their most obvious logical diffi-
culties, Cairnes did little to test the evidential basis of these
arguments. He accepted as proven Olmsted's contentions
that southern slave and white labor were less efficient than
northern labor. He also accepted as proven the rapid and
steadily declining fertility of lands worked by slaves. These
"facts" implied the general inefficiency of slave agriculture
and the steady decline in output per capita within the
agricultural sector. Hence, he also accepted the last two
points as proven.

It was Cairnes's failure to consider seriously the validity
of this set of alleged facts that constitutes the basic flaw in

his analysis of the economics of slavery. Correction of Olmsted's logic by itself was not enough to warrant the economic indictment of slavery. Cairnes simply never came to grips with the basic empirical issues on which that indictment must stand or fall.

Only on the question of the interregional slave trade did Cairnes attempt to extend the body of evidence supplied by Olmsted, Helper, and the other works on which he drew. His effort to infer the scope of this trade from demographic data in the census of 1850 was quite amateurish. He incorrectly assumed that differences in the age structure of whites and blacks necessarily implied that the westward migration rate of slaves was much greater than that of whites. He also assumed that these differences had to imply that the bulk of the slaves sent west had been sold in the market. "If a planter, with his family and its following of slaves, removed from Virginia to Arkansas, the young and old of both races would go together, and the proportion between the two populations would remain unchanged." However, as shown in chapters 2 and 3, the size of the differences in the age and sex structure in the two subregions implies that the number of traded slaves was a small rather than a large share of total interregional movement.

It may seem odd to some readers that we have paid so much attention to books written more than a century ago — that on the issues of efficiency and growth we have chosen to cross swords with evidence supplied by Helper and Olmsted rather than that supplied by more recent writers. Surprising as it may be, between the time of the architects of the economic indictment and the appearance of the cliometricians, there were very few additions to the evidence bearing on efficiency and growth. Most discussions during the intervening century have been aimed not at adding to the body of evidence supplied by Helper and Olmsted but at reinterpreting the significance of their evidence by emphasizing or de-emphasizing one or another of its aspects.

Perhaps the most substantial new additions of economic information during the intervening century were made by Ulrich B. Phillips and by the authors of the various state studies of slavery. But Phillips's series on slave prices were more relevant to the issue of the profitability of slavery to planters than to the issues of efficiency and growth posed by Clay, Helper, Olmsted, and Cairnes. While Phillips and the authors of the state studies did much to unearth information on the operations of the very large plantations — generally those with more than one hundred slaves — these findings pertained mainly to the question of the material conditions of the lives of slaves, although some light was shed on the managerial qualities of planters. Other significant precliometric additions to the underlying corpus of knowledge about the operation of the slave economy are described in appendix C. These other additions, like those discussed here, did not fundamentally alter the case for the deleterious effects of slavery on efficiency and growth made by the architects of the economic indictment.

As a consequence, the writings of these men, particularly those of Olmsted and Cairnes, have never been allowed to slip into the category of intellectual history. Continual reliance on their arguments and their evidence by modern writers has kept their indictment alive, has maintained their position as the principal antagonists on the issues of efficiency, growth, and even on the issues of the profitability and viability of slavery. Their work is the core around which the traditional interpretation of slavery has been molded.

Six

Paradoxes of Forced Labor

The Relative Efficiency of Slave Agriculture

Since 1968 a group of cliometricians has been working on the measurement of the relative efficiency of input utilization in the agricultural sectors of the North and South for the year 1860. The construction of an appropriate measure is an arduous and complex task, both because the raw data which enter into such a measure are difficult to obtain, and because of the many adjustments which need to be made in the raw data. Despite more than five years of work, this project, which now involves over a score of economists and their assistants, is still less than half complete. Nevertheless, even at this stage, a number of important findings have emerged which directly contradict the central assertions in the economic indictment of slavery. While some of these findings are still preliminary and subject to change, it is unlikely that future revisions will overturn the main interim conclusions.

The primary instrument used to measure and compare

the relative efficiency of the agriculture in the North and South is called the "geometric index of total factor productivity." With this index, efficiency is measured by the ratio of output to the average amount of the inputs. The higher the output per average unit of input, the greater the efficiency. The geometric index of total factor productivity was originally devised in the early 1940s. It was used, in a celebrated paper published in 1957, to measure the growth in the efficiency of the American economy between 1909 and 1949. It has been widely used since that time to evaluate and compare the economic performances of various sectors of the economy within the U.S. during many different time periods, as well as to compare the economic performance of various nations. The equation for the index is presented in appendix B, along with a discussion of the characteristics of this measure and the way in which it has been applied to determine the relative efficiency of slave agriculture.

The following are the main interim findings:

1. Southern agriculture as a whole was about 35 percent more efficient than northern agriculture in 1860; that is, on average, a southern farm using a given amount of labor, land, and capital could produce about 35 percent more output than a northern farm, or group of farms, using the same quantities of these inputs.

2. Both southern farms using free labor and southern farms using slave labor were more efficient than northern farms. Compared with each other, however, southern slave farms were 28 percent more efficient than southern free farms. Compared with northern farms, southern free farms were 9 percent more efficient, while slave farms were 40 percent more efficient.

3. There were economies of scale in southern agriculture. This means that a single large farm using given quantities of inputs could produce more output than a group of small farms which together used the same quantities of inputs. Not all of the superior efficiency of slave farms was due

Figure 42

A Comparison of the Efficiency of Southern Farms with Northern Farms in 1860

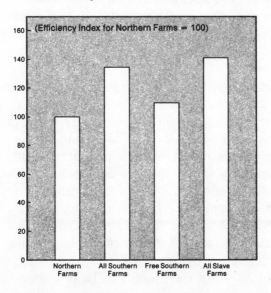

(Efficiency Index for Northern Farms = 100)

Figure 43

A Comparison of the Efficiency of Large and Small Southern Farms in 1860

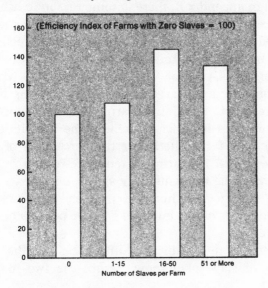

(Efficiency Index of Farms with Zero Slaves = 100)

to economies of scale. And not all economies of scale were in production. Our measures indicate that plantations of moderate size in the New South (sixteen to fifty slaves) may have had certain advantages in production over very large plantations.

In general, however, the larger the farm, the greater the role of economies of scale. Economies of scale contributed only 6 percent to the efficiency of fairly small plantations with from one to fifteen slaves. Scale led to a 15 percent gain in efficiency for moderate-sized plantations with between sixteen and fifty slaves. And the average scale at which the largest plantations operated — those with over fifty slaves — raised their efficiency by just over 23 percent. In other words, plantations with just a few slaves were not really able to take advantage of the benefits of large-scale organization. Moderate-sized plantations were able to achieve most, but not quite all, of the benefits of large-scale organization which accrued to the very large plantations.

It should be emphasized that the work thus far measures economies of scale only in the process of production. As is indicated in appendix B, there is some reason to believe that there were scale effects in the marketing and other aspects of plantation activity besides production. These effects are not captured by the present indexes.

4. Economies of scale were achieved only with slave labor. There were no large-scale southern farms based on free wage labor. Small free farms did not combine into large enterprises in order to achieve the benefits of scale. The larger the farm, the larger the percentage of persons who were slaves. On farms of ten or fewer persons, about 11 percent of the residents were slaves, on average. But on farms of fifty to one hundred persons, 90 percent were slaves. On farms of one hundred or more persons 94 percent were slaves.

5. There were significant differences in the relative efficiency of slave plantations within the two major sub-

Figure 44

The Percentage of Farm Residents Who Were Slaves, by Size of Farm

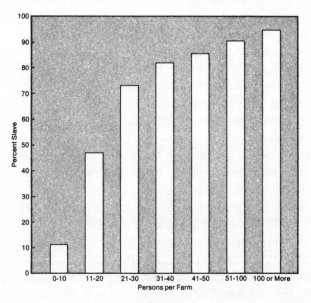

Figure 45

A Comparison of the Efficiency of Old South Farms with Northern and New South Farms

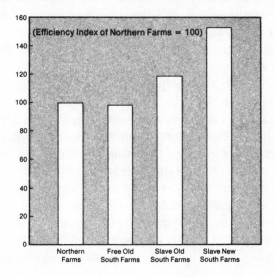

regions of the South. On average, the plantations of the newer, or slave-buying, states were 29 percent more efficient than those of the older, slave-selling states. The free farms of the Old South virtually matched the efficiency of free northern farms. The slave plantations of the Old South exceeded the efficiency of free northern farms by 19 percent, while the slave plantations of the newer southern states exceeded the average efficiency of free northern farms by 53 percent.

It therefore appears that the main assumptions of the economic indictment of slavery were without foundation in fact. Southern agriculture was more, not less, efficient than northern agriculture. While it is true that large plantations using slave labor made better use of their resources than the small southern farms that relied exclusively on free labor, this was not because the whites of these small enterprises were "driven to indolence, carelessness, indifference to the results of skill, heedlessness," and "inconstancy of purpose." For family-sized southern farms, and those who labored upon them, were more efficient in 1860 than their northern counterparts. It was, rather, because the large slave plantations had achieved, on average, a degree of efficiency that was unmatched by any other major subsector of American agriculture, North or South, during the antebellum era.

Similarly, the superiority of farms in the slave-buying states relative to those in the selling states does not imply that the farms of the older states were inefficient. The farms of Virginia, North Carolina, Tennessee, and the other selling states were more efficient than those of the North, but they were not able to capture the benefits of large-scale organization to the same degree as those in the buying states.

There is a sense in which this failing may be attributed to differences in land quality. But these were not the differences in land quality that were emphasized by Olmsted and Cairnes. There is no clear evidence that land in the older states was being depleted, that the average quality of soil or land yields was declining. The statistical analyses of data on land yields and land values that have thus far been performed are ambiguous. But even if one interprets these findings in a manner most favorable to the hypotheses of Olmsted and Cairnes, they indicate only a slight deterioration in yields as plantations aged — on the order of one half of one percent per annum. This deterioration was more than offset by investment in farm capital, transportation improvements, and other factors which affected the overall productivity of agriculture in the selling states. In other words, the assertions of Olmsted and Cairnes on these matters were unfounded. Far from declining, between 1850 and 1860 the average value of farm lands and improvements in the three chief exporting states (Virginia, North Carolina, and South Carolina) increased by 60 percent — nearly as much as the increase (79 percent) experienced by the three chief slave-importing states (Alabama, Mississippi, and Louisiana). This is not to say that there were no abandoned farms in the selling states. There were abandoned farms in all states — North and South — as changing economic conditions led farmers to leave enterprises on marginal land which had been profitable under one set of relative prices but did not remain profitable under later sets of relative prices. Olmsted and Cairnes exaggerated the extent of abandonments, converting the atypical into the general case.

To some extent Olmsted and Cairnes were misled by the widespread concern among southern planters with the problem of maintaining land fertility. This concern was not misplaced. For, as already noted, the sandy nature of southern soils, the heavy rainfalls, and the relative absence of winter freezes all worked toward undermining the fertility of southern soils. Great care was therefore necessary to maintain soil fertility. This point was continually emphasized by leading southern agriculturalists as well as by southern political leaders. Much attention was paid to this problem in southern agricultural journals. Many planters experimented with various types of fertilizers, methods of plowing, and regimens of crop rotation. Successful experiments were regularly reported. All farmers were urged to follow such practices. Those who did not were severely criticized and held up to scorn by agricultural and political leaders, some of whom overdramatized and exaggerated the extent of the problem. Olmsted and Cairnes completely misunderstood the nature of the running discussion among Southerners on this issue. Confusing rhetoric with reality, they assumed that the agricultural leaders were losing the battle to maintain land fertility. However, the available evidence on the course of the value of land and improvements as well as on land yields indicates that they were wrong.

In what sense are the subregional differences in land quality relevant to an explanation of the interregional differences in productivity and to the interregional redistribution of the slave population? The soils and climate of the various states were not equally advantageous to all southern crops. The Atlantic Coastal Plain just below the Mason-Dixon line and the Central Piedmont Plateau were favorable for raising tobacco and general farming, but could not support a cotton culture. Rice had its greatest advantage in the swamplands along the southeastern coastal flatwoods of Georgia and South Carolina and in the lower Gulf Coastal Plain. Sugar production was confined largely to a handful of parishes in the Mississippi Delta. Cotton could be grown successfully in a long belt stretching mainly from South Carolina through Texas. The bounds of this belt were determined largely, but not exclusively, by climatic conditions since the cotton culture requires a minimum of two hundred frostless days and ample rainfall. Temperature set the northern boundary and rainfall the western boundary. Not all land within this boundary is equally suitable. The black-belt lands of Alabama and Texas were more congenial to cotton than the sandy loams of the Piedmont or the marshes of the coastal plains, except for long-staple cotton. Perhaps the best cotton lands of all were the alluvial soils of the Mississippi flood plain.

Thus, the distribution of southern labor among the states was in large measure determined by the changing structure of the demand for southern crops. As long as tobacco and wheat were the principal crops of the South, as they appear to have been through the end of the eighteenth century, it was most efficient to concentrate labor and the other resources in regions which bordered on Chesapeake Bay. But as the demand for cotton grew, relative to other southern commodities, efficiency dictated a reallocation of labor and other resources to the lands of Alabama, Mississippi, Louisiana, and later, Texas. In other words, the westward movement of southern farming was due, not to the depletion of soils, but to the increase in the demand for products whose relative advantage was on western rather than on eastern soils.

The westward shift was also stimulated by certain technological advances which appear to have increased the relative productivity of western lands. Two of the most important of these took place in the transportation sector rather than within the agricultural sector. One was the development of the steamboat and its diffusion throughout the South during the 1820s and 1830s. Steamboats drastically reduced the cost of transportation into the interior of the South along rivers which had been too shallow or had currents too swift to permit their navigation by sailboats. The accessibility of lands in the interior of various states, and hence the *economic* productivity of these lands, was further enhanced by the development of the railroad and its construction through the South, especially during the decade of the 1850s.

Perhaps the most important technological advance within the agricultural sector of the South after 1800 was in the realm of management, particularly in the development of organizational methods which permitted southern planters to capture the potential benefits of economies of large-scale operation. It must be remembered that the shift from the production of grain and tobacco to cotton, sugar, and rice coincided with a substantial increase in the average size of slaveholdings. The optimal farm size appears to have differed by crop. There is little evidence of economies of scale in grain production; and economies of scale appear to have been fairly limited in tobacco production. Thus, farms located in counties specializing in these crops grew little between 1790 and 1860. On the eve of the Civil War the average size of Virginia slaveholdings was still only 18.8, while the county averages in the alluvial regions of short-staple cotton production ranged as high as one hundred and twenty-five slaves per holding. By the last decade prior to the Civil War the optimal size (minimum size of the most efficient farms) had increased to approximately fifty slaves in the cotton lands of the black belt and to over two hundred slaves in counties of the alluvial lands along the Mississippi. Indeed by the last decade of the slave era, the ability to provide efficient management appears to have become the main constraint on the optimal size of plantations.

One should not leap to the conclusion that this finding supports the stereotype of planters as a class of "idlers" who lacked "steady habits and frugal instincts," and who usually entrusted the primary management of their plantations to inept, cruel overseers while they indulged their taste for pleasure in various cities of the South, the North, or of Europe. No doubt such planters existed. But they were a distinct minority. Among moderate-sized holdings (sixteen to fifty slaves) less than one out of every six plantations used a white overseer. On large slaveholdings (over fifty slaves) only one out of every four owners used white overseers. Even on estates with more than one hundred slaves, the proportion with white overseers was just 30 percent,

Figure 46

The Percentage of Farms with White Overseers, by Size of Farm

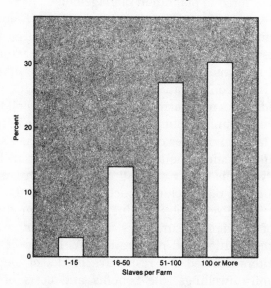

and on many of these the planters were usually in residence.

The continual discussions of problems of plantation management in the agricultural journals of the South were not evidence of the failure of southern planters but of the earnestness with which they approached their tasks. Far from being cavalier fops, the leading planters were, on the whole, a highly self-conscious class of entrepreneurs who generally approached their governmental responsibilities with deliberation and gravity — a manner which accorded with their self-image. They strove to become steeped in the scientific agricultural literature of the day; they organized agricultural societies as a means of disseminating information on the "best practices" in various aspects of farming, and in order to encourage experimentation in animal husbandry, agronomy, horticulture, and related matters; and they established journals in which they could report their findings as well as debate the full range of problems that they encountered in plantation management.

No question was treated with more gravity than that of labor management. Planters recognized that this was the critical issue. Economic success rode or fell with it. No aspect of slave management was considered too trivial to be omitted from consideration or debate. Details of housing, diet, medical care, marriage, child rearing, holidays, incentives and punishments, alternative methods of organizing field labor, the duties of managerial personnel, and even the manner or air to be assumed by a planter in his relationship with his slaves were all deemed worthy of debate. Discussions of diet included such matters as the balance between meat, vegetables, grains, and dairy products, the virtues of fat versus lean meats, and the optimum method of food distribution and preparation. With respect to housing, planters debated the respective merits of single- and multi-family dwellings, the benefits and costs of various types of building materials, the design of chimneys, and the optimum spatial distribution of slave houses and other buildings. On marriage and the family, the debate included such issues as whether or not slaves should be permitted to marry across plantations, and the latitude to be allowed to drivers and overseers in the mediation of intra- as well as interfamily disputes. Debates around the incentive structure turned on such matters as the relative advantages of gifts or cash bonuses versus allotments of plots of land, the types of crops that slaves could grow on their individual plots, whether or not slaves should be permitted to have quasi-property rights in the small livestock, and whether slaves should be permitted to market their own crops and livestock or should be required to sell them to the planter at prevailing market prices.

Whatever the differences among planters in the resolution

of these particular issues, there was widespread agreement that the ultimate objective of slave management was the creation of a highly disciplined, highly specialized, and well-coordinated labor force. Specialization and interdependence were the hallmarks of the medium- and large-sized plantations. On family-sized farms, each worker had to fulfill a multiplicity of duties according to a pace and pattern which were quite flexible and largely independent of the activities of others. On plantations, the hands were as rigidly organized as in a factory. Each hand was assigned to a set of tasks which occupied him throughout the year, or at least through particular seasons of the year. There were drivers, plowmen, hoe hands, harrowers, seed sowers, coverers, sorters, ginners, packers, milkmaids, stock minders, carpenters, blacksmiths, nurses, and cooks — to give only a partial listing.

With respect to field labor, the various hands were formed into gangs or teams in which the interdependence of labor was a crucial element. During the planting period the interdependence arose largely from within each gang. A planting gang consisted of five types of hands who followed one another in a fixed procession. Leading off the procession were plowmen who ridged up the unbroken earth; then came harrowers who broke up the clods; then drillers who created the holes to receive the seeds, each hole a prescribed distance apart from the next one; then droppers who planted the seeds in the holes; and finally rakers who covered up the holes. The intensity of the pace of these gangs was maintained in three ways:

First, by choosing as the plowmen and harrowers who led off the planting operation the strongest and ablest hands.

Second, by the interdependence of each type of hand on the other. (For as on an assembly line, this interdependence generated a pressure on all those who worked in the gang to keep up with the pace of the leaders.)

Third, by assigning drivers or foremen who exhorted the

leaders, threatened the laggards, and did whatever was necessary to ensure both the pace and the quality of each gang's labor.

During the period of cultivation, this interdependence, and the productive tension which it created, stemmed to a considerable extent from the interaction between gangs. Field hands were divided into two groups: the hoe gang and the plow gang. The hoe hands chopped out the weeds which surrounded the cotton plants as well as excessive sprouts of cotton plants. The plow gangs followed behind, stirring the soil near the rows of cotton plants and tossing it back around the plants. Thus the hoe and plow gangs each put the other under an assembly-line type of pressure. The hoeing had to be completed in time to permit the plow hands to carry out their tasks. At the same time the progress of the hoeing, which entailed lighter labor than plowing, set a pace for the plow gang. The drivers or overseers moved back and forth between the two gangs, exhorting and prodding each to keep up with the pace of the other, as well as inspecting the quality of the work.

This feature of plantation life — the organization of slaves into highly disciplined, interdependent teams capable of maintaining a steady and intense rhythm of work — appears to be the crux of the superior efficiency of large-scale operations on plantations, at least as far as fieldwork was concerned. It is certainly the factor which slaveowners themselves frequently singled out as the key to the superiority of the plantation system of organization. Although Olmsted repeatedly reported that planters preferred slave labor to white labor because slaves "could be driven," the significance of these statements completely eluded him. White men, said one planter, "are not used to steady labour; they work reluctantly, and will not bear driving; they cannot be worked to advantage with slaves, and it is incon-

venient to look after them, if you work them separately."
A slaveholder who listened to Olmsted's report of his con-
versation with Griscom, the Northerner who claimed that
slave laborers produced only one fourth as much output per
day as northern laborers, responded that these slaves "could
not have been well 'driven.'" Another reported that "he
would never have white people at ordinary work, because
he couldn't drive them." Still another said: "You never could
depend on white men, and you couldn't *drive* them any;
they wouldn't stand it. Slaves were the only reliable laborers. . . ." The conclusion that Olmsted drew from such reports
was not that slave labor in the plantation context was of
a superior quality, but that southern free laborers must have
been extremely lazy, inept, and of low quality compared to
northern laborers.

Even on those few occasions when Olmsted actually
witnessed gangs working in the field, he failed to appreciate
the significance of slave teamwork, coordination, and intensity of effort, although he faithfully recorded these
features of their work. The hoe gang, he reported on one
of these instances, "numbered nearly two hundred hands
(for the force of two plantations was working together),
moving across the field in parallel lines, with a considerable
degree of precision. I repeatedly rode through the lines at a
canter, with other horsemen, often coming upon them
suddenly, without producing the smallest change or inter-
ruption in the dogged action of the labourers, or causing
one of them, so far as I could see, to lift an eye from the
ground." What conclusion did Olmsted draw from this experience? Did he view it as a remarkable demonstration of
the teamwork of black laborers and of the intensity of their
concentration on the task at hand? The "stupid, plodding,
machine-like manner in which they labour," said Olmsted,
"is painful to witness." While Olmsted was willing to concede that these slave hands probably worked "harder, and

more unremittingly," than northern laborers, he still doubted that "they accomplish as much in the same time as agricultural labourers at the North usually do."

Harvest operations in cotton do not appear to have offered the opportunities for division of labor and specialization that existed during the planting and cultivation seasons (although such opportunities do appear to have existed in sugar harvesting). In the absence of an interdependence that could be exploited to promote an intense rhythm of work, planters attempted to achieve the same objective by dividing harvest hands into competing groups. There were daily as well as weekly races, with prizes (bonuses) offered to the winning team and to the leading individual picker. There were daily weigh-ins of the cotton picked, and those who did not respond to the positive incentive had to face the abuse, verbal or physical, of the driver, if they fell too far below the expected pace.

The so-called "task method" was still another means of promoting the intensity of labor during the harvest season. Under this method, slaves were assigned given plots of land which were to be picked each day. Intensity of labor was promoted by permitting the slave to use his time for his own purposes when the task was completed. One way of ensuring that the work was done well under this system was to reassign the same plot to the same slave in each of the successive rounds of picking. Daily weighing of cotton also served as a check on performance.

Specialization and division of labor were not limited to fieldwork. They carried over into domestic aspects of plantation life. Certain domestic tasks were socialized to a considerable extent. This was true of child rearing and, to a lesser extent, of the production of clothing and of cooking. It was women, predominantly, who specialized in these employments. Most large plantations maintained nurseries. These were supervised by one or more of the older women, depending on the size of the plantation, who generally were assisted by older children. Women who worked in the fields, or at other assignments, deposited their children in the morning and picked them up in the evening. Nursing mothers returned to the nursery three or four times per day for feedings.

The production of clothing was, in varying degrees, carried out on most plantations. Some had loom houses in which most of the cloth consumed on plantations was woven. Others limited production to the sewing of purchased cloth. Sometimes these tasks were carried out by women in their own houses, when the weather was inclement or during slack seasons. In other cases, a permanent staff was assigned to a special building. Olmsted described the loom-house staff on one very large plantation. Of the dozen hands so employed, one "was insane, and most of the others were crippled, invalids with chronic complaints, or unfitted by age, or some infirmity, for field work."

Olmsted's description points to another aspect of the efficiency of plantations — the extraordinarily high labor-force participation rate (share of the population in the labor force). In the free economy — North and South — approximately one third of the population was in the labor force. Among slaves, the labor-force participation rate was two thirds. Virtually every slave capable of being in the labor force was in it. This was due largely to the inability of slaves, particularly women and children, to choose leisure, education, or work at home, if they preferred it, to work in fields or other assigned tasks. It was partly due to institutional arrangements which permitted plantations to find methods of employing those who would, to a large extent, be unemployable in free societies, particularly in free urban societies — the mentally retarded, the crippled, the aged.

Plantations not only brought a larger share of the population into the labor force, but they were also able to move closer to "full-capacity" utilization of the labor potential than was true of the free economy. This was not because slaves worked more hours per day or more days per week than free farmers. The best available evidence is that both slaves and free farmers averaged approximately 70–75 hours of work per week during the peak labor periods of planting, cultivation, and harvesting. Nor does it appear that slaves worked more days per year. In addition to having Sundays off, slaves had all or part of half of their Saturdays free, most of these being concentrated in the off-peak periods of farming. There was also up to a week or so of additional holidays, some at predesignated times, as during Christmas or in the interstice between the end of cultivation and the beginning of the harvest, some as unscheduled rewards for work well done. About a dozen days per year were lost due to illness. Thus the work year appears to have consisted of roughly 265–275 days.

The higher rate of the utilization of labor capacity was partly due to what was, by the usual standards of farmers, an extraordinary intensity of labor. Far from being "ordinary peasants" unused to "pre-industrial rhythms of work," black plantation agriculturalists labored under a regimen that was more like a modern assembly line than was true of the routine in many of the factories of the antebellum era. It was often easier for factory workers to regulate the pace of machines to their accustomed rhythm than for slaves to regulate the pace set by drivers. For much of antebellum manufacturing was still operated on the work patterns of the handicrafts. Division of labor was still at relatively low levels and interdependence of operations was still limited. Just as the great plantations were the first large, scientifically managed business enterprises, and as planters were the first group to engage in large-scale, scientific personnel management, so, too, black slaves were the first group of workers to be trained in the work rhythms which later became characteristic of industrial society. It was not the slaves but men like Olmsted who retained a "pre-industrial peasant mentality," who viewed the teamwork, coordination, and intensity of effort achieved by black field hands as "stupid, plodding, machine-like," and "painful to witness." While Olmsted's revulsion is quite understandable, he was nevertheless wrong in concluding that the gang system was inefficient, and his belittling of the quality of slave labor was unwarranted.

The high rate of the utilization of labor capacity was also abetted by the large scale of plantation enterprises in another respect — greater flexibility in being able to match occupations to abilities. This was most apparent in the case of the elderly. On free farms as well as on plantations, child rearing was a task assigned to the aged. But whereas a grandmother on a free farm devoted herself to only a few children, her plantation counterpart cared for a score of children in plantation nurseries. Planters with relatively large numbers of superannuated slaves, or others whose mental or physical ability limited their capacity for work, found that it paid to promote less demanding enterprises, such as weaving, to make use of their labor. This feature of plantation life helps to explain one of the findings of chapter 3, the positive average net earnings from slaves down to ages in the middle or late seventies.

The Quality of Slave Labor and Racism

The large slave plantations were about 34 percent more efficient than free southern farms. This advantage was not due to some special way in which land or machinery was used, but to the special quality of plantation labor. It is true that large plantations used more land and equipment (by value) per worker than small plantations. However, this feature was taken into account in computing the efficiency indexes. In other words, even after one adjusts for the fact that on large plantations slaves generally worked on better land than free southern farmers and had more equipment, large plantations were still some 34 percent more efficient than free farms.

The advantage of plantations, at least that part which has been measured thus far, was due to the combination of the superior management of planters and the superior quality of black labor. In a certain sense, all, or nearly all, of the advantage is attributable to the high quality of slave labor, for the main thrust of management was directed at improving the quality of labor. How much of the success of this effort was due to the management, and how much to the responsiveness of the workers is an imperative question, but its resolution lies beyond the range of current techniques and available data.

Whatever the contribution of management, however, it should not all be assigned to white planters and overseers. For blacks — though slaves, though severely limited in the extent to which they could climb the economic ladder of antebellum society — were a vital part of the management of plantations and, in this capacity, of the economic successes of the plantation.

Slaves entered into plantation management at two levels. As drivers or gang foremen they were ubiquitous on medium and large plantations. In the fields the drivers were responsible for ensuring that each gang achieved its daily objectives and, if the gang was operating on the task system, for determining the daily tasks of particular hands. Gang objectives were sometimes established either by the plantation owner or overseer. In other instances the establishment of these objectives was left to the discretion of the drivers.

Slaves also operated at the highest level of plantation supervision, short of actual ownership, as overseers or general managers. When acting as overseers, slaves were responsible not only for the overall direction of the labor force but for various entrepreneurial decisions, including the scheduling of the particular field operations and the purchasing of supplies. In such cases the burden of the success or failure of the entire production side of plantation operations rested on these slaves. Much of the attention of owners was directed to the commercial aspects of operations — the marketing of the crops, the purchase of equipment, the acquisition of new lands, the construction of new buildings, the negotiation of loans — or to other nonagricultural enterprises in which they were engaged.

Various scholars have recognized that slaves *sometimes* acted as overseers or general managers. But it has been assumed that this was rare, that on most large plantations the general management *of production* was in the hands of white overseers. The white overseer is assumed to have been a ubiquitous figure, present on virtually all plantations of one hundred or more slaves and on the majority of those with fifty to one hundred slaves. As pointed out previously, data in the census manuscripts clearly invalidates this assumption. Only 30 percent of plantations with one hundred or more slaves employed white overseers. On smaller plantations the proportion was even lower.

It might be thought that on many of the large plantations sons of planters took over the functions of the overseer. The data in the manuscript schedules of the census rules this possibility out in most cases. Among large plantations without overseers, 61 percent had only one adult male over age nineteen in the planter's family. In these cases the planter was the only adult male in his family who was in residence, or else the father was absent or dead and his only resident son was running the plantation. In any event there was no second male family member to take up the duties of the overseer. On 6 percent of the large plantations there were two adults over age nineteen, but the second of these persons was at least seventy years of age, and hence was probably too old to be actively involved in the business affairs of the plantation. Another 9 percent of the plantations had no male at all over age nineteen in residence. Thus, for 75 percent of the plantations without overseers, there were no sons or other males who could have assumed the duties of the overseer. The conclusion indicated by these findings is startling: On a majority of the large plantations, the top nonownership management was black.

The question that begs to be explained is how so many scholars could have been so badly misled on this issue? Part of the explanation turns on a methodological consideration. To a considerable extent, the views of historians regarding the nature of plantation management are based on inferences from correspondence between owners and overseers. However, such correspondence (including instructions to overseers) was most likely to arise when owners did not reside on their plantations. Thus, previous historians based their conclusions on a biased sample of evidence, on a relatively small group of plantations which were unrepresentative of the whole. It is probable that absentee owners relied on white overseers to a much greater extent than did resident owners, among other reasons, because laws made it illegal to leave slaves exclusively under their own supervision.

Part of the explanation also turns on the way in which many historians have accepted the arguments of the authors of the economic indictment of slavery. One would hardly expect a system in which even the masters were cavalier fops and idlers to produce a high-quality class of slave managers. Nor was a mass of blacks "incapable of all but the rudest forms of labour," "evasive," incapable of maintaining "a steady routine," "incorrigibly indolent," "wanting in versatility," and unsuited for any activity that requires "the slightest care, forethought, or dexterity" likely to throw up any considerable number of able managers. If one accepts the premise that the system crushed all opportunity for the personal and intellectual development of slaves, mere consistency requires one also to expect to find that slaves were debarred from virtually all positions of responsibility. Interestingly enough, Olmsted did not show such consistency of mind. Despite his low opinion of the quality of the black masses, he had a high opinion of the quality of blacks who functioned as drivers.

In the selection of drivers, regard seems to be had to size and strength — at least, nearly all the drivers I have seen are tall and strong men — but a great deal of judgment, requiring greater capacity of mind than the ordinary slave is often supposed to be possessed of, is certainly needed in them. A good driver is very valuable and usually holds office for life. His authority is not limited to the direction of labour in the field, but extends to the general deportment of the negroes. He is made to do the duties of policeman, and even of police magistrate. It is his duty, for instance, on Mr. X's estate, to keep order in the settlement; and, if two persons, men or women, are fighting, it is his duty to immediately separate them, and then to "whip them both."

Before any field of work is entered upon by a gang, the driver who is to superintend them has to measure and stake off the tasks. To do this at all accurately, in irregular-shaped fields, must require considerable powers of calculation. A driver, with a boy to set the stakes, I was told, would accurately lay out forty acres a day, in half-acre tasks. The only instrument used is a five-foot measuring rod. When the gang comes to the field, he points out to each person his or her duty for the day, and then walks about among them, looking out that each proceeds properly. If, after a hard day's labour, he sees that the gang has been overtasked, owing to a miscalculation of the difficulty of the work, he may excuse the completion of the tasks; but he is not allowed to extend them. In the case of uncompleted tasks, the body of the gang begin new tasks the next day, and only a sufficient number are detailed from it to complete, during the day, the unfinished tasks of the day before. The relation of the driver to the working hands seems to be similar to that of the boatswain to the seamen in the navy, or of the sergeant to the privates in the army.

Having generally had long experience on the plantation, the

advice of the drivers is commonly taken in nearly all the administration, and frequently they are, *de facto*, the managers. Orders on important points of the plantation economy, I have heard given by the proprietor directly to them, without the overseer's being consulted or informed of them; and it is often left with them to decide when and how long to flow the rice-grounds — the proprietor and overseer deferring to their more experienced judgment. Where the drivers are discreet, experienced, and trusty, the overseer is frequently employed merely as a matter of form, to comply with the laws requiring the superintendence or presence of a white man among every body of slaves; and his duty is rather to inspect and report than to govern. Mr. X considers his overseer an uncommonly efficient and faithful one, but he would not employ him, even during the summer, when he is absent for several months, if the law did not require it. He has sometimes left his plantation in care of one of the drivers for a considerable length of time, after having discharged an overseer; and he thinks it has then been quite as well conducted as ever. His overseer consults the drivers on all important points, and is governed by their advice.

"Mr. X" was not the only planter who frequently consulted with his slave managers and who deferred to their judgment, or insisted that his overseers do so. Nor was Olmsted the only one to note the high quality of black managers. When McBride, the owner of the Hickory Hill plantation, left on a long trip, he wrote detailed instructions to his overseer on the method of planting and cultivating various crops. In the case of rice, however, McBride said he was too ill-informed on that crop to offer advice and suggested that the overseer consult the driver who was "an old rice planter." Similarly, Charles Manigault instructed his overseer to "be careful not to interfere too much with the beating and management of the Rice Mill" since "the Negroes in charge have much experience therein." Indirect testimony of the high regard which planters had for the intelligence and good judgment of their slave drivers and other lower echelon personnel comes from the frequent complaints of white overseers that direct consultations between planters and drivers or other respected slaves were undermining their authority. No doubt some drivers deliberately provoked tests of strength between themselves and the overseers. In many such instances they were successful, and the overseer was fired or left of his own volition. On many of those plantations which did make use of white overseers, the turnover rate of overseers was quite high.

That the quality of slaves, both as ordinary workers and as managers, could have been so completely misrepresented by the antebellum critics of slavery is testimony to the extent of their racist myopia. What bitter irony it is that the false stereotype of black labor, a stereotype which still plagues blacks today, was fashioned not primarily by the oppressors who strove to keep their chattel wrapped in the chains of bondage, but by the most ardent opponents of slavery, by those who worked most diligently to destroy the chains of bondage.

While keenly aware of the torment which these false stereotypes of incompetence have helped to impose on blacks for more than a century, we are, as social scientists, impressed by this exceptional demonstration of the power of ideology to obliterate reality, and we view it as an unparalleled opportunity to investigate the complex interrelationships between ideas and the material circumstances of life. What is at issue here is not only how these false stereotypes regarding blacks came into being, but how they could have persisted for so long. Resolution of the first issue involves consideration of the intricate ways in which variations of racist viewpoints among critics and defenders of slavery, among northern and southern whites — for with very few exceptions they were all racists — interacted with each other to create an almost indestructible image of black incompetence. Resolution of the second issue involves consideration of why it has been so difficult for the many historians and social scientists who have studied slave society to penetrate this image and to discover the reality which it hid.

Much as we desire to do so, we cannot settle these issues — not merely because they lie beyond the scope of this book, or even because they require skills which go beyond our special areas of expertise, but because much research is still required before the various aspects of these questions can be treated adequately. Nevertheless, we cannot resist the opportunity to suggest some considerations which we believe ought to enter into the ultimate resolution.

One point on which there can be little doubt is that the belief in Negro incompetence was given a powerful fillip by the racial theories that came into prominence during the first half of the nineteenth century. These theories were embraced by Northerners as well as Southerners, by critics of slavery as well as its defenders. The theories asserted that blacks and whites were of different species or at least that blacks were an "inferior variety" of the human species. The African origins of blacks were thought to have contributed to the biological defects. Some attributed the racial differences to geographic factors. Thus, Negroes had "a dull torpid brain," a feature thought to be characteristic of "inhabitants of the warmer climates." Others saw Negro backwardness as being rooted in their savage ancestry. Whatever the cause, the innate inferiority of the Negro race was said to manifest itself in laziness, limited intellectual capacity, a childlike simplicity, docility, sensuousness, and tempestuousness. It is important to stress that these racist views were not embraced merely in popular thought. They were the reigning tenets of mid-nineteenth-century anthropology, in Europe as well as in the United States.

Although both critics and defenders of slavery believed in the innate inferiority of Negroes, there were important differences between them in assessing the effect of slavery on the natural endowments of Negroes. Critics of slavery believed that bondage had not only retarded the development of blacks but had exacerbated the baser features of their nature. Slavery had encouraged blacks to be slovenly, to prefer indolence to industry, to be evasive, to lie, and to steal. Abolitionists believed that slavery retarded black development because it was incapable of recognizing individual accomplishment and rewarding it, because it relied on the lash to elicit effort, thus identifying labor with pain. They also believed that the plantation form of organization kept blacks relatively isolated from contacts with whites and hindered their capacity to assimilate the higher white culture. Hence they drew a distinction between house servants and field hands, assuming the former were more highly developed intellectually and culturally because of their more intimate association with whites.

Defenders of slavery argued that their system not only had a beneficial development on blacks but was, indeed, pushing them to the outer limits of their capacity. Despite the fact that they were of an inferior race, under the slave system of labor organization blacks were induced to work harder and produce more than white labor. Not only was the natural indolence of blacks thus thwarted, but the most talented of their number were trained in the handicrafts and in other higher arts, thus achieving a status under slavery which was not only "elevated from the condition in which God first created them" but was clearly more lofty than anything that might be obtained under freedom. For everybody knew that slave labor was "vastly more efficient and productive than the labor of free blacks."

Obviously a debate cast along the lines just described could only serve to reinforce the stereotype of Negro incompetence. For neither side ever called the alleged natural incompetence of the Negro into question. Quite the contrary — each new round of debate served to raise the proposition of natural incompetence to the status of an axiomatic truth. Critics of slavery emphasized the failings of southern production, attributing these to a system which was not only based on an inferior variety of human labor but which degraded all labor, reducing in quality not only the effort of blacks but of whites as well. Defenders of slavery attributed outstanding accomplishments in production not to the high quality of black labor but to the success of the system of slavery which enabled the South to achieve as much as it did from what was basically inferior human material.

That Olmsted fully accepted the racial views of his day is clearly evident in his books. The Germans appear as the only whites in the South capable of resisting the degrading effects of slavery on white labor. They are invariably portrayed as industrious and efficient — the very models of enterprising, thrifty, and ambitious small proprietors. On the other hand, the only Jews that Olmsted encountered in the South were moneylenders "of no character" who charged extortionate interest rates ("often . . . not less than 25 per cent per annum"), who lived in squalid homes, and who engaged "in an unlawful trade with the simple negroes." Similarly, the Irish were "dumb Paddies" who easily succumbed to the degrading southern attitude toward labor and usually fell to a level that made their labor even less desirable than that of slaves. Olmsted's northern chauvinism came to the fore whenever he compared the quality of northern and southern laborers. Few northern employers would have recognized their employees from his description of them. Northern workers were almost invariably portrayed as highly motivated, diligent, self-propelled, and polite, even when being fired for some infraction of their normally high standards of behavior. There can be little doubt that Olmsted's jaundiced views of black relative to white labor, and of southern relative to northern labor, were influenced by the racial presuppositions that he brought with him on his travels through the South.

But to leave the matter there is to grossly oversimplify the issue. For whatever his prejudices, Olmsted was an extremely keen and diligent observer who was striving to discover those characteristics which distinguished the system of slave labor and which differentiated it from the system of free labor. While his prejudices undoubtedly predisposed him toward misinterpreting what he in fact observed, or had reported to him, it is not likely that he would have fallen into these errors if there had not been mitigating circumstances that made his misinterpretations plausible — if there had not been substantial elements which lent support, or at least appeared to lend support, to his conclusions.

One of the features of slavery which confused Olmsted was the extremely high labor-force participation rate. With 67 percent of all slaves in the labor force, nearly a third of the labor force was composed of untrained, awkward children. A smaller but significant proportion consisted of elderly persons and others who were crippled or disadvantaged in some respect. Women, whose physical capacity for heavy work was more limited than that of men, were also overrepresented in the slave labor force as compared with the free labor force. With such large differences in the age-sex-health structure of the two work forces, there is a sense in which the "average" output of a slave worker might have been less than that of an "average" free worker.

Olmsted recognized that for a valid comparison of the relative efficiency of slave and free workers, one had to adjust for differences in the age-sex-health composition of the two labor forces. He accepted the legitimacy of the planters' practice of rating children, the aged, and disabled persons as one eighth, one quarter, or some other fraction of a prime-aged, healthy hand. In his formal discussion of the issue of the relative efficiency of free and slave labor he attempted to avoid the problem of the age-sex-health composition by comparing slaves and free laborers "man with man, with reference simply to equality of muscular power and endurance."

While Olmsted, in principle, recognized the need for the adjustment, he never quite overcame, it appears, the psychological effect of seeing so many children, women, aged persons, and handicapped persons in the labor force. Many of his examples of the inefficiency of slave labor are drawn from these categories of workers. This was particularly true during his first visit to the "Seaboard States" where many of his direct encounters with slaves were in hotels or in the homes of slaveowners or overseers. In these places his contacts with slaves would have been to a disproportionate extent with children and the aged. He frequently described the ineptness of servants, their bungling attempts to light a fire, and their frequent interruptions of the master. "[T]hey came to him [the master] like children," said Olmsted, "who have been given some task, and constantly are wanting to be encouraged and guided, simply and confidently." And why not? These servants were, to a considerable extent, children not yet old enough to begin their tenure as field hands.

The last point deserves to be stressed because it exposes a fallacy in the argument of those who make such heavy distinctions between the cultural development of house servants and field hands. Analysis of data in the probate records and plantation registers indicates that there were few men in the ages between fifteen and forty who functioned as house servants. Servants were generally youngsters under fifteen or persons in the late forties, fifties, sixties, and seventies. Thus it appears likely that the children who began as house servants soon took their places among the field hands, while the elderly who were house servants came largely from among the field hands. The most outstanding male slaves in the prime ages were the drivers. Top male field hands tended to be shifted into crafts as they aged. Outstanding women received the more choice domestic jobs. If some house servants seemed more capable than the average field hand, it may have been due to encounters with slaves whose past performances in the field had been recognized with a choice domestic assignment. The views of travelers in the South may also have been affected by the relatively greater ages and maturity of these servants. The issue which probably confused Olmsted more than any other one came to the fore during his very first visit to a slave plantation — a wheat farm in Maryland which he examined on December 14, 1852. The slaves he saw there were not engaged in the fields but were at work in the neighborhood of the plantation buildings. The owner of the plantation told Olmsted that while he had employed white laborers on several occasions for digging ditches, he would not think of using whites "for common farm-labor, and made light of their coming in competition with slaves. Negroes at hoeing and any steady field-work, he assured me, would 'do two to their one'. . . ."

Olmsted did not press the planter further. He clearly did not accept such a high appraisal of the quality of the planter's black labor force. Olmsted characterized the slaves on this farm as "stupid and dilatory in executing any orders given to them." "Those I saw at work," he said, "appeared to me to move very slowly and awkwardly, as did also those engaged in the stable."

This Maryland wheat plantation was not a run-down, piddling farm operated by a "mean white." It was, in Olmsted's words, a "fine farm," over two thousand acres in extent, run under "excellent management," with a main house which had "somewhat the look of an old French chateau," with "well-secured, wire fences," with a "nicely graveled and rolled" road, with "thorough-bred Shorthorns" as the milking stock ("I have seldom seen a better lot of milkers," said Olmsted), and with drains on the farm's lowlands that were so well built that they lasted "twenty years without failing." The planter's experiments with fertilizers so impressed Olmsted that he singled them out. How could so keen a planter, a man whose excellence in farm management had won him "a national reputation," have deceived himself so badly about the quality of his laborers? And how had he been able to prosper with workers who were "stupid and dilatory," who moved "very slowly" and who "must" have been "very difficult to direct efficiently"?

The mistake was Olmsted's. What he observed on this plantation was the easy-going rhythm of slaves during the winter interstice. The planting of winter wheat had been completed more than a month before Olmsted's arrival and the fall harvesting of other crops, such as corn, had also been completed well before his visit. This was a period for putting things in order — repairing fences, thoroughly cleaning stables, rerolling of roads — important tasks all, but not the type that called for intensive effort. The high-pressure tasks of planting, cultivating, and harvesting were either over, or not yet at hand. As we have previously stated, Olmsted's itinerary during his first trip kept him squarely in the interstice between harvesting and planting. As he moved south and westward into cotton country, he generally moved toward both later completion of the harvest and later resumption of the date of planting. By the time he arrived in Georgia, Alabama, and Louisiana, states in which he might still have observed the picking of cotton in mid-December, he was already into February. He left Louisiana well before the onset of the new planting season, which began during the last days of March or early in April.

Thus, Olmsted's opinion of the typical work rhythms of slaves, an opinion in which he gained more and more confidence as he traveled through the "Seaboard States," was once again based on an unrepresentative sample of evidence. Olmsted appears to have made the mistake of assuming that the leisurely work pace of slaves during the southern agricultural interstice prevailed throughout the balance of the year. In his subsequent two trips, Olmsted did, of course, witness the typical rhythms of planting and cultivating. But by then he had become so convinced that the pace he had observed during his first trip was the norm, that he invariably classified his later encounters with intense labor as exceptions.

Toward an Explanation for the Persistence of the Myth of Black Incompetence

The principal cause of the persistence of the myth of black incompetence in American historiography is racism. Perhaps no single history book written during the twentieth century has had a greater impact on the interpretation of slave life than U. B. Phillips's *American Negro Slavery*. To point out that this volume was deeply marred by its author's adherence to the proposition that Negroes were racially inferior to whites would hardly evoke controversy among historians today. This point is now emphasized not only by the critics of Phillips but also his defenders.

How different the situation was when *American Negro Slavery* was published in 1918. Of the principal reviewers of the book, only two attacked Phillips's treatment of Negroes — and they were not in the mainstream of the historical profession as it was then constituted. One of these reviewers was W. E. B. Du Bois, the director of publicity and research for the N.A.A.C.P. and the editor of its journal, *Crisis*. Du Bois found *American Negro Slavery* "curiously incomplete and unfortunately biased."

The Negro as a responsible human being has no place in the book. To be sure individual Negroes are treated here and there but mainly as exceptional or as illustrative facts for purposes outside themselves. Nowhere is there any adequate conception of "darkies," "niggers" and "negroes" (words liberally used throughout the book) as making a living mass of humanity with all the usual human reactions. . . .

Mr. Phillips recurs again and again to this inborn character of Negroes: they are "submissive," "light-hearted" and "ingratiating" (p. 342), very "fond of display" (pp. 1, 291), with a "proneness to superstition" and "acceptance of subordination" (p. 291); "chaffing, and chattering" (p. 292) with "humble nonchalance and a freedom from carking care" (p. 416). From the fourteenth to the twentieth century Mr. Phillips sees no essential change in these predominant characteristics of the mass of Negroes; and while he is finishing his book in a Y.M.C.A. army hut in the South all he sees in the Negro soldier is the "same easy-going amiable serio-comic obedience," and all he hears is the throwing of dice (pp. viii, ix). This Negro nature is, to Mr. Phillips, fixed and unchangeable. A generation of freedom has brought little change (p. ix). Even the few exceptional Negroes whom he mentions are of interest mainly because of their unexpected "ambition" and not for any especial accomplishment (p. 432). The fighting black maroons were overcome by "fright" (p. 466), and the Negroes' part in the public movements like the Revolution was "barely appreciable" (p. 116); indeed his main picture is of "inert Negroes, the majority of whom are as yet perhaps less efficient in freedom than their forbears were as slaves" (p. 396)!

Brilliant as it was, Du Bois's critique fell largely on deaf ears. It could hardly have been otherwise during an era when the pseudoscientific racial theories which still dominated anthropology were widely accepted in scholarly circles. Indeed, more than two decades elapsed before scholars in the mainstream of the history profession began to press the theme enunciated by Du Bois.

While not unanticipated by others, the flag of general revolt against the Phillips school was raised by Richard Hofstadter in a 1944 paper entitled "U. B. Phillips and the Plantation Legend." Hofstadter attacked Phillips for exaggerating the paternalistic impulses of the planter, for painting too "rosy" a portrait of the material conditions of slave life, and for depicting the Negro as "a singularly contented and docile 'serio-comic' creature." The real nature of the treatment of slaves, said Hofstadter, was far more cruel than admitted by Phillips, slave health was much poorer than Phillips admitted, and slaves were more often left to the mercy of harsh overseers by their absentee owners than Phillips admitted. Hofstadter also charged Phillips with having underestimated the extent, and having distorted the nature of, "the slave's resistance to slavery." He chided Phillips for stressing a benign type of "give-and-take process between master and slave," for failing to appreciate "the extent to which the easement of the slave's condition came not from the master's benevolence but from the slave's resistance." Hofstadter ended his essay with a call for the rewriting of the history of slavery from the "viewpoint of modern cultural anthropology"; by this he meant the new view on race, pioneered by Franz Boas, which held that racial factors were unimportant in determining intellectual capacity.

Hofstadter's rebellion was far less sweeping than might appear. Hofstadter did not challenge Phillips on the general profitability and viability of slavery. Neither did he take issue with him on the quality of slave labor, on the economic efficiency of slavery, or on the effect of slavery on southern economic growth. Indeed, Hofstadter confined his attack to just four of the twenty-three chapters of *American Negro Slavery*, specifically excluding from consideration those which dealt with the issues of profitability, efficiency, and growth.

The limited nature of Hofstadter's attack on Phillips is not difficult to explain. Like so many others, Hofstadter's conception of slavery was developed largely from his reading of Olmsted. Hofstadter excoriated Phillips for not having made greater use of the work of this witness and critic. "Olmsted was not only an honest but an unusually acute observer," said Hofstadter, "and I believe that a fuller and more accurate knowledge of the late antebellum South can be obtained from the volumes of Olmsted than from Professor Phillips's own writings." But Phillips, despite his mistrust for the man, had read Olmsted with care and made great use of him. On the issues of the profitability and efficiency of slavery, as well as on the quality of slave labor and the effect of slavery on southern economic growth, Phillips was pure Olmsted. And on some of these issues Phillips merely paraphrased Olmsted. (Olmsted: "slaves thus get a fictitious value like stocks 'in a corner.' " Phillips: "when the supply [of slaves] was 'cornered' it was unavoidable that the price should be bid up to the point of overvaluation.")

Despite Phillips's pretensions to a revolutionary break with James Ford Rhodes, the dominant historian in the interpretation of southern slavery at the time Phillips was a graduate student, and despite Hofstadter's claims to a revolutionary break with Phillips, all three men — and the schools of historical writing on the antebellum South which they symbolize — were adherents to what we have termed the "traditional interpretation" of the slave economy. That interpretation is the one which emerged from the economic indictment of slavery described in chapter 5. It consists of five main propositions. These are: 1, that slavery was generally an unprofitable investment, or depended on a trade in slaves to be profitable, except on new, highly fertile land; 2, that slavery was economically moribund; 3, that slave labor, and agricultural production based on slave labor, was economically inefficient; 4, that slavery caused the economy of the South to stagnate, or at least retarded its growth, during the antebellum era; 5, that slavery provided extremely harsh material conditions of life for the typical slave.

Phillips accepted all of these propositions except the last. When he claimed he was revolutionizing the interpretation of the antebellum South, he was referring only to point five, the harsh treatment of slaves, and to the shadow which that treatment cast on the character of slaveholders. Phillips did not have to overturn Rhodes on the character of blacks and the quality of their labor. Rhodes's views on the character of slaves and on the quality of their labor were fully congenial to Phillips. Rhodes described slaves as "indolent and filthy"; their expression was "besotted and generally repulsive"; on their "brute-like countenances . . . were painted stupidity, indolence, duplicity, and sensuality"; their labor was "stupid, plodding, machine-like"; licentiousness and indifference to chastity were "a natural inclination of the African race" which was further fostered by slavery; as women displayed "an entire lack of chastity," the men displayed "an entire lack of honesty"; and slave women yielded "without objection, except in isolated cases, to the passion of their master." In Rhodes's view the error of southern apologists was not in the claim that blacks were inferior, but in the manner in which they sought to cope with the problem created by this inferiority. "So long as Southern reasoners maintained that the negro race was inferior to the Caucasian, their basis was scientific truth, although their inference that this fact justified slavery was cruel as well as illogical."

The irony of Hofstadter's call for a rejection of the Phillips position on treatment, without a simultaneous attack on the other four points, is that it led in the direction of the re-establishment of the pre-Phillips or "pure" version of the traditional interpretation of the economics of slavery. As long as historians remained locked in combat on the issue of treatment, explicitly accepting all other aspects of the economic indictment of slavery, the myth of Negro incompetence continued to reign supreme — just as it had in the antebellum era when critics of slavery and apologists debated over whether slavery had exacerbated or ameliorated the "natural" inferiority of blacks.

We do not mean that Hofstadter, or that scholars who responded to his call, aimed to re-establish the theories of the racial inferiority of Negroes as they existed in Rhodes or as in Clay, Helper, and Olmsted. Quite the contrary, as both Hofstadter and those who rallied to his banner have made clear, their aim was the unequivocal and complete rout of the racist myths that lingered on in the historiography of the antebellum South. What they failed to appreciate was that these racist myths drew sustenance not merely from one of the five points in the traditional interpretation of slavery but from each of them.

This was true even of Kenneth Stampp who, as is pointed out in appendix C, went further than any other post-Phillips scholar, except perhaps Lewis C. Gray, in rejecting the traditional interpretation of slavery. In *The Peculiar Institution,* Stampp argued that investments in slaves were quite generally profitable, indeed, highly profitable for most planters. He also rejected the contention that economic forces would by themselves have led to the demise of slavery, even in the upper South. Nor did Stampp find any evidence to support the claim that slavery prevented industrialization and economic growth. He pointed to "innumerable experiments" which "demonstrated that slaves could be employed profitably in factories," arguing that slaveholders preferred to operate in agriculture because, for the South, agriculture "seemed to be the surest avenue to financial success."

Stampp even expressed doubts about the fourth proposition in the traditional interpretation — that slavery was less efficient than an economic system based on free labor. "Slavery's economic critics overlooked the fact," he said, "that physical coercion, or the threat of it, proved to be a rather effective incentive, and that the system did not prevent masters from offering tempting rewards for the satisfactory performance of assigned tasks."

At this point, however, Stampp faltered. He hesitated to go on to the conclusion that slaves were equal to free men in the efficiency of their labor. He conceded that slave productivity was sharply reduced by "the slave's customary attitude of indifference toward his work, together with the numerous methods he devised to resist his enslavement." Stampp was able to hold on to his contention that slavery was profitable only by arguing that there were other "advantages" which "more than compensated for whatever superiority free labor had in efficiency." These "advantages" included longer hours of work, more complete exploitation of women and children, and lower real wages for slaves than for free men.

Why did Stampp, who broke with so much of the traditional interpretation and who came so close to rejecting the myth of the incompetence of slave labor, fail to do so? Why did he, as it were, pull back just as he seemed about to do so?

The answer lies in Stampp's preoccupation with the refutation of Phillips on point five, the nature of the treatment of slaves. Surely Phillips's idyllic portrait needed correction. In reacting against the Rhodes treatment of plantations as houses of immorality and unmitigated terror run by men who were not only brutal but corrupt, Phillips substituted a near-paradise — at least as much of a paradise on earth as was reasonable to expect from a "primitive" race whose "savage" instincts had to be kept in check and which had to be trained to overcome a "natural ineptitude" and "indolence." In Phillips's reconstruction, planters emerged not merely as good men but, to use Du Bois's word, as supermen. Slavery became "less a business than a life." The objective of planters was not so much to make a profit as to make men.

Recoiling from such apologetics, Stampp provided testimony that cruelty was indeed an ingrained feature of the treatment of slaves. The cases of cruelty which Phillips regarded as unusual, as outside the unwritten rules of the master class, emerged as a common pattern of white behavior in *The Peculiar Institution*. Cruelty, Stampp said, "was endemic in all slaveholding communities"; even those "who were concerned about the welfare of slaves found it difficult to draw a sharp line between acts of cruelty and such measures of physical force as were an inextricable part of slavery." For Stampp, cruelty arose not because of the malevolent nature of the slaveholders but because of the malevolent nature of the system — because a master could brook nothing less from his slave than "perfect" submission. To achieve that goal masters were impelled, regardless of their humanity in other respects, to develop in the Negro "a paralyzing fear of white men," to "impress upon him his innate inferiority," and to "instill in him a sense of complete dependence." While Stampp did not employ the concentration camp analogy later set forth by Stanley Elkins, his plantation strongly suggested a prison with cruel wardens.

From this point the argument could have gone — and did in fact go — in two directions. One was the direction taken by Elkins, who argued that a system as cruel as the one described by Stampp must have had a devastating impact on the personality of slaves. No one could live under so brutal a regime without succumbing to it. Negroes were not supermen, any more than were the Jews in Hitler's concentration camps. Although plantations were not concentration camps, the masters who ran the plantations had as much absolute power over slaves as Hitler's gauleiters had over the Jews, and as much determination to crush their spirit. What emerged from the process was "Sambo, the typical plantation slave . . . docile but irresponsible, loyal but lazy, humble but chronically given to lying and stealing." Sambo's "behavior was full of infantile silliness" and his "relationship with his master was one of utter dependence and childlike attachment."

Stampp decided to move in a direction that, on the surface, appears quite different from the one Elkins chose. He argued that slaves did not succumb; they resisted. Resistance did not generally take the form of revolution or strikes. Such open forms of resistance were sheer suicide. There were no rebellions among U.S. slaves comparable to those in Jamaica or Brazil; there was no protracted guerrilla warfare.

Resistance in the U.S. took a much more subtle form; it came in guises so innocent that masters and overseers failed even to recognize it. The participants in this resistance movement "were the meek, smiling ones whom many thought were contented though irresponsible."

They were not reckless rebels who risked their lives for freedom; if the thought of rebellion crossed their minds, the odds against success seemed too overwhelming to attempt it. But the inevitability of their bondage made it none the more attractive. And so, when they could, they protested by shirking their duties, injuring the crops, feigning illness, and disrupting the routine. These acts were, in part, an unspectacular kind of "day to day resistance to slavery."

What, of course, is common to both Stampp and Elkins is agreement on the characteristic of slave behavior: slaves lie, steal, feign illness, behave childishly, and shirk their duties. Indeed, this characterization has been one of the enduring constants in the literature on slavery. By whatever path they moved, writers on slavery usually returned to the theme of the inferiority of slave labor. To Olmsted, Rhodes, and Phillips the inferiority was due to racial factors. To Cairnes, inferiority was sociological in origin. To Elkins, the cause was psychological. To Stampp, the inferiority was due to "day to day resistance." Paradoxically, it was the slaveholders who were least inhibited in acknowledging that blacks were better workers than whites, although they attributed this superiority to themselves rather than to their bondsmen.

Stampp hesitated to make the leap required to recognize the superior quality of slave labor because he remained too enmeshed in the debate between the critics of slavery and the apologists, and he overestimated the cruelty of the slave system. The logic of his position made it difficult to acknowledge that ordinary slaves could be diligent workers, imbued like their masters with a Protestant ethic, or that, even though they longed for freedom, slaves could strive to develop and improve themselves in the only way that was open to them.

Still, Stampp came remarkably close to discovering the true nature of the slave system, the true advantage of bondage to the agricultural capitalists who dominated antebellum society. What was crucial to the system was not cruelty but force. Force could, and often did, lead to cruelty, but not as much cruelty as Stampp then believed. For what most planters sought was not "perfect" submission but "optimal" submission. These are two very different concepts. If Stampp blurred the distinction, it was because, like so many before him, he tended to confuse rhetoric with reality. "Perfect" submission was the rhetorical position of the master class, not its practical objective. The shrewd capitalistic businessmen who ran the slave plantations were not usually psychological perverts who gloried in the exercise of unlimited force for its own sake. They generally used force for exactly the same purpose as they used positive incentives — to achieve the largest product at the lowest cost. Like everything else, they strove to use force not cruelly, but optimally.

The Economic Significance of Property Rights in Man

In recent years economists have extended the use of the concept of capital beyond its usual application to machines, buildings, and other inanimate objects. They have applied the concept of capital to the wealth inherent in the capacity of human beings to perform labor, calling such wealth "human capital." This extension of the concept seemed odd at first because it was applied not to explain behavior in nineteenth-century slave societies but in twentieth-century free societies. Nobody doubts that human beings were a form of capital in slave society. Slaves who were traded commanded prices as specific and well-defined as those on land, buildings, or machines. Since prices of slaves varied by age, health, skill level, and geographic location, it is clear that the vocational training of slaves or their relocation from one region to another were just as much forms of investment as the erection of a building or extension of a fence.

What made the application of the concept of human capital to free societies seem odd is that free people are not traded in well-defined markets and hence do not command market prices. However, the absence of explicit market prices on human beings does not mean that free men do not actually have capital values, but only that the absence of a trade in human beings usually prevents their capital values from being made explicit. Legal recognition of the fact that free people continue to have capital values takes place whenever courts grant cash awards to the widows of men killed in industrial accidents. The amount of such an award usually turns on a debate regarding the capital value of the deceased at the time of his death.

Viewed in this light, the crucial difference between slave and free society rests not *on the existence* of property rights in man, in human capital, but on who may hold title to such property rights. Under freedom, each person holds title, more or less, to his own human capital. He is prevented by law from selling the title to this capital except for quite limited periods of time and then only under a very restricted set of conditions. Moreover, one generally cannot sell the title to the human capital of others, or if such sales are permitted (as in the cases of the contracts of movie and athletic stars, or as in the case of the parents or guardians of minors), the title is transferred only for relatively short intervals of time and under strictly defined limitations. In slave societies, however, a large number of individuals were permanently deprived of the title to their own human capital. Those who held the titles (the masters) were virtually unrestricted by law in the ability to sell them. And ownership of a female slave brought with it title, in perpetuity, to all her descendants.

How did the special way in which the antebellum South treated the matter of property rights in man affect the economic behavior of that society? What special economic advantage, if any, did the system of property rights which prevailed under slavery give the slaveowners? How did this system of property rights affect the real income of the masters, of slaves, of free Southerners, and of free Northerners? While these are not new questions, certain of the findings of the cliometricians suggest new answers. Two findings of particular importance are that:

1. Economies of scale in southern agriculture were achieved exclusively with slave labor.
2. While the urban demand for slave labor was quite elastic, the agricultural demand was very inelastic.

The first finding is not new. Olmsted realized that economies of scale were achieved only with slave labor, and specifically addressed himself to that question. Characteristically, Olmsted concluded that the failure of small free farmers to combine into large units through the medium of "a joint-stock cotton plantation" was due to their ignorance and lack of enterprise. But as we have seen, small free southern farmers were not bunglers. Nor were they lacking in enterprise. Many small free farmers became the masters of large slave plantations. If there had been no special advantage to slave labor, one would expect at least some of these enterprising individuals to have based their plantations on free labor. The fact that economies of scale were achieved exclusively with slave labor clearly indicates that in large-scale production some special advantage attached to the use of slaves.

Interestingly enough, there is no evidence that slaves possessed any special advantage or disadvantage for large-scale production in urban industries. While some large-scale factories were based exclusively on slave labor, others were based exclusively on free labor. Many urban firms, perhaps most, employed a combination of the two types of labor. For example, in the Tredegar Iron Works, the largest iron manufacturer in the South and the fourth largest in the nation, slaves sometimes made up as much as half of the labor force. The second finding — the relatively high urban elasticity of demand for slaves — means that in the urban context slaves and free laborers were quite good substitutes for each other. When the price of slaves rose relative to free wages, urban enterprises shifted away from the employment of slave labor and increased the employment of free labor. And when the prices of slaves fell relative to free wages, these urban enterprises shifted back into slave labor.

In agriculture, however, the demand for slaves was highly inelastic. This means that in the slave-using agricultural sector, free labor was a very poor substitute for slave labor. Variations in the ratio of slave prices to free wages had virtually no effect on the preferences of large plantations for slave labor. Even when slave prices rose quite sharply relative to free wages, the labor force of the large plantations remained overwhelmingly slave. Whatever special advantage attached to slave labor was, therefore, confined exclusively to the use of that labor in large-scale agricultural enterprises.

To identify the unique advantage of slaves to large-scale agricultural enterprises, it is necessary to make use of the economists' distinction between "pecuniary" and "nonpecuniary" income. Pecuniary income is tangible income of some sort, whether received in money or in kind. Pecuniary income enters into national income accounts and hence is also referred to as "measured" income. Nonpecuniary income is of an intangible nature and it is not measured in national income accounts. Nonpecuniary income can be either positive or negative. For example, it is generally thought that the nonpecuniary income earned by most members of the faculty of Harvard University is large and positive, since these faculty members usually prefer to stay at Harvard even when they have been offered much larger pecuniary incomes by other institutions. The difference between the pecuniary income actually received by professors at Harvard and what they could earn elsewhere is a first approximation of the value that these academics attach to the nonpecuniary benefits of being located at Harvard.

It is not necessary to belabor the point that for free men, work in gangs on plantations involved large nonpecuniary disadvantages. Nevertheless, it seems reasonable to suppose that if planters offered free laborers large enough pecuniary payments, they could have attracted a sufficient number of free laborers to run their plantations. How big a premium would they have had to offer to induce free agriculturalists to forego the tempo and life-style of small farms and to accept a much more intense, more highly regulated, more interdependent regimen? And did the plantations have the capacity to pay that premium? For as competitive firms, there was a well-defined upper limit to the premium that they could afford. The ceiling on the potential premium to free labor for plantation work was given by the increase in output that could be achieved through combining small-scale farms into large-scale farms. Thus, if a would-be planter tried to bribe a typical group of white farmers into forming a large-scale plantation based on gang labor, he would not be able to offer more than a 50 percent increase over what they were already earning through their labor on small farms. The failure of free small-scale farmers to combine into large-scale plantations is *prima facie* evidence that the nonpecuniary disadvantages of gang labor — and all that it entailed — were greater than 50 percent of the wages of free farm laborers.

It might be thought that the preceding argument implies

that since slaves did work on plantations, the nonpecuniary disadvantages of gang labor to them was less than 50 percent of the wages of free labor. That conclusion would be warranted only if the conditions under which labor was elicited from slaves corresponded to those for free men. Obviously they did not. In general, the labor of free men could only be elicited through wage bargains. However, ownership of the human capital of blacks carried with it the right to use force to obtain labor. Ownership of the title to a slave gave a master the right to use whatever force was necessary — including such force as might eventuate in death — to compel his chattel to engage in the normal work routine of the plantation. From the master's viewpoint, the advantage of force, when *judiciously* applied, was that it produced desired behavior, in certain realms of activity, at a lower cost than could have been achieved through financial inducements. The analogy to the parental use of force today is striking. Parents often find that it is cheaper (easier) to *compel* children to go to bed at a given hour rather than to attempt to bribe them into doing so. But one should not leap from this analogy to the unwarranted conclusion that force necessarily resulted in the infantilization of mature slaves.

Force was not an incidental feature of slavery. Without force, the alienability of the title to the human capital of blacks would have been worthless, at least insofar as it affected the plantation's capacity to produce. For it was only by applying force that it was possible to get blacks to accept gang labor without having to pay a premium that was in excess of the gains from economies of scale. The validity of this contention is demonstrated by the experience of the immediate postemancipation period. After the slaves were freed, many planters attempted to reconstruct their work gangs on the basis of wage payments. But such attempts generally foundered, despite the fact the wages offered to freedmen exceeded the incomes they had received as slaves by more than 100 percent. Even at this premium, planters found it impossible to maintain the gang system once they were deprived of the right to apply force. Freedmen generally preferred renting land and farming it, usually for shares, to working in gangs, although the payments being offered for gang labor were more than 100 percent greater than the average earnings of freedmen through sharecropping. Thus whether one compares immediate postwar gang wages with income from sharecropping or prewar pecuniary payments, available evidence shows that the application of force made it possible to obtain labor from slaves at less than half the price that would have had to have been offered in the absence of force. The nonpecuniary disadvantage of gang labor was no less to blacks than to whites.

The special advantage of slavery for agricultural production, then, is that it was a very cheap way of "compensating" slaves for the nonpecuniary disadvantages of gang labor. This discovery makes it possible to explain why the advantage of slave labor was much less in urban industry than in agriculture. The nonpecuniary disadvantage of accepting the monotonous and intense routine of factories appears to have been offset by nonpecuniary benefits which both black and white workers attached to life in the cities. In other words, the net nonpecuniary disadvantage of work in urban industry was quite low, perhaps even negative (see appendix B). The scope of the benefits that could be obtained from the application of force was thus much more limited in urban industry than in plantation agriculture.

For a given amount of labor, there was an optimum amount of force — an amount that would make the total cost (cost of force plus the pecuniary payment to the slave) of procuring the desired labor a minimum. Planters worried about what that optimum was. They realized that there were limits on the extent to which force could be substituted for pecuniary payments, that if they resorted to too much force they would increase rather than reduce the cost of labor. That is why they generally restricted the amount of force that their overseers or drivers were permitted to impose on hands, why they felt it was necessary to give explicit instructions on when, how, and to what degree force could be applied.

It has been widely assumed that slaveholders employed force because it permitted them to push pecuniary payments to the subsistence level, or at least close to that level. This assumption is false. Odd as it may seem, the optimal combination of force and pecuniary income was one that left slaves on large plantations with *more* pecuniary income per capita than they would have earned if they had been free small farmers. The explanation of this paradoxical finding turns on the fact there were definite costs to the generation of force. After a certain point, the cost of obtaining an additional unit of labor with force became greater than the cost of obtaining it through pecuniary payments. To use the language of economists — there were rapidly diminishing returns to force. The analysis of the trade-off which faced planters in choosing between force and pecuniary payments is a complex but standard problem of economics. Because of its complexity we have relegated it to appendix B, where it is shown that the average pecuniary income actually received by a prime field hand was roughly 15 percent greater than the income he would have received for his labor as a free agricultural worker. In other words, far from being kept at the brink of starvation, slaves actually shared in the gains from economies of scale — so far as purely pecuniary income was concerned. Slaves received approximately 20 percent of the increase in product attributable to large-scale operations.

This finding underscores the importance of the system of pecuniary incentives discussed in chapter 4. It is not correct to say, as one leading historian did, that though pecuniary "rewards were much used," force was the "principal basis" for promoting the work of slaves. Pecuniary incentives were no more an incidental feature of slavery than force. Both were indispensable to the existence of the plantation system. The absence of either could have made the cost of production under the plantation system greater than the gains from large-scale production.

Planters recognized that both forms of economic inducement were essential, and they expected their managers to be adept at employing both. "Nothing," said the *Instructions to Managers* in a widely used plantation account book,

is more important in the right government of negroes, than the feeling and deportment of the manager towards them. And whilst he must be strict and impartial in carrying out his rules amongst them, and in requiring the performance of their labor, 'tis but just and humane, when they have done their duty, to treat them with kindness, and even sometimes with indulgence. In all government rewards and encouragements are as necessary as punishment, and are often more effective. Notice, then: encourage and reward such as best perform their duties. Even a word of kindness, if judiciously used, will effect much. At other times respite from labor for a few hours of any day, or at the end of the week, may be granted, and when such loss of time will not materially affect the plantation operations; and at others, some additional allowances of provisions and indulgencies at the holydays, etc.

The good opinion of a good master is always desired by his negroes, and the manager should, therefore, make it a point to report to the proprietor the names and characters of all those who are deserving on account of faithful attention to duty, that they may be further rewarded. . . .

The object of all punishment should be, 1st, for correction to deter the offender from a repetition of an offence, from the fear of the like certain punishment; and, 2nd, for example to all others, shewing them that if they offend, they will likewise receive certain punishment. And these objects and ends of all just punishments can be better attained by the certainty than by the severity of punishment.

Never fail, therefore, to notice the breach of an established rule, and be equally unfailing in punishing the offender justly, according to the nature and circumstance of the offence. Never inflict punishment when in a passion, nor threaten it; but wait until perfectly cool, and until it can be done rather with sorrow than in anger.

Olmsted repeatedly ran into examples of the heavy use made of pecuniary incentives by slaveholders and of the effectiveness of such incentives. On a sugar plantation in Louisiana he was surprised to find that slaves worked "with greater cheerfulness" during the grinding season than any other, although during this season they averaged eighteen hours of work per day. The reason, he discovered, was that at grinding time the hands were "better paid." In the Carolinas he reported that slaves on hire to fisheries as divers also revealed a surprising Protestant ethic. "What! slaves eager to work, and working cheerfully, earnestly, and skilfully?" The reason Olmsted, again reported, was that they were receiving extra pay for "skill" and "perseverance."

Olmsted was also aware of how high such extra pay could go. "One of the largest manufacturers [of tobacco in Virginia]," he said, in the course of trying to demonstrate how much dearer slave labor was than free labor, "informed me that he paid seldom less than $60 a year, and sometimes over $300, to each slave he used, in addition to the rent paid to their masters, which was from $100 to $150 a year." On a rice plantation in Georgia, Olmsted encountered a slave engineer who received "considerably higher wages, in fact [in the form of presents], than the white overseer."

On the issue of pecuniary incentives, however, as on so many others, Olmsted badly misinterpreted the evidence. In each of the foregoing instances, except the case in which he was arguing for the high real cost of slave labor, Olmsted treated the use of pecuniary incentives as an exception, employed only by "[m]en of sense" who had "discovered that when they desire to get extraordinary exertions from their slaves, it is better to offer them rewards than to whip them; to encourage them, rather than to drive them." Olmsted's preconceptions prevented him from realizing that pecuniary rewards were as integral a part of slavery as punishment.

Discovery of the relatively high average level of pecuniary payments to slaves not only calls into question the traditional interpretation of the incentive system, but also the traditional explanations for the relatively low incidence of rebellion on the part of slaves. The failure to recognize the flexible and many-faceted character of the slave system, and the widely held assumption that systematic employment of force precluded the use of pecuniary incentives in any significant way, have led historians to exaggerate the cruelty of slavery. This in turn led them to expect slaves to be pushed frequently, if not continuously, to the point of rebellion. The relative absence of rebellion thus posed a dilemma. In the attempt to resolve the dilemma, some historians have stressed the overwhelming odds against the success of attempts at rebellion, depicting, or suggesting, that the South was an armed camp.

Available evidence does not sustain this hypothesis. If physical power was the explanation for the absence of rebellion, one would expect to see government expenditures rise with the density of the slave population. Analysis of census data shows no such correlation. It might be argued that police power was supplied not by the state but by the planters themselves. If that were the case, one would expect to see the number of white males per plantation increase with plantation size. No such correlation exists. Regardless of the plantation size there were roughly six white persons per plantation — slightly over the average family size. On a plantation of one hundred slaves, the ratio of adult slaves to adult white males was roughly thirty to one. It strains credulity to believe that men armed with just pistols, if at all, could so cower slaves pushed to the point of rebellion that they would be unable to act against their oppressors. White planters and overseers were not supermen. Two or three strong, young slaves lurking behind some building surely could have disposed of a brutal overseer or planter, as sometimes happened, without anyone being the wiser as to the identity of the perpetrators of the deed.

Concern of planters with "abolitionist agitators" was not paranoia but hard-headed business. Planters were able to produce the needed force to maintain their system at exceedingly low costs. A small group of determined revolutionaries might well have pushed the cost of force to prohibitive levels. Similarly, the frequent discussions, in instructions to overseers, of the need for moderation in the application of force are not *prima facie* evidence of widespread brutality — proof that too much force was in fact being applied. As pointed out in chapter 4, overseers' instructions focused on the issues that planters considered most crucial to successful operations. That they would caution against the abuse of force is no more of a basis for assuming that slaves were generally treated cruelly by overseers than their instructions on feeding of livestock is proof that animals were being starved. Interestingly enough, the instructions reveal that the main fear of planters regarding the misuse of force was that it would raise costs, not by provoking general rebellion, but by leading to the flight of the individual slaves who were being abused.

One factor which undoubtedly reduced the cost of the force required to maintain the system of slavery was the ubiquity of racist attitudes among whites, and the embodiment of these attitudes in laws which severely reduced the value of freedom to blacks. For blacks, the alternative to slavery was not freedom but, as one scholar has put it, "quasi-freedom." This term applies to the North as well as to the South. In both sections of the country free blacks led a precarious existence. While northern Negroes were usually spared the threat of reinslavement because of infractions of the law, they were barred from testifying in ten states, prevented from assembling in two, and excluded from voting in ten. Illinois, the "Land of Lincoln," banned the migration of free Negroes into the state. Those who entered and stayed more than ten days were guilty of a "high misdemeanor." Data in the 1850 census suggest that the economic condition of the average free northern Negro may have been worse than that of the average free Negro in the South. A comparison between New York and New Orleans reveals that New York Negroes lived in more crowded housing, had a lower proportion of craftsmen, and less wealth per capita than free Negroes in New Orleans.

For blacks during the antebellum era, then, freedom and slavery were not separated by a sharp dividing line. One gradually shaded into the other. To some blacks, especially among the talented whose opportunities were most constricted by slavery, even quasi-freedom was worth nearly any price — and they risked everything for it. But for the average slave, who in any case expected his lot to be that of a laborer, the costs of revolution, or even flight, were not worth the gains of quasi-freedom — except under special circumstances such as the separation of a man from his wife or parents from their children.

That slaves received higher pecuniary incomes than they would have as free agricultural laborers does not mean that their real incomes were higher. For, as previously noted, there were large nonpecuniary disadvantages to the gang system, equal to at least $75 per year per adult male hand. Table 3 shows that for the southern slave population as a whole, gang labor imposed a nonpecuniary loss of at least $90,000,000. Against this very large loss, slaves received a relatively small pecuniary offset of $6,000,000. Thus their net loss was $84,000,000.

Although it may be surprising to some readers, the main gainers from the gang system were not slaveholders but consumers of cotton. Since cotton plantations had the characteristics of a competitive industry, all gains in productivity that did not go into the form of higher wages would normally have been passed on to consumers in the form of lower prices of cotton. Indeed, under normal circumstances, the extra profits to slaveholders which arose from the gang system would have been transitory. That they persisted was not due to any special behavior on the part of planters. It was due to the behavior of consumers of cotton whose demand for the fiber increased more rapidly than the labor force and total factor productivity. In this sense, even the extra profit of slaveholders was due to the behavior of consumers of cotton. Table 3 shows that of the total pecuniary gain from gang labor, consumers received nearly half, or $14,000,000, while slaveowners received about $10,000,000.

Table 3

Approximate Income Gains and Losses from Large-scale Operations in 1850 (in millions of dollars of 1850)*

	1 PECU- NIARY GAIN	2 NON- PECU- NIARY LOSS	3 NET GAIN OR LOSS (COL. 1 − COL. 2)
Slaves	6	90	−84
Consumers of Cotton	14	0	14
Slaveholders	10	0	10
TOTALS	30	90	−60

* See appendix B for the method of computation.

Slaves as a class, therefore, suffered a net loss in 1850 of at least $84,000,000 so that the rest of the world could benefit by $24,000,000. (The use of the term "rest of the world" was deliberate. For most U.S. cotton was consumed not in the United States but abroad). It is of some interest to note that the pecuniary benefits of gang production were much more widely diffused than the losses suffered by slaves. For every slave working in the cotton fields, there were hundreds of consumers of cotton. This means that the average annual gain to a consumer was quite small. Indeed, for every dollar gained by a typical consumer of cotton cloth, there was a slave laboring somewhere under the hot southern sun who would lose at least $400.

Some antebellum critics of slavery recognized that the system was being perpetuated by the greed of consumers. Robert Russell, one of the most acute of the British travelers to the South, believed that slavery was "a necessary evil attending upon the great good of cheap cotton." How indignant Olmsted was at this charge. That claim, he retorted, was sheer nonsense. He devoted a full chapter in *The Cotton Kingdom* to the refutation of Russell, arguing that slavery raised rather than lowered the price of cotton. How widespread this self-delusion was, is difficult to ascertain. Certainly not all of the antislavery politicians who railed against southern bondage, while they continued to consume cotton and resisted attempts to tax it, were naïve. At least some of these politicians thought that a total boycott of southern cotton, sugar, tobacco, and rice would have brought an end to slavery. Russell was not the only one who held this view. While Senator James H. Hammond undoubtedly overestimated how far the South could go before it provoked war, he clearly understood the hypocrisy in the position of many critics of the South when he proclaimed:

No, you dare not make war on cotton. No power on earth dares to make war upon it. Cotton *is* king. Until lately the Bank of England was king, but she tried to put her screws as usual, the fall before the last, upon the cotton crop, and was utterly vanquished. The last power has been conquered. Who can doubt, that has looked at recent events, that cotton is supreme? . . .

The Course of Economic Growth in the South, 1840–1860

The construction of regional income accounts for the nineteenth century, like the estimation of regional efficiency indexes, is an arduous task. Work on these accounts for the census years between 1840 and 1860, which was launched in the early 1950s, is still going on today. Table 4 presents the regional income estimates which have now been in use for about half a decade. A recent paper has suggested that the estimate of southern income for 1840 may be too low; the same criticism may also apply to the figure for 1860. If these proposed corrections hold up, it will be necessary to alter some of the details of the analysis that follows, but the main thrust of the argument will not be affected. Rather, the proposed corrections will merely serve to strengthen the argument.

Table 4 shows that in both 1840 and 1860 per capita income in the North was higher than in the South. In 1840 the South had an average income which was only 69 percent that of the North's. In 1860 southern per capita income was still only 73 percent as high as in the North.

These figures might appear to sustain Helper's contention that the South was a poverty-ridden, stagnant economy in the process of sinking into "comparative imbecility and obscurity"; that under the burden of slavery the South had been reduced to the status of a colonial nation — "the dependency of a mother country." No such inference is warranted, however, merely because of the existence of a 25 percent gap between the North and the South in the level of per capita income in 1860. Before any conclusion can be drawn, it must first be determined whether the gap means that, by the standards of the time, the South was poor or that the North was extraordinarily rich.

Progress toward the resolution of this issue can be made

Table 4

**Per Capita Income by Region for 1840 and 1860
(in 1860 prices)***

	1840	1860	AVERAGE ANNUAL RATES OF CHANGE (PERCENT)
National Average	$ 96	$128	1.4
North:	109	141	1.3
Northeast	129	181	1.7
North Central	65	89	1.6
South:	74	103	1.7
South Atlantic	66	84	1.2
East South Central	69	89	1.3
West South Central	151	184	1.0

* See appendix B for a discussion of the construction of these estimates. The per capita income figures are for the entire population, free and slave.

by disaggregating the North into two subregions: the Northeast, and the north central subregions. This is done in table 4, which shows that the northern advantage over the South was due entirely to the extraordinarily high income of the Northeast. Per capita income in the north central states was not only less than half as high as in the Northeast; it was 14 percent lower than per capita income in the South. If the South was a poverty-ridden "colonial dependency," how are we to characterize the states that occupy the territory running from the western border of Pennsylvania to the western border of Nebraska — states usually thought of as examples of high prosperity and rapid growth during the antebellum era?

Far from being poverty-stricken, the South was quite rich by the standards of the antebellum era. If we treat the North and South as separate nations and rank them among the countries of the world, the South would stand as the fourth richest nation of the world in 1860. The South was richer than France, richer than Germany, richer than Denmark, richer than any of the countries of Europe except England (see table 5). Presentation of southern per capita income in 1860 dollars instead of 1973 dollars tends to cloak the extent of southern economic attainment. The South was not only rich by antebellum standards but also by relatively recent standards. Indeed, a country as advanced as Italy did not achieve the southern level of per capita income until the eve of World War II.

The last point underscores the dubious nature of attempts to classify the South as a "colonial dependency." The South's large purchases of manufactured goods from the North made it no more of a colonial dependency than did the North's heavy purchases of rails from England. The true colonial dependencies, countries such as India and Mexico, had less than one tenth the per capita income of the South in 1860.

The false image of the South as a land of poverty emerged out of the debates on economic policy among southern leaders during the 1850s. As sectional tensions mounted Southerners became increasingly alarmed by federal policies which they thought were giving economic advantage to the North. They also became increasingly impatient with what they thought was an insufficiently active role by their state and local governments to promote internal improvements and to embrace other policies that would accelerate the southern rate of economic growth. To generate a sense of urgency southern newspapers, journals, economic leaders, and politicians continuously emphasized every new economic attainment of the North and every unrealized objective of the South, every northern advantage and every southern disadvantage. The abolitionist critique on the issue of development was lifted — lock, stock, and barrel — from southern editorials, speeches, and commercial proclamations, sometimes with acknowledgments (as in Olmsted), sometimes without (as in Helper).

Table 5

The Relative Level of the Per Capita Income of the South in 1860

(*Southern per capita income level* = 100)

Australia	144	Belgium	92	Italy	49
North	140	France	82	Austria	41
Great Britain	126	Ireland	71	Sweden	41
South	100	Denmark	70	Japan	14
Switzerland	100	Germany	67	Mexico	10
Canada	96	Norway	54	India	9
Netherlands	93				

The myth of southern backwardness and stagnation thus arose not because of any lack in the southern economic achievement but because the northern achievement was so remarkable, and because the continuous comparisons between the North and South were invariably unfavorable to the South. Compared with any country of Europe except England, however, the South's economic performance was quite strong. That comparison was never invoked by the abolitionists because it made the wrong point. It was rarely invoked by the Southerners because it would encourage complacency when urgency was called for.

Table 4 also shows that far from stagnating, per capita income was actually growing 30 percent more rapidly in the South than the North. The South's rate of growth was so rapid (1.7 percent per annum), that it constitutes *prima facie* evidence against the thesis that slavery retarded southern growth. Since few nations have achieved a rate of growth as high as 1.7 percent per annum over sustained periods, those who continue to advance the retardation thesis are implying that in the absence of slavery, the progress of the antebellum South would have exceeded virtually all recorded experience over the past 150 years. France, for example, experienced an average growth rate of 1.55 percent per annum over a 103-year period ending in 1960. Over similar periods the growth rate of the United Kingdom was 1.2 percent and Germany's was 1.43 percent. The long-term annual growth rate for the U.S. as a whole has averaged 1.6 percent. Only Sweden and Japan have been able to sustain long-term growth rates substantially in excess of that achieved by the antebellum South between 1840 and 1860.

When one disaggregates the southern rate of growth by subregions, it turns out that growth within each of the three subregions was less than the growth rate of the South as a whole. This is because part of the South's growth was due to the redistribution of southern population from the older states to the newer ones, particularly to Texas and the other rich states of the west central subregion. It will be noted that this subregion enjoyed an even higher level of per capita income than the Northeast. Approximately 30 percent of the annual growth in per capita income was due to the redistribution of population among subregions and the balance to the growth of per capita income within each of the subregions.

One scholar has recently argued that only the growth within subregions is meaningful, that the proportion of the growth rate which is due to the redistribution of the population from east to west is a statistical illusion that ought to be exorcised. The people within each subregion, he states, "could hardly see the realities, advantages, or even any meaning in such economic development."

This viewpoint reflects a fundamental misconception of the process of economic growth. The various industries or subregions of a nation never grow at even rates. Shifting demand for iron, for example, led the U.S. iron industry to grow much more rapidly than cotton textiles between 1842 and 1848, but much more slowly than textiles between 1848 and 1858. Technological progress also proceeds at uneven rates among industries and regions. The capacity of an economy to grow depends not only on its luck in the marketplace, and its luck or creativity with respect to technological breakthroughs, but on the capacity of the economy to respond to such developments. The ability of an economy to shift labor and other resources from one sector or subregion to another is always a major determinant of its growth. This was true in the North as well as the South. Roughly 16 percent of the northern growth rate between 1840 and 1860 was due to the shift of labor and other resources from agriculture to manufacturing. In other words, if we consider only growth rates within sectors, the rate of growth of northern per capita income between 1840 and 1860 would have been not 1.3 percent but less than 1.1 percent.

To argue that the people within subregions "could hardly see the realities" of growth which could be obtained through shifts between subregions is to misunderstand completely the meaning of figure 11, which showed the dramatic shift of the slave population from a concentration along the Chesapeake Bay in 1790 to a concentration in the cotton belt in 1860. It is precisely because Southerners could perceive the benefits to be achieved from interregional migration, because they could perceive the "meaning in such economic development," that so many of them moved. The large share of the southern growth rate due to interregional migration underscores the point made at the end of chapter 2, the extreme flexibility of the slave economy and the ease with which it "adjusted to the rapidly changing labor requirements of various southern firms and localities."

Equally fallacious are the arguments that the skewed (unequal) income distribution of the South made its markets too small to support a large-scale, modern manufacturing industry, and reduced the rate of investment in physical capital by reducing savings. The assumption that the inequality of the southern income distribution lowered its aggregate savings rate is probably false. This assumption is based on the mistaken belief that large consumption expenditures by the rich necessarily imply low savings. In the fairly typical year of 1925, the per capita consumption of the top one percent of income earners in the United States was about $4,800, while that of the remaining 99 percent was under $550. Certainly this is a pronounced difference, and given normal human reactions this could (and did) lead to discussions of wasteful expenditures by the rich. Yet in 1925 the top one percent had a savings-income ratio of 42.9 percent, and accounted for over 50 percent of estimated personal savings. This suggests the possibility that the effects of large consumption expenditures on southern capital formation may be overstated. Whatever conspicuous consumption did exist was probably carried on mainly by planters who were wealthy by the standards of the times. Their conspicuous consumption probably absorbed only part of their incomes, and their savings rates were probably far in excess of the national average. Given what we now know about the relationship between income and savings, it is quite possible that savings in the South were higher than they would have been with a less skewed income distribution.

In any case, recent work on the southern wealth distribution reveals that previous scholars have generally exaggerated the degree of inequality. Certainly the Cairnes contention that 70 percent of nonslaveholding whites lived at the border of starvation is untenable. While the wealth distribution among southern farmers was more unequal than among northern farmers, it was less unequal than the wealth distribution in urban areas. Since the North had a much larger proportion of its population in the cities than in the countryside, the overall inequality of the wealth distribution was roughly the same above and below the Mason-Dixon line for the free populations.

This finding strikes at the heart of the claim that the skewed southern income distribution made the southern market too small to support large-scale manufacturing firms of the type which existed in the Northeast. Even if the income distribution had been more unequal than it was, the fact that planters purchased large quantities of clothing and shoes for slaves from northern firms suggests the existence of a large market for manufacturing goods on plantations. It can, indeed, be argued that the products ordered by planters were more standardized and amenable to mass production techniques than would have been the situation if slaves were themselves the source of demand.

Manufacturing appears to be the only area in which the antebellum South lagged seriously behind the North in physical capital formation. The South did not falter in the financing of railroad construction. The region had 31 percent of the nation's railroad mileage, with per capita mileage only slightly below the national average. This network was financed predominantly by indigenous capital. While the track-to-area ratio was lower in the South than in the rest of the nation, the southern economy was endowed with an unusually favorable system of navigable streams and rivers. Nor were planters lagging behind the rest of the nation in the application of machinery to farming. Expenditures on farming implements and machinery per improved acre were 25 percent higher in the seven leading cotton states than they were for the nation as a whole.

To draw the conclusion that the South was industrially backward, merely because it compared unfavorably with the North, is to repeat the error referred to in the discussion of income levels. Table 6 helps to put the South's position as an industrial nation into perspective. In railroad mileage per capita she was virtually tied with the North, and both were far ahead of their nearest competitor. As a manufacturer of cotton textiles, the South ranked sixth in the world, well below Great Britain and the northern United States, but ahead of Germany, Austria-Hungary, and Russia. Of the available indexes of industrial production, the South ranked poorly only in the output of pig iron, falling behind all of the leading nations of Western Europe. The poor showing in iron production, was, of course, due to the South's relatively meager endowments of iron ore and coal. Her resources in these minerals came nowhere near those of the North, Great Britain, France, or Belgium. Thus the South's lag behind the North in industrialization is fully consistent with the proposition that during the antebellum era the South's comparative advantage was in agriculture rather than in manufacturing.

For the most part, it was natural resource endowments which gave the South a comparative advantage in agriculture. But the existence of slavery may also have played a role. To the extent that slavery permitted economies of large scale and raised agricultural productivity, it might have created an economic incentive to shift resources away from

Table 6

The Relative Level of Southern Industrialization in 1860 as Revealed by Three Partial Indexes

| | Southern Index Levels = 100 | | |
	INDEX OF RAILROAD MILEAGE PER CAPITA	INDEX OF COTTON TEXTILE PRODUCTION PER CAPITA	INDEX OF PIG IRON PRODUCTION PER CAPITA
South	100	100	100
North	108	401	637
Great Britain	43	1,055	2,728
France	16	136	425
Germany	21	87	231
Russia	1	26	60
Austria-Hungary	9	64	152
Italy	6	23	16
Netherlands	7	41	
Belgium	25	142	1,191
Denmark	5		
Sweden	9	92	779
Switzerland	28	270	
Spain	8	74	
Canada	68		
India	1	2	
Australia	21		

industry and into agriculture. But this is not a necessary consequence of the productivity gain. Similarly, while the gain in productivity might have raised southern per capita income, this too is not a necessary consequence of economies of scale. The resolution of these issues depends on the values of certain parameters of the demand and supply equations for cotton and other traded goods. The parameters are quite difficult to estimate. Preliminary work suggests that slavery both retarded industrialization and increased per capita income. However, it will probably require several years of additional work before the validity of these preliminary findings is known.

Epilogue.

Implications for Our Time

During the past decade we frequently presented papers to scholarly conferences or to faculty colloquia, both in the United States and abroad, on various aspects of our research into the economics of slavery. Sometimes, after the end of a discussion, one of our colleagues would come up to us and, with a nervous smile, ask, "What are you guys trying to do? Sell slavery?" We answered: "No. And even if we were, you wouldn't buy it. No one would buy it."

We have attacked the traditional interpretation of the economics of slavery not in order to resurrect a defunct system, but in order to correct the perversion of the history of blacks — in order to strike down the view that black Americans were without culture, without achievement, and without development for their first two hundred and fifty years on American soil. We have tried to show that this false portrait of black history was originally the consequence of a debate between critics and defenders of slavery, a debate which rested on the racist premise that blacks were biologically inferior to whites. Whether the history of the South was written by Northerners or Southerners, that premise was carried forward, by all but a few historians, throughout the post–Civil War period and down to the eve of World War II. The revulsion against racism which coincided with World War II led not to a rejection of the racist depiction of black history, but rather to the elimination of its most crass features. What emerged was a subtle refurbishing of the traditional interpretation, which left Negroes as a people who were still deprived of the opportunity for cultural, intellectual, social, and personal development for 250 years. Now, however, the explanation for this stunted development was not biological inferiority, but unfortunate sociological circumstances. Blacks were the pitiful victims of a system of slavery so repressive that it undermined their sense of family, their desire for achievement, their propensity for industry, their independence of judgment, and their capacity for self-reliance. In the place of a discredited biological justification for the inferiority of blacks, there was enthroned a respectable and acceptable sociological justification.

Some historians tried to avoid the worst implications of the new line of argument by asserting that although the cruelty and repression of the slave system were unbounded, blacks were stronger than the repression. But in the absence of evidence of massive resistance, the argument was hardly convincing. The most that proponents of this view were able to conjure up were a handful of abortive conspiracies and ineffectual attempts at "day-to-day resistance." Thus blacks were made to be failures even at resistance — sympathetic failures, but failures nevertheless. The image of black incompetence was unintentionally extended to still another dimension of life.

To what levels of achievement did the refurbished interpretation permit blacks to climb? While white America produced heroes of the struggle against tyranny who were honest, courageous, and industrious, the refurbished interpretation offered black rebels whose greatest achievements were such proficiency at stealing, shirking responsibilities, and feigning illness — and who were possessed of such sly capacity for lying — that they could trick their masters into believing that they were contented. And what of the Levens, who managed large plantations more successfully than "any white man," the Ahams, whose industry permitted them to accumulate large sums of capital, the slave-engineers who were so adept at their profession that their incomes exceeded those of their white overseers? In the refurbished version they, of course, are held to have been exceedingly rare, and in any case are depicted as "Uncle Toms" (how else could they have risen to such rank?).

One of the worst consequences of the traditional interpretation of slavery is that it has diverted attention from the attack on the material conditions of black life that took place during the decades following the end of the Civil War. By exaggerating the severity of slavery, all that has come after it has been made to appear as an improvement over previous conditions. The relatively low levels of wages of freed blacks, the relatively low-skill composition of the black labor force, the relatively poor condition of black health, the relative shortness of black life expectations — these and other conditions of the post–Civil War decades have been explained largely as the unfortunate inheritance of the era of slavery. While many have recognized that obstacles continued to be placed in the path of blacks struggling for self-improvement, it has been widely assumed that the primary factors in the slow pace of progress were the disabilities with which blacks emerged from slavery. Only time would overcome the lack of black skills and the unfortunate habits toward work and morality inculcated in blacks by the conditions of slavery. Whatever blame there was for the unsatisfactory conditions of blacks after the Civil War thus rested with a class which no longer existed (the master class) or, unfortunately, with blacks themselves.

During the last few years, the attention of cliometricians has begun to shift from the antebellum to the postbellum era. While the findings thus far are extremely tentative, the evidence that is beginning to accumulate suggests that the attack on the material conditions of the life of blacks after the Civil War was not only more ferocious, but, in certain respects, more cruel than that which preceded it. It appears that the life expectations of blacks declined by 10 percent between the last quarter century of the antebellum era and the last two decades of the nineteenth century. The diet of blacks deteriorated. Studies of the diet of black sharecroppers in the mid-1890s indicate that they were protein- and vitamin-starved. The health of blacks deteriorated. Sickness rates in the 1890s were 20 percent higher than on slave plantations. The skill composition of the black labor force deteriorated. Blacks were squeezed out of some crafts in which they had been heavily represented during the slave era and were prevented from entering the new crafts that arose with the changing technology of the last half of the nineteenth century and the first half of the twentieth. The gap between wage payments to blacks and whites in comparable occupations increased steadily from the immediate post–Civil War decades down to the eve of World War II. It was only with World War II that this trend reversed itself. And it is only during the past fifteen years that the reduction in the differential has accelerated to an extent that equality in wage payments for blacks and whites in comparable occupations seems once again in sight.

We do not claim that these findings are entirely new. Although largely forgotten, some of the same points were made in 1944 by the Swedish economist Gunnar Myrdal, whose detachment from the American scene may have contributed to the insightfulness of his analysis of the "American Dilemma."

[I]n certain respects the surviving caste system shows even more resistance to change than did slavery. The main economic significance of slavery was that the employer really owned his labor. Because of that he also had a vested interest in its most profitable utilization. This fundamental unity of interest between capital and labor — as labor *was* capital — constituted a main point in the pro-slavery theory.

It is true that the slaves were robbed of their freedom to move on their own initiative. But as factors of production, they were moved by the economic interest of their owners to their "most advantageous uses." Before Emancipation the Negroes took part in the westward movement of production and people. From this point of view the fight of the South to widen the realm of slavery in the United States prior to the Civil War was also a fight to bring Negro labor to those places where it could be put to most advantageous use. After Emancipation the freedmen could move individually in the regions where they were already settled. But they were, as a group, practically blocked from entering new rural territory in the Southwest. Only the cities in the South and the North left them an outlet for migration.

Before Emancipation it was in the interest of the slave owners to use Negro slaves wherever it was profitable in handicraft and manufacture. After Emancipation no such proprietary interest protected Negro laborers from the desire of white workers to squeeze them out of skilled employment. They were gradually driven out and pushed down into the "Negro jobs," a category which has been more and more narrowly defined.

There is no doubt that, compared with the contemporary caste system, slavery showed a superior capacity to effectuate economic adjustment, even if the slave owners and not the slaves reaped the profits. Even to many Negroes themselves slavery, again in certain limited respects, was a more advantageous economic arrangement than the precarious caste status into which they were thrown by Emancipation.

How could it have happened? How could pecuniary income, diet, health, skill acquisition, and other aspects of the material conditions of life have been worse for blacks during so many years after emancipation than it had been under slavery? That the proposition seems absurd is due partly, as we have tried to show in this book, to an exaggeration of the severity of slavery. But it is also due to an exaggeration of the extent of the moral reform sought by the antislavery crusaders. Few of the antislavery critics had equality of opportunity for the races as the goal of their crusade. Since they conceived of blacks as members of an inferior race, equality of opportunity had little meaning to them. Most expected that freed Negroes would have to be constrained in various ways if an "orderly" society was to be maintained. For as Olmsted said, it was not possible to "suppose that in one generation or two the effects of centuries of barbarism and slavery are to be extinguished."

What antislavery critics generally objected to was not the fact that slavery constrained the opportunities open to blacks, but the form which these constraints took. While physical force was unacceptable, legal restrictions were not. Thus many one-time crusaders against slavery sat idly by, or even collaborated in passing various laws which served to improve the economic position of whites at the expense of blacks. Licensure laws helped to squeeze blacks out of some crafts. Educational restrictions helped to exclude them from others. Meanwhile, taxation and fiscal policies were used to transfer income from blacks to whites, perhaps more effectively, certainly more elegantly, than had been possible under slavery.

Time on the cross did not come to an end for American blacks with the downfall of the peculiar institution. For they were held on the cross not just by the chains of slavery but also by the spikes of racism. It is one of the bitterest ironies of history that the antislavery critics who worked so hard to break these chains probably did as much as any other group, perhaps more, to fasten the spikes that have kept blacks in the agony of racial discrimination during their century of freedom. The spikes are fashioned of myths that turned diligent and efficient workers into lazy loafers and bunglers, that turned love of family into a disregard for it, that turned those who struggled for self-improvement in the only way they could into "Uncle Toms." Three hundred and fifty years on the cross are enough. It's time to reveal not only to blacks but to whites as well, that part of American history which has been kept from them — the record of black achievement under adversity.

Afterword 1989

Except for the correction of a few typographical errors and the addition of the sources of direct quotations, the text of this edition of *Time on the Cross* remains as it was originally published in 1974. We have resisted the temptation to revise the text for several reasons. First, *Without Consent or Contract*[1] presents more completely than we could possibly achieve through revisions of *Time on the Cross* what we have learned during the past sixteen years. Second, the main deficiencies of *Time on the Cross*, which was an early report on preliminary findings, are not errors of commission but of omission. We were not far off the mark on the main issues that we addressed but we concentrated on only a small part of the range of issues that ought to be covered by a history of American slavery. Indeed, the book was designed, not to present a new consensus on the slave economy, but to challenge what we perceived as the prevailing consensus, which we referred to as "the traditional interpretation." This approach led us to concentrate on certain key issues.

The fact that *Time on the Cross* was designed to challenge views that prevailed in the late 1960s and early 1970s is still another reason for resisting the temptation to revise it. The book is now part of intellectual history in the sense that many of the findings that astonished us and outraged some critics were subsequently confirmed and have become part of the current consensus on the operation of the U.S. slave system. Similarly, the

---

1. *Without Consent or Contract: The Rise and Fall of American Slavery* by Fogel (Norton, 1989); Fogel, Galantine, and Manning (1990); and Fogel and Engerman (1990), vol. I and II.

quantitative methods that we employed and that seemed so alien and threatening to the historical discipline are now accepted as a standard feature of historiographic training. From the perspective of 1989, the defensive and awkward way in which we dealt with key issues and championed cliometric methodology has a dated quality that cannot be eliminated merely by rephrasing some sentences here or there. That quality is inherent in the architecture of the book, and explains the aggressive tone in the prologue and in other chapters.

The public debate set off by the publication of *Time on the Cross* greatly accelerated the pace of research on the economics and demography of slavery. It was a debate in which there were no losers. The detailed scrutiny of our preliminary findings pointed up numerous gaps that required additional data or different analytical techniques, and also broadened the range of issues under investigation. Much of the debate was focused on the three questions that had been at the center of cliometric work on slavery before 1974 and that were also central topics in *Time on the Cross*: the profitability and economic viability of slavery, the rate of southern economic growth between 1840 and 1880 and the factors that influenced it, and the relative productivity of slave and free agriculture.[2] Not only was there a searching re-examination of the conceptual bases for many of the earlier computations, but many aspects of the operation of slave markets and of antebellum agriculture, of commerce, and of manufacturing were more deeply probed than ever before. New bodies of relevant data were uncovered which made it possible to estimate variables and parameters bearing on aspects of the slave economy that previously had to be left to conjecture. Although the new work has not dramat-

---

2. Cliometric work on profitability was initiated by Conrad and Meyer (1958). Work on the issue of profitability prior to 1974 is summarized in Fogel and Engerman (1974), 2: 54–79. Estimation of the levels and relative rates of growth of northern and southern per capita income between 1840 and 1860 stems from the work on national income accounts by Easterlin (1960, 1961), Gallman (1966), and Engerman (1967). The early attempts to measure the relative efficiency of slave and free agriculture are described in Fogel and Engerman (1974), 2: 126–149.

ically revised the basic estimates of profitability, of the rate of southern economic growth, or of the relative productivity of slave agriculture that were reported in *Time on the Cross*, it has produced a far more detailed and textured picture, not only of the nature of the slave economy and of the forces that influenced its development, but also of the free economy.[3]

Consider, for example, the way in which the debate over the length of the work year of free farmers and slaves served to extend knowledge about the operation of both labor systems during the antebellum era. The issue arose when initial efforts to compare the productivity of free and slave farms revealed that the latter were more efficient. This unexpected result raised questions about the way in which the labor input had been measured, particularly about the decision to measure the labor input in man-years rather than in man-hours. The plausibility of the criticism touched off an extensive search for data bearing on the length of the northern and southern work years, and on labor schedules generally, in order to determine if the hypothesized differences in annual work hours could account for the differences in productivity.

The results of the effort to test the hypothesis about work schedules were surprising and highly informative. As it turned out, free northern farmers worked about ten percent more hours than southern slaves, and not fewer hours as had been hypothesized. Specialization in livestock and dairying not only led to longer workdays than crop production but also increased the number of hours worked on Sundays. The principal reason for the work year's being longer in the North than on slave plantations was that the North specialized in livestock and dairying, but on the large slave plantations hardly 5 percent of output originated in these activities. The new data revealed other unsuspected features of the slave mode of production, such as the highly regular pattern of days worked per week (and hours worked

---

3. Work on these issues since 1974 is described in Fogel (1989), ch. 3 and 4; Fogel, Galantine, and Manning (1990), parts III and IV; Fogel and Engerman (1990), I: parts I–III.

per day) over the seasons. It soon became evident that the greater intensity of work per hour, rather than more hours of labor per day or more days of labor per year, was the prinicpal form of the exploitation of slave labor. The gang-system played a role comparable to the factory system or, at the later date, the assembly line, in regulating the pace of labor. It was, in other words, an early device for labor speed-up.[4]

The implications of the new discoveries about work schedules have not yet run their full course. Current research touched off by these discoveries, and by concomitant discoveries about manufacturing, is leading to wide-ranging reconsideration of the initial phases of the Industrial Revolution. New hypotheses are being formulated that emphasize, not mechanization and labor saving, but the more efficient exploitation of the existing labor supply as the principal result of the factory system. More particularly, it is argued that factory technology was designed to make use of forms of labor, particularly the labor of women and children, that could not be as effectively employed as the labor of adult males in certain agricultural contexts. According to this hypothesis, the relative effectiveness of women and children in the production of cotton inhibited the growth of the factory system, while the inability of grain farming to effectively exploit such labor spurred the factory system. These hypotheses have led to a deeper search for the information locked away in previously examined censuses and factory reports and to searches for new bodies of data capable of revealing the sources of increased productivity in the early factories, and for data bearing on the relationship between factory growth and the relative productivity of women and children in agriculture.[5]

The most dramatic new cliometric findings since 1974 have to do with the health and demography of slave populations, which were still infant subjects when we dealt with them in *Time on*

---

4. For further information on the issues in the two preceding paragraphs see papers #10, #11, and #12 in Fogel and Engerman (1990), vol. I.

5. See Goldin and Sokoloff (1982, 1984); Sokoloff (1984, 1986); Fogel (1989), 107–113, and the sources cited in the notes to these pages.

the Cross. No other fields of slavery research have grown more explosively than these have, and the sophistication of the investigators in demography, nutrition, and general biomedical knowledge has grown apace. The analysis of immense bodies of demographic and anthropometric data for slave populations in the United States, the British West Indies, Cuba, Brazil, and various ethnic groups in Africa became feasible as the cost of data processing declined. These developments have produced better explanations of both the high fertility rates of U.S. slaves and the differences between their fertility and mortality rates and those of the slave populations in the Caribbean and South America.[6]

The breakthrough on health and demographic issues was spawned largely by the attempt to test the abolitionist charges that slaves were severely malnourished. In *Time on the Cross* we sought to address this issue by making use of data in the Parker-Gallman sample of the manuscript schedules of the U.S. census for 1860 to estimate nutrients available for consumption by slaves on large plantations. There were, however, numerous questions raised about our data source and estimation procedures, as well as about the inferences that could be drawn from our findings.[7]

That debate helped to stimulate an intense search for other types of data bearing on the slave diet. Stephen C. Crawford turned to the ex-slave narratives and found information that enabled him to characterize the diffusion of various foods among slaves as well as the association between the variety of the diet and such matters as plantation size and the opportunity of slaves to supplement the master's ration.[8] Archaeologists and medical anthropologists investigated the fauna in excavations of the slave quarters of twenty plantations in five states.[9] Economic and social historians searched plantation records, legal records, prison

---

6. See Fogel (1989), ch. 5 and the sources cited there.

7. See, for example, Sutch (1975); Kiple and King (1981). For a response to these criticisms see Fogel (1989), 132–138; and Fogel, Galantine, and Manning (1990), entries #43–#45.

8. See Crawford (1980); Fogel, Galantine, and Manning (1990), entries #43, #51; Fogel (1989), 123–138, 161, 195–196.

9. Gibbs et al. (1980); Reitz, Gibbs, and Rathbun (1985).

records, and similar documents for information either on actual consumption or on rations specified in orders to overseers or in public decrees.[10]

Information on diet only reveals nutrient intake (gross nutrition) and by itself still leaves open the issue of whether a given diet was adequate to sustain rapid physical development and good health in the face of heavy claims on that diet. Consequently, some investigators turned to height and body mass indexes, which are measures of net nutrition, to assess the nutritional status of slaves.[11] Others searched journals for reports of nutritional diseases among slaves and analyzed frequency distributions of causes of death for clues about the prevalence of nutritional deficiency diseases.[12]

The new data not only made it possible to resolve points that were at issue in 1974–1976, but have revealed aspects of slave nutritional status and health that were not even contemplated during these debates. It now appears that children rather than adults were the principal victims of malnutrition. Despite the fact that they were worked quite hard, the relatively good health of adolescent and adult U.S. slaves is reflected in their mature stature, their high body mass indexes, and their life expectancies.[13] In order to sustain their heavy levels of work, adult slaves were relatively well fed, clothed, and housed. Much of the new story turns on the overwork of pregnant women, which diverted nutrients from the development of the fetus. As a consequence slave mothers produced very small babies, which, even

10. Van den Boogaart and Emmer (1977); Savitt (1978); Higman (1984); Sheridan (1985).

11. A body mass index gives the ratio of weight (usually measured in kilograms) to height (usually measured in meters squared). See the papers by Trussell, Steckel and Margo in Fogel and Engerman (1990), 2: parts IV and V; Fraginals (1977); Higman (1979 and 1984); Fogel et al. (1978); Friedman (1980 and 1982); Margo and Steckel (1982); Eltis (1982); Fogel, Galantine, and Manning (1990), entry #47.

12. Kiple and King (1981); Kiple (1984).

13. Fogel, Galantine, and Manning (1990), entries #41 and #47; Fogel (1989), 138–142; Fogel and Engerman (1990), 2: #23; Fogel et al. (1983); Fogel (1987).

if not neurologically impaired, were vulnerable to infections that sturdier infants could have survived. Infant death rates were exceedingly high, running about 30 percent, and, partly because of poor weaning diets, about 20 percent of the survivors died between ages one and five.[14]

We are pleased that the various trains of new research stimulated by *Time on the Cross* have advanced knowledge. We also take comfort in the fact that the new research has more often amplified or extended our preliminary findings than it has contradicted them. However, our pride in the achievements of the book does not prevent us from recognizing its deficiencies.

On rereading the book in 1989 we were struck by a certain insularity that characterized the treatment of economic issues in *Time on the Cross*. Economic issues are almost invariably detached from their political context. This feature of the book was not an accident. It was a general characteristic of cliometric work on the economics of slavery down to the end of the 1970s. Indeed, during the 1960s and 1970s we assumed that such compartmentalization was a precondition for a "scientific" treatment of the economic and demographic issues—a necessary precaution for the protection of our work from contamination by the ideological disputes of political historians. Consequently, we formulated our research agenda by focusing on the summaries of economic doctrines such as those set forth in U.B. Phillips (1918, ch. 18), Lewis C. Gray (1933, ch. 20), Kenneth M. Stampp (1956, ch. 9), and Eugene D. Genovese (1965).

That decision led us to misunderstand the origins and nature of the economic issues. Summaries of doctrine tended to juxtapose the opinions of such outstanding figures as Montesquieu, Hume, Franklin, Smith, Turgot, Say, Tocqueville, and Mill. We thought that their views were merely the highlights of a widespread, intense joining of issues when in fact they were isolated footnotes to other points or obiter dicta that were separated from

---

14. See Fogel, Galantine, and Manning (1990), entries #41, #42, #49; Fogel (1989), 142–147; Fogel and Engerman (1990), 2: #18, #23; Steckel (1979; 1986a, and 1986b).

one another by decades of inattention. We now know that the prevailing opinion from the seventeenth through the mid-nineteenth century was that the slave system was a highly successful and highly profitable one that had displaced free labor in its areas of hegemony. That assumption was so deeply ingrained for two and a half centuries that it was rarely challenged and it is these rare challenges that were given exaggerated attention in the doctrinal histories.[15]

Our misunderstanding of the origin of the economic issues became clear to us only after we immersed ourselves in the history of the ideological and political struggles against slavery. In the United States, as it had been in Great Britain, the antislavery struggle was conducted primarily on moral and humanitarian grounds from pre-Revolutionary times until the mid-1850s.[16] Indeed, such abolitionist leaders as William Lloyd Garrison adamantly resisted all proposals to shift the basis of their assault from religious to economic grounds, proposals that emanated from the more worldly leaders of the movement. Nevertheless, the principal basis of the antislavery appeal did suddenly shift from "Christian duty" to "the pocketbook."[17] The shift took place between 1854 and 1856 and the political success was immediate and spectacular. The new approach transformed the antislavery movement from a minor political factor into a powerful political force that could control the national agenda. This relatively brief and successful struggle for power tossed up a complicated set of economic issues that since the 1850s have been at or near the center of debate on the nature of the slave system and the cause of its downfall.[18]

Would the research on economic issues have proceeded more smoothly if the political context of the economic issues had been better understood from the outset? We doubt it. Indeed, it is likely

---

15. Davis (1984), part I: Drescher (1977 and 1986); Fogel, Galantine, and Manning (1990), entries #2, #14–#22; Fogel (1989), 61–72, 81–98.

16. See Drescher (1977 and 1986); Fogel (1989), ch. 7–10 and the Afterword.

17. The quotations are from Thomas (1963), 326.

18. See Fogel (1989), ch. 10.

that deeper understanding of the politics of the antislavery struggle at the outset of our research, ironic as it may appear, would have inhibited the investigation of key aspects of the economics of slavery. In that case very important but unexpected aspects of the operation of the slave economy, which resulted from the pursuit of the concocted issues, might still be undisclosed.[19] We do not mean to argue that ignorance of politics was a virtue, but only to comment on the actual history of the accumulation of knowledge about the slave economy during the past thirty years. Eventually the discoveries about the workings of the slave economy forced us to come to grips with a wide range of political issues. It was only after the integration of both fields of knowledge was achieved that the economic issues could be understood in their proper context. Although the technical findings on the operation of the slave economy reported in *Time on the Cross* have stood up reasonably well, the failure to set them in an appropriate political context gives them a certain disembodied character.

Perhaps the most serious deficiency in *Time on the Cross* is its failure to provide a new moral indictment of slavery that is consistent with the new empirical knowledge on the actual operation of the slave system, as we understood it in 1973. We do not, however, agree with some critics who have charged that the book is "amoral." From the day that we began work on the book we realized that our new findings on the operation of the slave economy raised urgent moral issues and we grappled with these issues continuously. Our comments on moral questions are scattered throughout both volumes of *Time on the Cross*. On rereading these passages we believe that although some of our points were salient, they fell short of an adequate reformulation of the moral problem of slavery.

The principal contribution of *Time on the Cross* to the reformulation of the moral problem was its identification of the "myth of black incompetence"; of the way that exaggerations of the mate-

---

19. Fogel (1989), ch. 3–4 and pp. 116–123, 276–280, 326–329, 343–354; Fogel, Galantine, and Manning (1990), entries #2, #15, #23, #32, #50, #71.

rial severity of slavery promoted the view that Afro-Americans were without culture, without achievement, and without development during their first 250 years on American soil; and of the way that exaggerations of the severity of slavery had been turned from an antislavery weapon into apologetics for the continued discrimination and injustices against blacks in our own time.

Yet important as these points are, they do not come to grips with some of the most morally disturbing aspects of the new findings about the operation of the slave economy, particularly the ominous paradox between a system that is horribly retrogressive in its social, political, and ideological aspects, yet highly profitable and quite advanced by the standards of the time in its technology and economic organization. We also failed to deal with moral issues arising out of the discovery that slaves were effective workers who had developed a much stronger family life, a more varied set of occupational skills, and a richer, more distinct culture than convention dictated. As a result we seemed to be diminishing the moral horror of slavery and providing (no matter how innocent the intention) an apologia for centuries of exploitation. To some readers we were also robbing blacks of a history of resistance to slavery and casting them instead in the role of collaborators in their own oppression.

We have addressed these and many additional moral issues at length in *Without Consent or Contract*.[20] We have refrained from summarizing these points here, since such important and complex issues cannot be dealt with adequately in summary. But one additional observation seems appropriate. We do not believe that we could have dealt adequately with the full range of moral issues in 1973 because we had not yet immersed ourselves in the history of the religious movements that spawned the antislavery ethic or in the history of the political struggle against slavery, which transformed the religious appeal against slavery into a politically popular secular appeal. Understanding the economics and demography of slavery, or even slave culture, did not by itself provide

---

20. Fogel (1989), esp. the Afterword; Fogel, Galantine, and Manning (1990), entries #54, #70–#74.

an adequate basis for coming to grips with the moral problem of slavery. We had to, as Perry Miller put it in another context, overcome our "obtuse secularism" and understand the role of religious inspiration in the shaping of the antislavery ethic.[21]

---

21. The quotation is from Essig (1982), xii.

Acknowledgments

We first became interested in the challenging problems connected with the economic analysis of the slave system while we were graduate students at the Johns Hopkins University. The appearance of the Conrad and Meyer article in 1958 touched off a debate in our department that raged for weeks and embraced most of the graduate student body and faculty of economics. One product of this stimulating debate was Yasukichi Yasuba's penetrating paper which, though published in 1961, was actually written in 1959. Another was our own deep and persistent interest in various analytical and empirical issues posed by the operation of the slave economy — an interest that was continually refueled through both research and teaching.

We did not return to intensive consideration of these issues, however, until 1965 when we began work on the essay which eventually appeared in *The Reinterpretation of American Economic History*. Since that time our investigation of the economics of slavery has evolved into a nearly all-consuming preoccupation.

Over the past decade and a half we have accumulated many obligations, some directly related to this book, some related to the various research projects on which we have drawn in writing the book, some of a quite general nature but which nonetheless significantly affected our approach to one or another problem considered in this book. The list that follows, although long, may well be incomplete; certain contributions to our work on the economics of slavery have probably eluded our memories.

It should not be assumed that those whose assistance we acknowledge necessarily agree with our findings. Some have been highly critical of the main thrust of our research — even passionately so. Others, enthusiastic about both our findings and methods, encouraged us to take up problems that we had not previously entertained. We have benefited from both types of responses.

Our oldest obligations are to the late Alfred H. Conrad and John R. Meyer and to our teachers and fellow students at Johns Hopkins, especially G. Heberton Evans, Jr., James K. Kindahl, Fritz Machlup, Edwin S. Mills, and Yasukichi Yasuba. Over the years we have learned much from discussions and debates with Eugene Genovese and Herbert Gutman, who constantly urged us to extend our research beyond narrowly defined economic issues.

We are most deeply indebted to those cliometricians who have been engaged in the arduous tasks of collecting, processing, and analyzing the data on which this book rests. The main data collection projects and their directors are listed in table B. 1 of the supplementary volume. Others who have generously made their unpublished data and findings available to us include William Calderhead, Robert Evans, Jr., Barry W. Higman, Abigail Curlee Holbrook, and Alice Hanson Jones. Most of these research projects, including our own on the relative efficiency of free and slave agriculture, were financed in whole or in part by the National Science Foundation.

A number of scholars have provided us with detailed comments on the various drafts of the manuscript, frequently causing us to revise our approaches on particular issues, to investigate matters that we had slighted, and to search for the resolution of inconsistencies in our evidence or arguments. Among these were Robert McC. Adams, Carl Degler, Albert Fishlow, Richard Freeman, Robert E. Gallman, Louis Gottschalk, Zvi Griliches, Ronald W. Jones, Stanley N. Katz, Donald N. McCloskey, Lionel W. McKenzie, Arthur Mann, Richard N. Rosett, Morton Rothstein, T. W. Schultz, Richard B. Sheridan, Harold Woodman, C. Vann Woodward, and Gavin Wright.

We wish particularly to acknowledge our debt to Kenneth M. Stampp, who provided us with forty-one single-spaced pages of commentary. His sharp and detailed criticism brought to our attention errors and ambiguities in our preliminary drafts, including insufficiently qualified statements, and instances of inadequate delineation between conjectures and reasonable well-confirmed findings. By bringing these matters to our attention he helped to strengthen our arguments, even where they clashed with his own work. In so doing, he set a standard of scholarship that we will strive to emulate when it is our turn to face the criticisms of our colleagues.

Among others who commented on all or part of the manuscript, pointed out errors, helped to clarify theoretical issues, brought particular articles or bodies of evidence to our attention, suggested improvements in exposition, assisted us in the establishment of research groups, or advised us on the canvassing of archives are: Hugh G. J. Aitken, Fred Bateman, Gary Becker, Lee Benson, Woodrow Borah, N. G. Butlin, Rondo Cameron, Loftus Carson, Elisabeth Case, Richard Caves, John Coatsworth, Bernard S. Cohn, Philip D. Curtin, Paul A. David, David B. Davis, Charles B. Dew, David Donald, Douglas F. Dowd, Seymour Drescher, Richard Easterlin, Clement Eaton, Stanley Elkins, Lloyd Fallers, Margaret Fallers, Enid M. Fogel, Charlotte Fogel, Ephim G. Fogel, Michael P. Fogel, Steven D. Fogel, James D. Foust, John Hope

Franklin, Joe B. Frantz, Herman Freudenberger, James Friedman, Eli Ginzberg, Richard Graham, Diane Griliches, H. J. Habakkuk, Neil Harris, R. M. Hartwell, D. Gale Johnson, Harry G. Johnson, Catherine Jones, Mary Karasch, Herbert Klein, Peter Laslett, Ronald Lee, Nathaniel H. Leff, H. Gregg Lewis, Richard C. Lewontin, Henry Manne, Edward Meeker, Sidney Mintz, Michael Mussa, Manning Nash, Marc Nerlove, Douglass C. North, Donald O'Hara, Walter Oi, William N. Parker, Douglas Price, Jacob Price, John Price, Laura Randall, Albert Rees, George Rieg, Jr., William Riker, Willie Lee Rose, Sherwin Rosen, Madelon Rosett, Henry Rosovsky, Jerome Rudolph, Barbara Solow, the late Robert S. Starobin, Stanley J. Stein, George Stigler, Richard Sutch, Dale E. Swan, Richard Sylla, Peter Temin, Stephan Thernstrom, Virginia Thurner, Charles Tilly, Thomas J. Weiss, John White, Harold Williamson, Joel Williamson, Larry Wimmer, E. A. Wrigley, Lionel Young, Joseph R. Zecher, Wilbur Zelinsky, and Joseph Zitomersky.

We have learned much from protracted debates with our students, during which we frequently found our roles reversed. Among those who taught us most are Claudia D. Goldin, David Haddock, Thomas Huertas, Phillip LeVeen, Jorge Marquez-Ruarte, Pedro de Mello, Jacob Metzer, Clayne Pope, Joe D. Reid, Jr., Ralph Shlomowitz, and Richard Steckel.

No one in our research group has been more indispensable than Marilyn Gore Coopersmith. In addition to serving as the administrative assistant for our research project on the relative efficiency of slavery, she was responsible for establishing our data collection team at the National Archives and also made a preliminary survey of the data resources at the Library of Congress and at several archives in Virginia. On many occasions she supplied the drive and determination that permitted us to achieve objectives that seemed beyond reach.

Keith Allred and Edwin Andrus directed the collection of

data at the Genealogical Society in Salt Lake City. David King was in charge of a data collection team in New Orleans and Nancy Jo Lestina played the same role at the National Archives. John Russel Daniel was responsible for the retrieval of data deposited at the State Department of Archives and History in Raleigh. Susan Groth assisted in bibliographic research. Forrest Nelson ably programmed most of our main computations. Others who assisted in the programming are Marjorie Crump, Chak Karuturi and John Olson. Most of the keypunching was efficiently performed by Stephania Zalitacz. Other research assistants include Allan Boles, Gary Eriksen, Tapan Mitra, and Allen Sanderson.

Most of the preliminary drafts and virtually the entire final draft of the manuscript was typed by Marjorie Adams. Martha Colburn also typed substantial portions of various drafts. Additional secretarial assistance was provided by Carol Bennett, Janet Chapin, and Janet Wood at the University of Rochester and by members of the secretarial pool of the Social Science Division at the University of Chicago.

Our search for data was facilitated by the assistance of Meyer Fishbein and William Lind of the National Archives, Frederick D. Nichols of the University of Virginia Library, John M. Jennings of the Virginia Historical Society, Randolph W. Church of the Virginia State Library, Paul Hoffman and George Stevenson of the North Carolina State Department of Archives and History, the late Virginia Gray of Perkins Library at Duke University, Charles S. Lee of the South Carolina Department of Archives and History, David E. Estes of the Woodruff Library of Emory University, Milo B. Howard, Jr. of the Alabama Department of Archives and History, L. M. Hawes and Charles Johnson of the Georgia Historical Society, W. Stanley Hoole of the University of Alabama Library, Chester Kielman of the University of Texas Archives, and members of the staffs of the Southern Historical Collection at the University of North

Carolina, the Georgia Department of Archives and History, the South Carolina Historical Society, the South Caroliniana Library of the University of South Carolina, the Mississippi Department of Archives and History, and the Department of Archives at Louisiana State University.

The completion of this volume was expedited by a research fellowship from the Ford Foundation and by research grants from the University of Chicago and the University of Rochester.

We are grateful to the following publishers and author for granting their permission to quote or to reproduce diagrams and tables (the numbers in parentheses refer to the pages in *Time on the Cross* or the companion volume, *Evidence and Methods: A Supplement*, on which the quotations, diagrams, or tables appear): American Political Science Association (I, 223–224), Hawthorn Books, Inc. (II, 173–174), Carnegie Institution of Washington (I, 45; II, 144, 146–148), Claudia Goldin (II, 152–155), Harper and Row, Publishers, Inc. (I, 261–262), United States Department of Agriculture (II, 92–93), and University of Chicago Press (II, 205–206, 211–212).

Sources of Direct Quotations

In the citations below, the first part of the note number indicates the page on which a direct quote appears in *Time on the Cross* and the second indicates the paragraph. If a paragraph is split onto two pages, the note for all quotes in the paragraph will attach to the page on which the paragraph ends.

Prepared by Ralph Shlomowitz and Martha Hoffman.

30.1 Davis (1966) 70.   30.2 Davis (1966) 92, 86, 165.   30.3 Davis (1966) 107.

31.1 Davis (1966) 106.   31.2 Davis (1966) 119, 118, 119.

48.1 Cairnes (1969) 124–127.

51.1 Phillips (1918) 369; Bancroft (1959) 208.

60.3 Phillips (1918) 150.

61.3 Phillips (1905) 266.   61.4 Phillips (1905) 271.

62.3 Ramsdell (1929) 169.

64.4 Genovese (1965) 19, 28.

65.2 Engerman et al. (1972) 34; Genovese (1965) 35.

66.1 Gray (1933) 1:469, 473.   66.2 Stampp (1956) 417, 245–246, 251.   66.3 Bancroft (1959) 68, 79–80.

67.1 Bancroft (1959) 79–80.   67.3 Conrad and Meyer (1964) 98.

68.1 Conrad and Meyer (1964) 106.

77.2 Taylor (1963) 81.

78.2 Conrad and Meyer (1964) 121.

80.1 Sutch (1974) 176.

84.4 Phillips (1918) 269.

86.1 Scarborough (1966) 75, 77.   86.3 Phillips (1918) 150.

90.1 Ramsdell (1929) 171.

98.2 Wade (1964), 3.

99.1 Wade (1964), 3.

103.1 Engerman et al. (1972) 35.

107.1 *Webster's Third New International Dictionary.*
109.1 Conrad, Dowd et al. (1967), 539; Jones (1965) 171–172; Stampp
     (1956) 340, 345, 346.   109.2 Elkins (1959) 82.
111.1 Sellers (1950) 55; Phillips (1910) 1:127.
119.1 *DeBow's Review* (1856) 376; Scarborough (1966) 71; Phillips
     (1910) 1:119.   119.2 Sydnor (1933) 48; Phillips (1918) 263;
     Scarborough (1966) 69.
121.1 Postell (1951) 8.
122.1 Sellers (1950) 55.   122.2 Stampp (1956) 293; Davis (1939) 79.
     122.3 Scarborough (1966) 70; Postell (1951) 111.
133.3 Jones (1965) 177.
134.3 Scarborough (1966) 77.
136.3 Kemble (1961) 95.
139.1 Rawick (1972) 5:18.
141.2 Stampp (1956) 343–344.
143.1 Rawick (1972) 17:108.   143.2 Rawick (1972) 17:161.
144.1 Kemble (1961) 95.
146.1 *Matthew's Bible.*   146.2 Scarborough (1966) 93.
147.2 Davis (1943) 41.
149.2 Seller (1950) 59.
158.1 Zilversmit (1967) 56; Davis (1966) 291; Zilversmit (1967) 73.
160.1 Greeley (1848) 205, 224, 205, 204, 224, 204.
162.1 Helper (1968) 27, 28.
163.1 Helper (1968) 35.   163.2 Helper (1968) 111, 116; Bailey (1965)
     42.
167.2 Helper (1968) 34.   167.3 Helper (1968) 81, 276.
170.1 Olmsted (1953) xliii.
171.1 Olmsted (1953) 477.
172.1 Olmsted (1953) 16, 17.   172.2 Olmsted (1953) 104–105, 98.
     172.3 Olmsted (1953) 104.
173.1 Olmsted (1953) 503.   173.2 Olmsted (1953) 508–509.
174.1 Olmsted (1953) 208, 209, 210.
176.1 Olmsted (1953) 15, 16.
179.1 Helper (1968) 8; Bailey (1965) 135.   179.2 Olmsted (1953) 82;
     (1960) 9.
180.1 Olmsted (1953) 467–468.   180.2 Olmsted (1953) 200.
183.1 Cairnes (1969) 44, 339, 340, 42, 46–47.   183.2 Cairnes (1969)
     81, 82, 95, 147.
184.1 Cairnes (1969) 55–56.   184.3 Cairnes (1969) 43–44.
185.2 Cairnes (1969) 53.   185.3 Cairnes (1969) 124–125.
186.2 Cairnes (1969) 165, 169.
187.1 Cairnes (1969) 162–163.

188.1 Cairnes (1969) 65, 70, 71–72, 70.   188.2 Cairnes (1969) 73, 142.
189.2 Cairnes (1969) 134.
196.2 Olmsted (1953) 104.
200.2 Greeley (1848) 204; Russel (1938) 49.
204.1 Olmsted (1953) 87.
205.1 Olmsted (1953) 87, 106; (1856) 84.
206.1 Olmsted (1953), 452,
207.2 Olmsted (1953) 449.
209.1 Genovese (1974); Olmsted (1953) 452.
213.1 Cairnes (1969) 46, 44, 46.
213.3–214.1 Olmsted (1953) 193-194.
215.1 *Southern Agriculturalist* (1830) 238; Phillips (1910) 1:124.
216.3 Gossett (1963) 63, 48.
217.2 McKitrick (1963) 123; Dew (1968) 422.
218.2 Olmsted (1953) 250, 196, 28.
219.3 Olmsted (1953) 91.
220.1 Olmsted (1953) 43.
221.2 Olmsted (1956) 10.   221.3 Olmsted (1956) 11.
222.1 Olmsted (1956) 5, 6, 7, 5, 11.
223.3–224.2 DuBois (1918) 722–723.
225.1 Hofstadter (1944) 123, 122, 124.
226.1 Hofstadter (1944) 121; Olmsted (1953) 14; Phillips (1905) 271.
227.1 Rhodes (1893) 307, 309, 318, 332, 335, 370.
228.2–3 Stampp (1956) 397, 399, 400, 399.
229.1 Stampp (1956) 399, 400.   229.3 Phillips (1918) 401.
230.1 Stampp (1956) 185, 148.   230.2 Elkins (1959) 82.
231.1 Stampp (1956) 108–109.
234.3 Olmsted (1860) 352.
240.1 Nevins (1947) 442.
240.2–241.1 *Plantation and farm instruction, etc.* (1852) 4–5.
241.2–4 Olmsted (1953) 255, 120, 119, 109, 188, 255–256.
244.1 Farnam (1938) 220.
246.2 Olmsted (1953) 494.   246.3 *Congressional Globe* (1858) 70.
247.3 Helper (1968) 25, 34.
252.2 Woodman (1972) 339.
261.2–262.1 Myrdal (1944) 222.
263.1 Olmsted (1860) 9.

References

Bailey, Hugh C. 1965. *Hinton Rowan Helper: Abolitionist-Racist*. University, AL: University of Alabama Press.

Bancroft, Frederic. 1959. *Slave Trading in the Old South*. Introduction by Allan Nevins. New York: Frederick Ungar.

Cairnes, J.E. 1969. *The Slave Power: Its Character, Career, and Probable Designs: Being an Attempt to Explain the Real Issues Involved in the American Contest*. Introduction by Harold D. Woodman. New York: Harper & Row.

Congressional Globe. 1858. 35th Congress, First Session, appendix.

Conrad, Alfred H. and Meyer, John R. 1958. The Economics of Slavery in the Antebellum South. *Journal of Political Economy* 66:95–130. Reprinted in their book, *The Economics of Slavery and Other Studies in Econometric History*. Chicago: Aldine, 1964, pp. 43–92.

Conrad, Alfred H. et al. 1967. Slavery as an Obstacle to Economic Growth in the United States: A Panel Discussion. *Journal of Economic History* 27:518–560.

Crawford, Stephen C. 1980. Quantified Memory: A Study of the WPA and Fisk University Slave Narrative Collections. Ph.D. dissertation, University of Chicago.

Davis, Charles S. 1939. *The Cotton Kingdom in Alabama*. Montgomery: Alabama State Department of Archives and History.

Davis, David Brion. 1966. *The Problem of Slavery in Western Culture*. Ithaca: Cornell University Press.

———. 1984. *Slavery and Human Progress*. New York: Oxford University Press.

Davis, Edwin Adams ed., 1943. *Plantation Life in the Florida Parishes of Louisiana 1836–1844, as Reflected in the Diary of Bennet H. Barrow*. New York: Columbia University Press.

De Bow's Review XXII.

Dew, Thomas R. 1968. *The Pro-Slavery Argument*. New York: Negro Universities Press.

Drescher, Seymour. 1977. *Econocide: British Slavery in the Era of Abolition*. Pittsburgh: University of Pittsburgh Press.

———. 1986. *Capitalism and Antislavery*. London: The Macmillan Press.

Du Bois, W.E. Burghardt. 1918. Review of *American Negro Slavery* by Ulrich Bonnell Phillips. *American Political Science Review* 12:922–26.

Easterlin, Richard A. 1960. Interregional Differences in Per Capita Income, Population, and Total Income, 1840–1950. In *Trends in the American Economy in the Nineteenth Century*. Conference on Research in Income and Wealth, vol. 24. Princeton: Princeton University Press (for NBER).

———. 1961. Regional Income Trends, 1840–1950. In *American Economic History*, ed. Seymour Harris. New York: McGraw-Hill.

Elkins, Stanley M. 1959. *Slavery: A Problem in American Institutional and Intellectual Life*. Chicago: University of Chicago Press.

Eltis, David. 1982. Nutritional Trends in Africa and the Americas: Heights of Africans, 1819–1839. *Journal of Interdisciplinary History* 12:453–475.

Engerman, Stanley L. 1967. The Effects of Slavery upon the Southern Economy. *Explorations in Entrepreneurial History* 4:71–79.

Engerman, Stanley L. et al. 1972. New Directions in Black History: A Forum Symposium on American Negro Slavery. *Forum*. University of Rochester, 1:22–41.

Essig, James D. 1982. *The Bonds of Wickedness: American Evangelicals against Slavery, 1770–1808*. Philadelphia: Temple University Press.

Farnam, Henry W. 1938. *Chapters in the History of Social Legislation in the United States to 1860*. Washington, D.C.: Carnegie Institution, 1938.

Fogel, Robert W. 1987. Biomedical Approaches to the Estimation and Interpretation of Secular Trends in Equity, Morbidity, Mortality, and Labor Productivity in Europe, 1750–1980. Typescript.

———. 1989. *Without Consent or Contract: The Rise and Fall of American Slavery*. New York: W. W. Norton.

Fogel, Robert W. and Stanley L. Engerman. 1974. *Time on the Cross: Evidence and Methods*. Boston: Little, Brown.

———, eds. 1990. *Without Consent or Contract: The Rise and Fall of American Slavery—Technical Papers*. Vol. I, *Markets and Production*. Vol. II, *The Conditions of Slave Life and the Transition to Freedom*. New York: W.W. Norton.

Fogel, Robert W., Stanley L. Engerman, Roderick Floud, Gerald Friedman, Robert A. Margo, Kenneth Sokoloff, Richard H. Steckel, James Trussell, Georgia Villaflor, and Kenneth W. Wachter. 1983. Secular Changes in American and British Stature and Nutrition. *Journal of Interdisciplinary History* 14:445–481.

Fogel, Robert W., Stanley L. Engerman, James Trussell, Roderick Floud, Clayne L. Pope, and Larry T. Wimmer. 1978. The Economics of Mortality in North America, 1650–1910: A Description of a Research Project. *Historical Methods* 11:75–109.

Fogel, Robert W., Ralph A. Galantine, and Richard L. Manning, eds. 1990. *Without Consent or Contract: The Rise and Fall of American Slavery—Evidence and Methods.* New York: W. W. Norton.

Fraginals, Manuel M. 1977. Africa and Cuba: A Quantitative Analysis of the African Population in the Island of Cuba. *Annals of the New York Academy of Science* 292:187–201.

Friedman, Gerald C. 1980. The demography of Trinidad slavery. Photocopy, Workshop in Economic History, Harvard University.

———. 1982. The Heights of Slaves in Trinidad. *Social Science History* 6:482–515.

Gallman, Robert E. 1966. Gross National Product in the United States. In *Output, employment and productivity in the United States after 1800.* Conference on Income and Wealth, vol. 30. New York: Columbia University Press.

Genovese, Eugene D. 1965. *The Political Economy of Slavery: Studies in the Economy & Society of the Slave South.* New York: Pantheon.

———. 1974. *Roll, Jordan, Roll: The World the Slaves Made.* New York: Pantheon.

Gibbs, Tyson, Kathleen Cargill, Leslie Sue Lieberman, and Elizabeth Reitz. 1980. Nutrition in a Slave Population: An Anthropological Examination. *Medical Anthropology* (Spring):175–262.

Goldin, Claudia and Kenneth Sokoloff. 1982. Women, Children, and Industrialization in the Early Republic: Evidence from the Manufacturing Censuses. *Journal of Economic History* 42:741–774.

———. 1984. The Relative Productivity Hypothesis of Industrialization: The American Case, 1820 to 1850. *Quarterly Journal of Economics* 49:461–487.

Gossett, Thomas F. 1963. *Race: The History of an Idea.* Dallas: Southern Methodist University Press.

Gray, Lewis Cecil. 1933. *History of Agriculture in the Southern United States to 1860.* 2 vols. Washington, D.C.: Carnegie Institution.

Greeley, Horace. 1848. *The Writings of Cassius Marcellus Clay: Including Speeches and Addresses.* New York: Harper & Brothers.

Helper, Hinton Rowan. 1968. *The Impending Crisis of the South: How to Meet It.* Edited by George M. Frederickson. Cambridge: Belknap Press.

Higman, Barry W. 1979. Growth in Afro-Caribbean Slave Populations. *American Journal of Physical Anthropology* 50:373–386.

———. 1984. *Slave Populations of the British Caribbean, 1807–1834.* Baltimore: Johns Hopkins Press.

Hofstadter, Richard. 1944. U.B. Phillips and the Plantation Legend. *Journal of Negro History* 29:109–124.

Jones, Bobby F. 1965. A Cultural Middle Passage: Slave Marriage and Family in the Ante-Bellum South. Unpublished Ph.D. dissertation, University of North Carolina.

Kemble, Frances Anne. 1961. *Journal of a Residence on a Georgian Plantation 1838–1839*. Edited, with an introduction, by John A. Scott. New York: Alfred A. Knopf.

Kiple, Kenneth F. 1984. *The Caribbean Slave: A Biological History*. Cambridge: Cambridge University Press.

Kiple, Kenneth F. and Virginia H. King. 1981. *Another Dimension to the Black Diaspora: Diet, Disease, and Racism*. Cambridge:Cambridge University Press.

Matthew's Bible. ("Wife Beater" Edition) The Gutenberg Exhibit of the Chicago Bible House, 310 N. Michigan Avenue, Chicago.

McKitrick, Eric L. 1963. *Slavery Defended: The Views of the Old South*. Englewood Cliffs, N.J.: Prentice-Hall.

Margo, Robert A. and Richard H. Steckel. 1982. The Heights of American Slaves: New evidence on Slave Nutrition and Health. *Social Science History* 6:516–538.

Myrdal, Gunnar. 1944. *An American Dilemma: The Negro Problem and Modern Democracy*. New York: Harper & Row.

Nevins, Allan. 1947. *Ordeal of the Union*. New York: Scribner's.

Olmsted, Frederick Law. 1856. *A Journey in the Seaboard Slave States*. New York: Dix & Edwards.

———. 1860. *A Journey in the Back Country*. New York: Mason Brothers.

———. 1953. *The Cotton Kingdom*. Edited, with an introduction, by Arthur M. Schlesinger. New York: Alfred A. Knopf.

Phillips, Ulrich Bonnell. 1905. The Economic Cost of Slaveholding in the Cotton Belt. *Political Science Quarterly* 20:257–275.

———, ed. 1910. *Plantation and Frontier Documents 1649–1863*. Vols. I and II of John R. Commons, et al. *A Documentary History of American Industrial Society*. Cleveland: The A.H. Clark Co.

———. 1918. *American Negro Slavery: A Survey of the Supply, Employment and Control of Negro Labor as Determined by the Plantation Regime*. New York: D. Appleton & Company.

Plantation and Farm Instruction, Regulation, Record, Inventory and Account Book. 1852. Richmond: J. W. Randolf.

Postell, William Dosite. 1951. *The Health of Slaves on Southern Plantations*. Louisiana State University Studies, Social Science Series, No. 2. Baton Rouge: Louisiana State University Press.

Ramsdell, Chas. W. 1929. The Natural Limits of Slavery Expansion. *Mississippi Valley Historical Review* 16:151–171.

Reitz, Elizabeth J., Tyson Gibbs, and Ted A. Rathbun. 1985. Archeological Evidence for Subsistence on Coastal Plantations. In *The Archaeol-*

ogy of Slavery and Plantation Life, ed. Theresa Singleton. Studies in Historical Archaeology. London: Academic Press.

Rhodes, James Ford. 1893. *History of the United States from the Compromise of 1850.* Vol. I: *1850–1854.* New York: Harper & Brothers.

Russel, Robert R. 1938. The General Effects of Slavery Upon Southern Economic Progress. *Journal of Southern History* 4:34–54.

Savitt, Todd L. 1978. *Medicine and Slavery: The Diseases and Health Care of Blacks in Antebellum Virginia.* Urbana: University of Illinois Press.

Scarborough, William Kauffman. 1966. *The Overseer: Plantation Management in the Old South.* Baton Rouge: Louisiana State University Press.

Sellers, James Benson. 1950. *Slavery in Alabama.* University, AL: University of Alabama Press.

Sheridan, Richard B. 1985. *Doctors and Slaves: A Medical and Demographic History of Slavery in the British West Indies 1680–1834.* Cambridge: Cambridge University Press.

Sokoloff, Kenneth L. 1984. Was the Transition from the Artisanal Shop to the Non-mechanized Factory Associated with Gains in Efficiency? Evidence from the U. S. Manufacturing Censuses of 1820 and 1850. *Explorations in Economic History* 21:351–382.

———. 1986. Productivity Growth in Manufacturing during Early Industrialization: Evidence from the American Northeast, 1820–1860. In *Long-term Factors in American Economic Growth,* Stanley L. Engerman and Robert A. Gallman, eds.

The Southern Agriculturist, Horticulturist and Register of Rural Affairs III May, 1830.

Stampp, Kenneth M. 1956. *The Peculiar Institution: Slavery in the Ante-Bellum South.* New York: Alfred A. Knopf.

Steckel, Richard H. 1979. Slave Height Profiles from Coastwise Manifests. *Explorations in Economic History* 16:363–380.

———. 1986a. A Peculiar Population. *Journal of Economic History* 46:721–741.

———. 1986b. Birth Weights and Infant Mortality among American Slaves. *Explorations in Economic History* 23:173–198.

Sutch, Richard. 1975a. The Breeding of Slaves for Sale and Westward Expansion of Slavery, 1850–1860, in Stanley L. Engerman and Eugene D. Genovese, eds., *Race and Slavery in the Western Hemisphere: Quantitative Studies.* Princeton: Princeton University Press.

———. 1975b. The Treatment Received by American Slaves: A Critical Review of the Evidence Presented in *Time on the Cross. Explorations in Economic History* 12:335–438.

Sydnor, Charles S. 1933. *Slavery in Mississippi.* New York: Appleton-Century.

Taylor, Joe Gray. 1963. *Negro Slavery in Louisiana.* Baton Rouge: Louisiana Historical Association.

Thomas, John L. 1963. *The Liberator: William Lloyd Garrison, a Biography.* Boston: Little, Brown.

Van den Boogaart, E. and P.C. Emmer. 1977. Plantation Slavery in Surinam in the Last Decade before Emancipation: The Case of Catherine Sophia. *Comparative Perspectives on Slavery in the New World Plantation Societies,* Vera Rubin and Artur Tuden, eds. New York: New York Academy of Sciences.

Wade, Richard C. 1964. *Slavery in the Cities, the South, 1820–1860.* New York: Oxford University Press.

Webster's Third New International Dictionary. 1966. Springfield, Mass.: G. and C. Merriam Company.

Woodman, Harold D. 1972. Economic History and Economic Theory: The New Economic History in America. *Journal of Interdisciplinary History* 3:323–350.

Zilversmit, Arthur. 1967. *The First Emancipation: The Abolition of Slavery in the North.* Chicago: University of Chicago Press.

Index

slaveowners, 36, 74, 79, 104–
107, 134, 162–163, 176, 188;
southern distribution of, 253–
254. *See also* income, slave;
real national income
income, slave, 40, 83–84, 148,
149, 237, 241, 260; and costs
of child rearing, 35–36; and
expropriation, 5–6, 56, 107,
153–157; and female slaves,
83–84; pecuniary and nonpecuniary, 238, 239, 244–246;
and profit-sharing, 149; size
distribution of, 151–152. *See
also* earnings of slaves; exploitation; rates of return on
slaves; real national income;
wages
India, 165, 249, T250, T256
industry, 5, 7, 126, 235, 238, 252;
development of, and slavery,
64, 160, 187–188, 228, 255–
257; and elasticity of demand
for slaves, 5, 101–102, 234;
slaves in, 5, 56–57, 98, 228,
235; southern lag in, 254–255,
T256; and work rhythms, 208.
See also urban society
inelastic. *See* demand for slaves;
supply of and demand for
slaves
"inferiority" (alleged) of Negroes.
See efficiency and quality of
slave labor; racism
Instructions to Managers (plantation handbook), 240–241
insurrections, slave, 37, 40, 55;
fear of, 98, 188; low incidence
of, 242–243, 259; and passive
resistance, 230–231
interest rates, 156–157
International Business Machines
Corporation, 73
international slave trade. *See*
slave trade
interregional redistribution. *See*
redistribution of population,
interregional
Ireland and the Irish, 218, T250
iron industry, 235, 252, 255,
T256
Italy and Italian peninsula, 6,
13, 14, 249, T250, T256

Jackson, Andrew, and Jackso-
nian administration, 7, 89
Jamaica, 19, 22, 23, 155–156,
230. *See also* West Indies
Japan, T250, 251
Jemison, William (plantation
owner), 149
Jesuits, 30
Jews, 218, 230
Jordan, Josie (former slave), 143

Kemble, Fanny, 136, 143–144

labor, free: age-sex-health structure in, 219; and cost of punishment, 147; demoralized by
slavery, 174, 218; and gang
labor, 236, 238; German, 173,
218; and housing, 116; and
northern shift to industry, 252;
vs. slave (*see* labor, slave);
and southern farms, 194, 205;
working hours of, 208
labor, gang, 141, 209, 210, 213;
free labor and, 236, 238; interdependence of, 203–206, 236;
nonpecuniary disadvantages
of, 236–238, 244–246; and use
of force, 237–239. *See also*
drivers; overseers
labor, slave: and age, 73–77; capacity, utilization of, 5, 75,
141–142, 202–209; children in,
42, 177; competition among,
206; discipline of, 127, 134,
146–147; division of (specialization), 141–142, 203, 206–
207; and economies of scale,
5, 61, 184, 185, 192, 194, 196,
200, 204, 234–237, 239, 240,
255–257; efficiency of, 60, 64,
160, 167, 172–177, 210, 220,
225; vs. free, 5, 65–66, 100–
102, 160, 172–178, 180–184,
188, 192, 204–206, 217–219,
221, 228, 231, 235, 241, 262;
growth rate of, 96; as human
capital, 147, 163, 174, 232–
234, 261–262; and labor-force
participation rate, 96, 176,
207–209, 219–221; -land ratio,
95, 97, 185; management of,